THE CARIBBEAN ECONOMIES IN AN ERA OF FREE TRADE

T0362198

The Caribbean Economies in an Era of Free Trade

Edited by

NIKOLAOS KARAGIANNIS and MICHAEL WITTER
The University of the West Indies, Jamaica

LONDON AND NEW YORK

First published 2004 by Ashgate Publishing

Reissued 2018 by Routledge
2 Park Square, Milton Park, Abingdon, Oxon OX14 4RN
711 Third Avenue, New York, NY 10017, USA

Routledge is an imprint of the Taylor & Francis Group, an informa business

First issued in paperback 2018

ISBN 13: 978-0-815-39754-0 (hbk)
ISBN 13: 978-1-138-62265-4 (pbk)
ISBN 13: 978-1-351-14752-1 (ebk)

Contents

PART III: COUNTRY-STUDIES

List of Figures

List of Tables

List of Contributors

Dillon Alleyne is Lecturer, Department of Economics, University of the West Indies, Mona, Jamaica.

Ian Boxill is Senior Lecturer and Head, Department of Sociology, Psychology and Social Work, University of the West Indies, Mona, Jamaica.

Anthony Clayton is Alcan Professor of Caribbean Sustainable Development, Sir Arthur Lewis Institute of Social and Economic Studies, University of the West Indies, Mona, Jamaica.

Marie Freckleton is Lecturer, Department of Economics, University of the West Indies, Mona, Jamaica.

Nikolaos Karagiannis is Fellow, Sir Arthur Lewis Institute of Social and Economic Studies, University of the West Indies, Mona, Jamaica.

Diaram Ramjee Singh is Lecturer, Department of Management Studies, University of the West Indies, Mona, Jamaica.

Robert Read is Senior Lecturer, Department of Economics, University of Lancaster, Lancaster, UK.

Carlos J. Rodriguez-Fuentes is Reader, Department of Applied Economics, University of La Laguna, Tenerife, Spain.

Christos D. Salvaris is Lecturer and Head, Centre for Hotel and Tourism Management, University of the West Indies, Nassau, The Bahamas.

Marjorie D. Segree is Economist, National Water Commission, Kingston, Jamaica.

Grahame F. Thompson is Professor, Department of Politics, Open University, Milton Keynes, UK.

Michael Witter is Senior Lecturer and Head, Department of Economics, University of the West Indies, Mona, Jamaica.

Foreword

Globalisation, the emerging process of international economic integration, which illustrates the present and future economic reality, is at one and the same time the most used and misused of concepts. Given its importance in shaping contemporary international economic and political relations, this phenomenon, which has been occurring for some time now, has become a powerful worldwide force. Indeed, globalisation has become both an ideological force (i.e., a conceptualisation of the world) and a material force (i.e., a process that has conferred immense power on transnational corporations, located mainly in the developed world, but with an increasingly global reach).

No country has been able to escape its influence. Its effect on less-developed and developing nations, including those of the Caribbean, has been particularly profound. The people of the Caribbean are not strangers to such global linkages, as the Caribbean region is arguably the most globalised of world regions having regard to its colourful colonial history. But it is this very historic familiarity with global integration, modernisation and industrialisation that underlies the region's abject dependency on outside authorities.

Decades after gaining political independence from a variety of European States, Caribbean States are still the victims of the historical legacy of dependency on outside suppliers, markets and geopolitical agendas. But today, we in the Caribbean are not alone. The whole world has entered the present era of globalisation, dominated now by the United States of America, but Caribbean States offer a chronicle of the impact produced by their exposure to the numerous previous rounds of the transformation of global capitalism.

This chronicle includes vast international gaps in income, competency and living standards. The region is economically stagnant with few realistic options by which Caribbean nations and their people can escape the constraints imposed by core states. While the world shrinks very unevenly in spatial and economic terms, the neoliberal reforms, the policy concessions to the United States, the pursuit of continuity of Lomé market access to the European Union and of NAFTA parity, appear to have largely fallen on deaf North Atlantic ears. To make matters worse, the region is inundated, unilaterally, by the consumerism of the North Atlantic region, especially the United States.

While Caribbean states and peoples are far from helpless and passive victims of exogenous forces beyond their control, they are under constant pressure to respond, adjust and cope while rapid and profound transformation of a variety of norms which govern society is taking place. Therefore, for these and countless other reasons, the present era of globalisation needs to be thoroughly analysed and its impact on the Caribbean carefully specified, given the very real constraints imposed by the global political economy.

The chapters of this book focus mainly on those local responses to globalisation associated with state policies, dynamic firms and the Caribbean people themselves, corresponding to the islands' struggle for development and economic survival. They represent a south-centric perspective on development. The book itself is essential reading for anyone who resists the intellectual blinkers of the current orthodoxy and the region's economic and political adversity.

Hon. Dr. Bernard J. Nottage
Chief Executive Officer
Coalition for Democratic Reform
Commonwealth of The Bahamas

Preface

In International Affairs, the strength of the English speaking Caribbean has always resided in its creativity and its ability to generate compelling intellectual ideas, which are universal in scope. It is therefore most likely that the region will have to summon up this expertise as it embarks on the intensive, complex, and critical negotiations which characterise this phase of globalisation.

The quality of the negotiating skills of the Caribbean representatives is a direct result of the region's ability to accurately assess its position in relation to the rest of the world and analyse the various phenomena which often consist of the twin factors of threat and opportunity, as well as its capacity to determine what options have to be exercised in order to ensure the unity and survival of the region. In other words, the region has converted its vulnerability into a source of strength.

It was the Caribbean, for example, which in the seventies persuaded the States of two other Continents, Africa and the Pacific, to take a united stand in the negotiations with the EEC. This unity gave birth to the four Lomé Conventions and the Cotonou Agreement. In the process, one of the more successful negotiating entities, the Asia, Caribbean and Pacific (ACP) group in modern international relations was fashioned. On this occasion, the Caribbean region faces the stern challenge of making its voice heard in the rush towards globalisation.

One of the striking features about the current phase of globilisation is the resolution of the global economy into a number of regional blocs and the attendant negotiations to work out their architecture. As a consequence, there are regional economical groupings in Asia, Europe, Africa, and Latin America and the Caribbean. In the latter case, the intention is to integrate all of the states of the American family of nations. The Free Trade Area of the Americas (FTAA) is a comprehensive trade negotiation process embracing the thirty four democratic nations of the Western Hemisphere.

The effort to unite the economies of the Western Hemisphere into a single free trade arrangement had its origin at the Summit of the Americas, which was held in Miami in December 1994. The Summit of the Americas can be said to be the culmination of the ideas contained in such concepts as the Enterprise for the Americas Initiative (EAI), the North American Free Trade Area (NAFTA) and MERCOSUR.

At the Miami meeting in 1994, the Heads of State and Government of thirty four democratic nations of the hemisphere reached agreement to create a free trade area of the Americas (FTAA). Barriers to trade and investment are expected to be progressively eliminated and the relevant negotiations completed for agreement by 2005. Since this meeting, four Ministerial Convocations have taken place in the preparatory phase of the FTAA process (1994-1998): the first was held in June 1995 in Denver, USA; the second in March 1996 in Cartagena, Colombia; the third in May 1997 in Belo Horizonte, Brazil; and the fourth in March 1998 in San José, Costa Rica. Out of these Ministerial Meetings the structure has emerged, including negotiating groups and a Consultative Group on small economies. In addition, four more FTAA Trade Ministerial Meetings (the fifth was held in Toronto, Canada in November 1999; the sixth in Buenos Aires, Argentina in April, 2001; the seventh in Quito, Ecuador in November 2002; and the eighth in Miami, USA in November 2003) and two more Summits of the Americas (in Santiago, Chile in April 1998; and in Quebec, Canada in April 2001) have taken place. The last Meeting of the Ministers responsible for Trade will be held in 2004 in Brazil. The FTAA is therefore well advanced and is likely to play a significant role in the emerging global economy.

The negotiations leading to the establishment of the FTAA will be intricate, complex and demanding. It will mean that Caribbean negotiators will have to have the skills and the knowledge to participate effectively in the creation of one of the biggest free trade areas of the globe. It will mean also that positions will have to be hammered out after analyses and studies have been done on the implications of the creation of the FTAA. In particular, the Caribbean Community will want the construction of an FTAA that takes into account its specific vulnerabilities and requirements for sustained economic growth and prosperity.

Karagiannis and Witter's book, *The Caribbean Economies in an Era of Free Trade*, has added to the body of information and knowledge from which the options and positions to be exercised by the Community can be extrapolated and acted upon. The publication of this book is timely. For, as already demonstrated, the process towards the establishment of the FTAA appears to be sailing under a full head of steam. The circumstances warrant, therefore, that the Caribbean be guided by all of the studies and analyses available which can inform its approach and negotiating posture towards the FTAA.

I believe Karagiannis and Witter's book will contribute to this process. It demonstrates that the region is strongest in the area of ideas. And it is this capacity to generate ideas which would ensure its survival and growth. The creativity that the Caribbean has displayed over a considerable period of time is the guarantee of its future. That is why this book must be essential reading for our Heads of State, our policy and opinion makers, and, above all, those involved in the intricate and complex negotiations which will lead to the creation of the FTAA.

I have no doubt that this book will contribute to the understanding and implications of the FTAA for the Caribbean Community and its peoples, and serve as a kind of guideline for the important FTAA negotiations which lie ahead.

Professor Kenneth O. Hall
Pro Vice-Chancellor and Principal
Mona Campus
University of the West Indies

Introduction

The political economy of development in the Caribbean is characterised by trade relations that take place in highly monopolised global markets; policy issues which serve the interests of transnational corporations and are influenced by multilateral agencies; a lack of focus and clear policies; and, 'pork barrel' policies and interference by the political directorates. Foreign capital controls the productive structures of the islands and territories - and particularly the most dynamic sectors of their economies -, repatriates a high volume of profits, and benefits very narrow sectors of the Caribbean population. Technological-industrial dependence has been consolidated, and export production is determined by demand from the main hegemonic centres of the world economy. Foreign financing has become necessary in two forms: to cover the existing fiscal and current account deficits, and to 'finance' development by means of loans. Caribbean nations encounter unyielding domestic obstacles to their self-determined self-sustained growth, which lead to the accumulation of deficits.

On the side of policy making, if we were to consider seriously the present state of mainstream analysis, we would find that there has been little of worth contributed to the concrete tasks of working out a rational strategy for coping with those problems which centre on raising the levels of development of the productive forces of Caribbean economies. Apart from the popular distinction between 'growth' and 'development', it is surprising how little attention has been paid to developing consistent strategies aimed at providing a planning frame to deal with the multidimensional problems of underdevelopment.

Retrospectively, during the last two decades or so, free market policies have been over-emphasised and presented as the 'panacea' for further development and prosperity, resulting in insufficient productive activity (e.g., through a lack of effective demand and inadequate levels of investment) and, thus, not effectively tackling the scale and diversity of problems that face Caribbean nations. Despite this shortfall in 'endogenous growth', many still maintain that the solution lies in a *laissez-faire* approach. Consequently, alternative development policy suggestions have been virtually ignored. A review of the global economy shows that all is not well, especially when one considers that global capitalism is experiencing one of its worst and most persistent crises.

Undoubtedly, the new millennium poses new challenges for national policy-making. Two challenges are fundamental. First, it is increasingly recognised that policy must be consistent, thorough and effective, and planning must be for the long-term, as well as for the short and medium-term. Second, governments, private sectors and social segments together must set the development agenda of tomorrow to meet the diverse and changing needs of consumers and producers (partly as a result of global competition). The 'appropriate' role of government in the new millennium, in particular, appears to be an interesting and challenging one. Thus, if the future of the Caribbean economies and societies needs to be very different from the past, it will require a much sharper focus on radical development policy agendas.

The book is composed of three parts (Parts I, II and III), which discuss theoretical issues, policy issues and country-studies respectively, or ten chapters, which are, to a greater or lesser extent, concerned with the tyranny of the recent neoliberal globalisation and the dangers that an unregulated global market system poses for Caribbean territories. In the opening chapter of Part I, Karagiannis utilises a variety of radical perspectives and argues that the recent globalisation project has been a calculus of inequality and unevenness as part of a repeated global capitalist record. In chapter 2, Thompson poses the question as to whether there are any limits to globalisation, considers trade and international flows as examples of international interdependency and integration, and contends that these may not expand in the future at the rate they have done in the past. In chapter 3, Read is concerned with the implications for the small states in the Caribbean of the proposed Free Trade Area of the Americas (FTAA), and discusses likely costs and benefits should Caribbean countries become members. In chapter 4, Clayton poses an urgent and interesting question: why some developing countries are capitalising on opportunities and adapting successfully to the new global environment, while others appear to be locked into patterns of underdevelopment. The author pays particular attention to factors such as technology, knowledge, specialisation and change.

Part II contains chapters 5, 6 and 7. In chapter 5, Rodriguez-Fuentes explores the possibilities of monetary policy in small island economies from a post Keynesian (interventionist) perspective. Although monetary policy may not solve structural problems of island economies, Rodriguez-Fuentes offers suggestions to overcome such problems and provide proper finance for long-run local profitable initiatives. In Chapter 6, Freckleton and Karagiannis seek to provide strategic options for CARICOM in the new trade environment. According to the authors, the mutually beneficial relationship between tourism and agro-industry can provide the foundation on which alternative endogenous development strategies can build. In chapter 7, Boxill, Ramjee Singh and Segree emphasise the 'Caribbean World' as a proposal that offers an alternative way of developing tourism in the region. For it to work, there has to be a radical departure from the way in which tourism is currently viewed, particularly in light of the many limitations associated with mass tourism in the Caribbean, and requires active intervention by governments, business sector and educational institutions across the region.

Finally, Part III is composed of chapters 8, 9 and 10. In chapters 8 and 9, Karagiannis and Witter analyse a number of problems, challenges and prospects for the Bahamian and Jamaican economic development respectively, in the era of the FTAA. In the last chapter of the book, Alleyne examines the demand for imports in Jamaica over the period 1972-2000. Since access to imports for most developing countries is limited by the availability of foreign exchange, the author contends that substitution possibilities between imports and domestic factors of production should be an important step in shaping economic policies that can help to conserve foreign exchange without constraining endogenous growth.

Overall, the contributions to this volume provide a rich menu for alternative economic policies in the Caribbean, at the turn of the Century. While there are differences between the proposals and different areas of concern are addressed, there are also some important common themes to the papers. These would identify as, first, the shortcomings of the current 'capitalism in the age of globalisation', and recommendations have been made towards rectifying these shortcomings. Second, the policy proposals are intended to shift policy concerns from a focus on promoting the interests of the rich and powerful nations to a greater concern for the interests of the dependent and less-developed countries (like the Caribbean territories). Third, the essays are informed, to a greater or lesser extent, by political economy analysis of the operations of international markets which stands in contrast to the starry-eyed view of economic orthodoxy.

This publication could not have been possible without the input of many persons. Special thanks go to the contributors for their willingness to participate and respond to our suggestions, as well as to Steve Pressman and the staff of Ashgate publishers who have provided excellent support throughout the period it took to prepare this book.

Nikolaos Karagiannis & Michael Witter
Kingston, Jamaica
June 2003

PART I
THEORETICAL ISSUES

Chapter 1

Dependence, Cumulative Causation and the Caribbean

Nikolaos Karagiannis

Introduction

Historically, the Caribbean territories have had long political and economic associations with developed Western countries as colonies, protectorates and/or departments. In fact the Caribbean case of underdevelopment (i.e., the plantation system) has been conditioned by the development and expansion of the 'Western' dominant countries through the mechanisms of the international market. Political independence established national sovereignty in older and newer nations of the Commonwealth Caribbean when both groups were integrated into the international system. Consequently, the political process of national independence converted states, societies, and nations that had evolved as integral parts of the international system of empire into nation-states. The effect was to legitimise their 'autonomy' based on concepts of self-determination rooted in Western culture.

In the case of the newer nations, independence coincided with the post-war intensification of the internationalisation of capital, labour, production, class relations, and the state and nation-state. However, the political independence of Caribbean nations has not been accompanied by any significant advances in their national economies: foreign ownership, management and control of production; dependence on metropolises' preferences for Caribbean services and exports; reliance on high levels of imports; and a dependent monetary system are among the outstanding features of Caribbean economies (i.e., the negative results of the foreign capitalist domination, and particularly the North American supremacy in the region). These Caribbean nations continue to be locked into a new economic oppression and rely on developed countries for transfers of income and capital, for banking and financial services, for business and technical skills, and even for ideas about themselves. The foreign trade sector is one of the spheres in which the dependence of Caribbean territories is most apparent. Largely, foreign decisions determine the growth of Caribbean economies while most Caribbean resources, natural, human and technological, remain basically underdeveloped.

The globalisation of modern-technology production is revolutionising the environment and conditions of international competition, and demands a rethinking of 'traditional' concepts of hegemony, national economic space and production, and the basic attributes of the nation-state - among other issues. Inadequate economic resources and skills, compounded by the size of scale on which Caribbean economies operate, and their high dependence on Western capitalist economies have convinced many that self-propelled economic development is not a feasible and realistic strategy.

The first main section of this chapter provides the main theoretical approaches to regional development and trade, and the second part evaluates these theoretical views while taking the reality into consideration. The final main section of the chapter provides notions for an alternative development policy framework while considering structural and functional problems of Caribbean economies.

Theory

It is possible to distinguish the following two main and very different sets of views on regional development: (1) orthodox views; and, (2) radical views.

Orthodox Views

The neoclassical approach suggests that, in equilibrium, there is an equalisation of returns to each factor of production. In the short run imbalances may exist; hence, resources may be unemployed because of unforeseeable random events or because market participants speculate that by holding resources off the market system today, they will get a better return tomorrow. Such considerations cause prices and quantities to deviate from their long-run equilibrium values (i.e., failure of prices to adjust). The geographical dimension of this view is based on the internal mobility of resources and implies that each region tends to specialise in producing what it is comparatively good at producing.

The neoclassical process focuses on the idea of marginal substitution between different factor inputs in response to relative prices. A depressed or under-developed region would face a low demand for labour and, consequently, would provide low wages. The equilibrating mechanism would include the movement of labour out of the depressed region(s) in search of high wages elsewhere and the inward movement of firms attracted by the low cost of labour. These movements would be expected to continue until wages were equalised across regions and, in effect, full employment restored through wage flexibility and factor mobility (Sawyer, 1989, pp.420-21). Hence, resources are viewed as moving in response to price signals, with resources moving into areas of high rewards and away from areas of low rewards (Sawyer, 1989, p.451).

Neoclassical theorists believe in the natural disappearance of spatial disparities. They generally assume perfect mobility of production factors between the regions of a given country or between nations. Wages will tend to equalise over regions or countries. A similar reasoning can be applied to capital movements, which will tend to equalise returns on capital over space. Hence, in the neoclassical analysis there is no room for spatial disparities, and disparities that may have occurred occasionally will be wiped out by movements of factors of production.

A similar result will be achieved even if factors of production are not mobile provided there is trade. In Heckscher-Ohlin analysis, exchange of goods between countries (or regions) leads to factor income equalisation: trade will equalise wages and capital income over space and provide convergence (this analysis assumes that all countries and, hence, their firms and regions, have equal access to technology and the rate of change of technology).

In the 'traditional' trade theory, regions or countries specialise in sectors and benefit equally from this specialisation, because all sectors are equally good for the economy. The 'new' theory of trade has provided a new argument for industrial targeting and added a concept of importance to this discussion: the notion of 'strategic sectors', i.e., strategic trade theory (Dixit, 1986; Krugman, 1986, 1991). Romer (1986) and Lucas (1985, 1988) consider that the national accumulation of knowledge, technology and R&D is basically *endogenous* (i.e., Schumpeterian 'creative dynamics'). According to Lucas (1985, 1988) effort and know-how are very important and the growth rate of human capital is proportional to the time spent in training. Romer (1987) treats effort and knowledge as two important inputs into the production of knowledge and his research produced results which were exactly the same as in Lucas' model. In addition, Becker *et al.* (1988) and Azariadis and Drazen (1988) offered similar contributions to the above literature by building models which were capable of several equilibrium paths while focusing on human capital investment.

In order to consider international trade, Lucas worked out a particular model to illustrate the 'endogenous progress of comparative advantage' and identified goods which are human capital intensive (i.e., high-technology products). His particular model suggests that the countries specialising in high technology sectors grow faster than others and thus reinforce their comparative advantage. Krugman (1990) added to these studies of endogenous innovation and concluded that international integration may encourage innovation and accelerate economic growth (see also Solow, 1991, 1994).

In summation, the neoclassical theoretical background of recent studies is either an extension of the traditional Solow model or the endogenous growth models. The former, the traditional view of differences in growth rates, suggests that the less advanced countries catch up to the leading ones and thus enjoy a faster rate of technological progress and growth. The latter supports the view that countries follow their own national growth paths and try to build their own technological capabilities with little tendency for convergence in income or productivity levels.

Radical Views

The dependency views of development and underdevelopment are different approaches to development and growth in which the expansion of the capitalist system is seen as an aspect of the movement of capital into areas of potentially high profits. Within the radical political economy tradition, this set of views finds expression in terms like 'dependency', the generation of 'under-development' and the relationships between the 'centre' and the 'periphery'. The discussion of dependency theory and the related unequal exchange theory by analysts such as Baran (1957), Samir Amin (1974), Cardoso and Faletto (1979), Emmanuel (1972), Frank (1971), Wallerstein (1974), among others, is based upon the concept that the world economy is divided into a 'core' of dominant nations and a 'periphery' of dependent ones. These theories share the common feature that they stress the unevenness of development as the product and consequence of the capitalist mode of production (i.e., 'the development of underdevelopment'), and that the relationship between the more developed and the less developed countries is one of the dominance of the former over the latter. This exploitative relationship takes place because advanced capitalist economies can use their economic and political power - and occasionally their military power - to structure the world economic system to their benefit.[1] As Baran (1957, p.28) argues, 'the economic development in under-developed countries is profoundly inimical to the dominant interests in the advanced capitalist countries'.

Radical analysts have focused on the forms, mechanisms, causes, and, to a lesser extent, on the social-structural consequences of imperialism for both the dominant and the dominated nations, and have acknowledged structural rigidities and market failure due to social, institutional and political factors which usually act as bottlenecks to the process of development (their advocacy of state intervention and regulation of foreign trade and investment as a way out of these bottlenecks is well known). It is not just a case that the more developed economies have higher income levels than the less developed ones, but it also includes economic, political and cultural domination. Dependency theorists have also stressed that,

> Dependency on foreign interests and foreign economic penetration keeps the state weak and prevents it from effectively playing its necessary role in protecting domestic industry and fostering economic growth (Barrett and Whyte, 1982, p.1072).

As a state's contact with the world capitalist economy grows, one might expect to see the government participating less in its economy.

Myrdal's well-known theory of 'cumulative causation' is another important, but quite different, contribution within the radical tradition. In fact, the process of cumulative causation can be advanced to account for the persistence of spatial differences in a wide variety of development indices including 'per capita income, rates of growth of industrialisation and trade, employment growth rates and levels of unemployment' (Myrdal, 1957, p.38).

According to Myrdal, the free working of the market system promotes an imbalance in regional resource use and the play of forces in the market normally tends to increase rather than decrease the inequalities between regions. Not only trade but also labour and capital are also attracted to some favoured areas - in what Myrdal describes as 'the power of attraction of a centre' (Myrdal, 1957, p.26). As a result, both economic and social forces tend to strengthen the disequilibrium situation by leading to cumulative expansion in the favoured region at the expense of other regions, which then become comparatively worse off, thus, preventing and/or retarding their future development. The process is cumulative, not in the sense that all market forces influencing the spatial distribution of factors of production work in the same direction, but that an initial push or pull of factors to one region or area rather than another will tend to move factors increasingly towards them and away from others, improving productivity and efficiency and widening still further the competitive advantage of the growing region over the lagging regions.

Cowling (1987, 1990) extended the above idea on the effects of cumulative causation into the social and political arena. According to the author, inequalities in economic terms generate inequalities in political power, cultural domination, etc. A region which is relatively rich does not only have more economic spending power but may be politically more powerful and exert cultural dominance over the less prosperous regions.

The phenomenon of cumulative causation at the level of the firm leads to industrial concentration. Centripetalism arises from the interaction of firms and markets and relates to 'the tendency for higher level activities and occupations to gravitate to the centre - to be lost to the regions; to be lost to the periphery' (Cowling, 1990, p.15). Furthermore, Cowling argues that strategic decisions with major implications for local, regional and national communities are being made outside those communities. The same centralising forces imply a transfer of resources to the centre, which reduces the capacity of the periphery to sustain its own economic, political and cultural development on which future self-determination is based. In fact the mode of production of material life conditions the general process of social, political and intellectual life. 'Centripetal economic tendencies become centripetal political and cultural tendencies and the community enters a vicious circle of relative decline' (Cowling, 1990, p.15). The prosperous regions and nations (i.e., centre) have economic power over the depressed regions and nations (i.e., periphery). Thus, production in the periphery may be controlled by the centre. In addition, this economic power is allied with political and cultural power and this cultural power may also be imposed on the periphery as a consequence of the economic power.

Facing the Reality: A Partial Critique

Historically, imperialism[2] (either economic concentration and centralisation of capital or the most 'progressive' mode of production) has resulted from capitalist economic necessity - structurally out of the economic imperatives of capitalism - a mode of production whose logic of internal development must inevitably lead to imperialist expansion, if it is to survive by warding off the unavoidable crises which quite often plague international capitalism. Sometimes, countervailing forces such as relative overpopulation, increasing depression and exploitation of labour power, the cheapening of elements of constant capital and foreign trade may result in a contemporary rise in profits. Nonetheless, there is an historical tendency for the rate of capitalist profits to decline generally or squeeze. It is this tendency that forces capitalists, or capitalist agents, agencies and corporations to search for profitable investment opportunities overseas. While searching for the 'super profits', the ruling classes of the dominant countries and their allies - i.e., social elites of less-developed and developing countries who have more in common with their counter-parts in the developed nations and with foreign corporations than their own people -, and/or large capitalist associations may establish cozy relations with (or even bribe) political leaders, diplomats, labour leaders, etc. 'in numerous different ways, direct and indirect, overt and covert' (e.g., deceit, fraud, corruption and other illegalities).[3] These are important issues in the Caribbean context. Although Caribbean states have thrown off colonial rule, they are still politically and economically dependent. This is reinforced by the dominant countries' direct ownership of assets in Caribbean territories, by technical domination, and by the dependency caused by the debts Caribbean countries owe to the West.

Moreover, the cumulative causation principle explains the unequal or uneven 'regional incidence' of development by endogenous factors resulting from the historical process of capitalist development itself rather than by 'exogenous' differences in resource endowment (Kaldor, 1978, p.148). This principle is essential for the understanding of the diverse trends of development as between different regions. It has to be remembered that market forces usually produce cumulative movements away from spatial equilibrium; once growth disparities occur, they tend to become cumulative and self-perpetuating. Hence, there is a strong tendency for the centripetal market forces to display cumulative causation, and for higher-level activities to gravitate towards the centre and the 'success' - the 'winners' (whether firms, regions or nations). Resources in the less developed areas have often been underutilised and the growth of resources has usually been slower than elsewhere (Sawyer, 1992, p.69).

Perhaps no word at present is used and misused more than globalisation. Although the term may obscure much more than it reveals, it generally serves to refer to various world-wide epoch-defining changes in the organisation of societies, economies and politics. In practice, globalisation provides a cover for a new form of imperialist exploitation and the institution of US hegemony over a global process of capital accumulation. In the last decade, capitalists in Europe and the USA have created favourable conditions for the takeover and recolonisation of economies across the less-developed and developing world. International capital (the most powerful business and financial magnates in the capitalist world *assisted by* political leaders, cultural and religious organisations, media and even some trade unionists) has managed to restore highly profitable returns on investments and operations in certain areas (such as IT, speculation, etc.) creating both opulent prosperity and growing poverty, inequality and misery. In effect, the terms globalisation and imperialism may be used as alternative frameworks for analysing the dynamics of the same worldwide developments and trends.[4]

More specifically, the globalisation project (or the 'New Liberal Order') of the 1990s was based on a coherent theoretical, ideological, political and institutional order. The argument is that globalisation carries the economic benefits of specialisation and the division of labour to the world level. An important corollary to this argument is that a minimalist state, which focuses on market support and regulatory activities, facilitates globalisation. Liberalisation on the other hand, - a process that promotes competitiveness - permits the reaping of economies of scale, secures economic restructuring and industrial reorganisation, provides for the wider availability of technology, and offers dynamic opportunities and gains for both businesses and countries. For this reason, unfettered globalisation coupled with political commitment to policies of liberalisation - as a major force driving global change - assures these outcomes (Thomas, 2000, pp.12-13).

Nevertheless, in this period of accelerated globalisation, markets have widened gaps in wealth, income, consumption, power, capabilities and access, both among countries and within them. It seems that the mechanisms of liberalisation are as uneven as the outcomes of global growth. This is not just a single unfortunate outcome, but part of a repeated global capitalist record (Thomas, 2000, p.14). Evidently, international markets have been skewed against the poorer countries of the world. Statistics illustrate very well some of the processes of unevenness and unequal exchange as well as a number of negative results in the contemporary world:

- Globalisation is proceeding apace, but largely for the benefit of the more powerful and dynamic countries. Uneven growth and development accompany this economic manifestation, and the major global economic performance indicators - output, trade, consumption, investment and prices - reveal this undesirable state of affairs (Thomas, 2000, p.12). The forthcoming FTAA is expected to enable the advanced North American countries to give new impetus to this unevenness of development that will set in motion all the other mechanisms of imperialist domination and exploitation.

- The poorest 20 per cent of the world's people saw their share in world income decline from 2.3 per cent to 1.4 per cent in the past three decades, while that of the richest 20 per cent grew from 70 to 85 per cent. The ratio of the shares grew from 30:1 in 1960 to 84:1 in 1995. Besides, the assets of the world's 358 billionaires exceeded the combined annual incomes of the 2.5 billion people who comprise the poorest 45 per cent of mankind (UNDP, *Human Development Report* 1996, p.8).

- The loss to the less-developed and developing countries from unequal access to trade, labour and finance is estimated at $500 billion a year, 10 times what they receive annually in foreign assistance (UNDP, *Human Development Report* 1997, p.87). In addition, as a former President and Chairman of the World Bank argues, foreign aid programmes constitute a distinct benefit to American business.[5] The three major benefits are: (1) Foreign aid provides a substantial and immediate market for the US goods and services; (2) Foreign aid stimulates the development of new overseas markets for US companies; and (3) Foreign aid orients national economies towards a free enterprise system in which the USA can prosper. In fact, capitalist aid appears to be a calculated business investment. Thus, it is not the imperialist countries which aid the developing and less-developed countries, but the latter which aid the former.

- Private foreign direct investment (FDI) is growing spectacularly, even though it is concentrated in a few economies and among a few firms, and is facilitated by the growth of cross-border mergers and acquisitions, inter-firm agreements, the world-wide introduction of liberalised FDI regimes, and the recent wave of privatisations, trade and exchange rate liberalisation, financial deregulation, labour markets reforms, social welfare reforms, and fiscal and monetary orthodoxy (Thomas, 2000, p.11; Girvan, 2000, p.68). Eighty three per cent of foreign direct investment goes to rich countries, and three quarters of the remainder goes to developing countries, mostly in East and Southeast Asia and in Latin America. Besides, the countries with the poorest 20 per cent of the world's people receive just 0.2 per cent of international commercial lending (*Human Development Report* 1992, p.48; 1996, p.9). In the Caribbean, in particular, the very nature, forms and uses of foreign capital inflows have frustrated the region's development potential and have not solved the crucial problem of material poverty and structural dependence.

- Financial capital plays a leading role in globalisation (i.e., growth in the volume and speculative character of global financial flows as well as the consolidation of huge concentrations of private finance capital - transnational corporations and institutional investors- as the dominant players in world production, trade and finance). This is reflected not only in the dramatic increase of financial flows across the foreign exchanges and higher levels of foreign direct investment, but also in the degree of integration between financial markets in different countries and regions and in the organisation of production on a transnational basis (Arestis and Sawyer, 1998, p.2). The volume of foreign exchange transactions worldwide reached $1,300 billion a day in 1995 (with the corresponding figure in the early 1970s being $18 billion), equivalent to $312 trillion a year of 240 business days (Tobin, 1996, p. xvi). By comparison, at the end of 1995, the annual global trade in goods and services was $5 trillion, the total reserves of central banks around $1.5 trillion and the annual global turnover in equity markets $21 trillion.

- The share in world trade of the world's poorest countries, with 20 per cent of the world's people, has declined from 4 per cent to almost 1 per cent during the last four decades. Given the uneven industrial development of trading nations, the structure of modern international trade is such that greatly favours the developed at the expense of the less-developed and developing countries. Indeed, cumulative terms-of-trade losses by the developing countries have exceeded $300 billion during the last two decades (*Human Development Report* 1996, p.9; 1997, p.84).

- There is a growing proliferation of various social problems, many of which are 'trans-boundary' and global in scope. Current global consumption has doubled since the mid-1970s. Consumer markets are integrated world-wide to a point where many fear a global 'addiction to consumption'. Furthermore, an unprecedented intensification of environmental problems and the rapid pace of environmental degradation threaten the sustainability of planet earth (Thomas, 2000, pp.10-11).[6]

Thus, the reality seriously challenges the neoliberal assumption that markets are 'free and fair' and lead to optimal outcomes, which is the theoretical underpinning of global and regional trade liberalisation.

Moreover, there has been exceptional growth of international production led by gigantic transnationals (TNCs). This growth of TNCs is the best demonstration of this trend that now occurs at a faster rate than either the growth of global trade or GDP. Far-reaching corporate reorganisation and changes in the structure of firm competition are very evident. But the growth in dominance, the global perspective and ambitions of the major industrial and financial corporations may cut across the interests of any particular nation. This is an important issue in the Caribbean case. The fundamental issue relates to the asymmetry of power between TNCs and national/local communities, which derives from the transnationality of these corporations and the international perspective and flexibility which that implies. To achieve their own objectives, transnationals can switch investment and production, or threaten to do so, whenever conditions in any one country or region appear disadvantageous, for example because specific taxes or wage costs are too high. As a result, economies can be relatively prosperous or relatively depressed by the actions (and huge impact) of transnational corporations - and the direct implication is that only when the environment becomes conducive to foreign investment will capital return. The power of these organisations can be used to secure their own objectives, often at the expense of communities (Cowling, 1990, p.12).

In addition, the financial institutions adopt a particularly short-term view with regard to investment - this is apparently true in the Caribbean - and impose their short-term perspective on firms, especially the small ones. Thus, small and/or new firms may be severely constrained in their investment ambitions by the short-term perspective of the financial institutions, since it is these firms which will find difficulties to fund their own growth (Cowling, 1990, p.14). This sort of financial environment is hardly conducive to the rational planning of the long-term future of the industrial base. Short-term decision making is crowding out long-term issues, and leaving firms weaker in the long term.[7]

Evidently, production has become more complicated, more fragmented, more specialised, more related to and dependent upon other firms and the 'accelerators' (i.e., quick and reliable access to highly specialised companies, skills, talents, R&D, communications, transportation, information, etc.). Changes in the structure of production usually increase the relative attractiveness of the more-developed areas. Economies of scale and learning effects might lead in certain sectors to the domination of some firms. There might be sectors which are more profitable than others, which would mean that specialisation (and free trade) does not benefit equally all regions or nations. For most, if not all, of the modern factors of growth and competitiveness, the most developed countries or regions are better, or much better, endowed than the lagging countries or regions. As an OECD report points out, 'manufacturing expertise grows by the cumulative effects of scale, learning, etc. and is - contrary to the assumptions of the orthodox theory of comparative advantage - geographically concentrated' (OECD, 1987, p.256).

Thus, instead of free trade being to the advantage of everyone, the countries or regions specialised in 'strategic sectors' are likely to benefit more from free trade and/or from increased trade. In fact, the more-developed countries or regions may reinforce their initial superiority thanks to trade. Furthermore, the revolution of knowledge, technology and innovation (i.e., acceleration in the pace of generation of new ideas) has brought new challenges: those countries without access, or even inadequate access, to modern knowledge and know-how to use it may fall even further behind. The trouble with the neoclassical analysis is that, in a world of static comparative advantage, free trade favours the rich and the strong (firms, regions and nations). Modern economies do not conform to perfect competition and full employment is not the usual outcome from the free operation of market forces. In addition, the allocation and reallocation of resources and, especially, the creation of them between sectors, industries, regions and nations has not been explained successfully by neoclassical equilibrium analysis.

Envisioning Alternative Development Perspectives

If we were to consider seriously the present state of mainstream economics, we would find that there has been little of worth contributed to the concrete tasks of working out a rational strategy for coping with those problems which centre on raising the levels of development of the productive forces of small dependent or underdeveloped economies. Apart from the popular distinction between 'growth' and 'development', it is surprising how little attention has been paid to developing a consistent strategy aimed at providing a planning frame to deal with the multi-dimensional problems of underdevelopment and material exploitation in the specific context of the small dependent economies. More specifically, neoclassical and neoliberal theories of growth, characterised by the absence of historical understanding and awareness, do not deal adequately with the problems of designing an economic strategy for transforming small dependent economies, which must undergo this transformation during the present neocolonial phase (the poverty of orthodox analysis). In this regard, geographical determinism seeks to explain underdevelopment as a product of the limitations of the physical environment (i.e., in terms of soil, natural resources and climate), while cultural notions may also be taken into consideration.

Nevertheless, 'smallness' is not the cause, but the spatial, demographic and resource context in which socio-political relations are formed and developed, and the mode of production is organised. Hence, smallness is interpreted simply as constituting, in a certain sense, an additional dimension to underdevelopment; to the nature of the structural dependence of the small underdeveloped economies on international capitalism. As a consequence, the strength of indigenous political, social, cultural and economic forces vis-à-vis international capitalism is vastly inferior. In fact, international trade and capital flows are penetrating deeper into the workings of the small, dependent Caribbean nations affecting their specific production structures in general, and income distribution, productivity growth and employment in particular. Hence, the notion of smallness has to be given a historical perspective which allows for dynamic changes in population, resources, output, technology and competency.

The conjunction of production relations and productive forces in the Caribbean is of such a character that the structural dependence and underdevelopment of the process of production is, on the one hand, the lack of an organic link between the pattern and growth of domestic resource use and the pattern and growth of domestic demand and, on the other, the divergence between domestic demand and the actual needs of the broad masses of the population. Consequently, the linkages between: resources-technology-production-labour-demand-needs are of such a character and are organised in such a way that these communities have internalised through their social relations of production and the use of their productive forces, a pattern of consumption that does not represent the needs of the community, and a pattern of production not oriented to either domestic consumption or domestic needs (which lead to the perpetuation of the neocolonial mode) (Thomas, 1974, pp.58-59).

Yet, industrial strategies have not been seen to be pivotal in Caribbean economies; thus, they have not been developed in a systematic or coherent fashion as a centrepiece of their governments' approach to economic policy making. State interventions have usually been seen as 'reactions' to pressing problems, and the policies which flow from these interventions appear to be consonant with the market failure analysis. Therefore, the general concept of a developmental role for the state is rather alien to the general economic and political culture in the region.

Further, fiscal budgets in the Caribbean via the political process often reflect the view of the political parties in power, and the class and interest group biases are usually maintained. Hence, although this deliberate policy is used, in fact the politicisation of the budgetary process in Caribbean states highlights programmes and policies which are akin to what is called 'pork barrel policies'. This process has a great deal of importance in shaping the fiscal policies of Caribbean governments (Jones-Hendrickson, 1985, pp.83-84).

While the state has survived as a democratic institution (largely so), it lost a great deal of its effectiveness as a development tool because it was transformed into a mechanism for winning elections and meeting populist demands. Because of the 'winner takes all syndrome' in Caribbean nations, the state became an instrument of disintegration rather than an institution around which society could cohere to deal with the development challenge. In a small society, the state is a large institution as an employer and dispenser of resources - hence the intense desire by various groups, not just special interests, to capture it.

During the last two decades or so, neoliberal policies have been the central routes to modern economic solutions in the region. But there are serious doubts about whether these economic policies have been translated into significant social and economic development, endogenous competency, industrial growth and competitiveness. While appropriate macroeconomic policies can contribute much towards enhancing the performance of local economies, nevertheless such policies only deal with the 'symptoms' of deeper structural problems. For this reason, the construction of a production-based approach to economic development and a much sharper focus on strategic industrial policy are seen to be necessary to resolve these deeper problems, and offer concrete alternative solutions to Caribbean economies. Some alternative policy suggestions for the Caribbean development discourse in general, and tourism industry in particular, are outlined below.

Appropriate Macroeconomic Policies

As macroeconomic management is very important, there are a number of measures that the government could take in an effort to facilitate conscious development efforts.[8] Appropriate macroeconomic policies should pay particular attention to:
- a faster, non-inflationary growth of domestic demand;
- the efficiency and effectiveness of government spending and taxation;
- sound government finances/investments;
- the role of FDI, as well as the management of the national debt, which should be designed in the context of the long-term strategy for overall development;
- competitiveness (the role of imports/exports and the growth of exports);
- the relationship between the financial sector and the productive sector; and,
- the social and political environment (or socio-political characteristics).

In the Caribbean region, the general instability in employment and national income levels as well as a lack of diversification have led a number of people to seek job security in the public sector. As a result, government institutions and public sector bodies have been absorbing as much labour as possible, and recurrent government expenditure levels in the Caribbean are under continuous upward pressure. It is noticeable that characteristically large percentages of (re)current government expenditure of Caribbean fiscal budgets has been dedicated to wages and salaries and debt repayments throughout the 1990s, while both the levels and the shares of government capital expenditure and social expenditure are low (or very low).

On the revenue side, an important feature of Caribbean states' public finance is the high dependence on international trade taxes (import duties) as a percentage of government revenue. Faced by the difficult realities of budgetary 'stress', a proactive fiscal policy would emphasise a 'prudent' government expenditure management and planning (i.e., long-term productive investments in human capital formation, skills, technological capacity, R&D, information and innovation) and would consider other alternative sources of government revenue (e.g., Tobin tax).

The consumption patterns of the Household sector of the Caribbean islands, due to their proximity to the large North American markets, are more reflective of a developed rather than a developing economy. Local demand has been created for products and services in advance of the domestic economies' productive capacity to deliver these items (Higgins, 1994, p.1). The direct result is an endemically exaggerated propensity to import throughout the region coupled with low actual levels of national savings (which are inadequate to finance higher levels of investment expenditure). In this case, higher levels of output and income ensuing from a higher degree of capacity utilisation and a better utilisation of equipment can be the source of higher levels of savings required to match higher levels of investment (which will bring about further increase in output and income levels).[9]

Moreover, to the general domination of Caribbean islands by foreign economic activity and foreign interests as well as development problems and limitations associated with the structure of Caribbean economies (e.g., few or weak linkages between economic sectors, the 'agricultural paradox of the periphery', etc.), must be added the weak capability of their real sector; the inevitable result is low levels of exports and high levels of imports, i.e., trade deficits, balance-of-payments constraints. Moreover, contrary to the 'current orthodoxy', it appears important to emphasise that it would not suffice to establish (a small) technologically modern export sector(s). The aim should be to bring about a general improvement in the competency and efficiency of Caribbean economies, in the level of technological infrastructure they rely on, and in the quality of workmanship and service, so that more and more activities may become increasingly competitive. For this reason, aggressive export strategies for Caribbean countries must seek to strengthen their national capability first, if these economies are to improve their ability to compete on international grounds (i.e., export growth). What is actually required is balanced development consolidating local production and emphasising diversification of exports.

Higher Levels of Investments

It has been repeatedly argued that the hotel sector's high operating costs in Caribbean islands is a serious barrier which may discourage productive investment. Investments in the Caribbean region have usually been insufficient to bring about the full utilisation of existing resources. Besides, most foreign corporations have developed a rentier-like appetite for short-run capital gains, and the developmental needs of local economies have taken a secondary place.

The real problems facing Caribbean economies are slow economic growth and high and persistent unemployment and under-employment caused by inadequate demand, which lead to low levels of investment expenditure and innovation and constrain potential supply. Therefore, fiscal spending must be directed to long-term investments in technological infrastructure and human capital formation, technical change and its implementation. At the same time, private investments on the accelerators of endogenous competency are essential and highly desirable. It is these higher levels of investment that can raise the rates of capital accumulation and the profit rates in the region.

Investments in education, health, and nutrition of the poor in particular, not only meet real, basic needs of a wide spectrum of the Caribbean population and increase their welfare directly, but also enhance their capacities for productive labour. Indeed, such investments and/or higher wages can affect the productivity of the poor, thereby enabling them to earn higher incomes, which in turn would permit them to purchase the bundle of goods and services they need with their own earnings (necessary to open up their access to opportunities for a full life). But, on the other hand, social programmes are likely to have limited impact on Caribbean countries' economic growth and competitiveness unless the overall development strategies also contain explicit consideration of growth-generating policies and competency-inducing plans.

Strategic Planning - Industrial Strategies

The growth in dominance, global perspective and ambitions of the major financial and industrial corporations pose a significant threat for any national economy, especially the small ones. Most trade is directly controlled by the transnational corporations, and much of the rest is indirectly controlled by them via licensing, sub-contracting and franchising arrangements. Consequently, national economies and communities in general may suffer from the unrestricted activities of TNCs (Cowling, 1990, p.13). The ultimate consequence of transnationalism is to tear loose the productive capacities of Caribbean territories. Also, the direction in which Caribbean economies are pointed at present seems to be somewhat random, depending on the current state of the global market rather than based on long-term development plans. Thus, we have a basis for recommending a framework of, and establishing a role for, strategic planning in Caribbean nations.

The second and related reason for requiring strategic planning is the systematic short-termism of the market system. In this context, it is often argued that financial institutions usually adopt a short-term perspective with regard to investment, and impose this perspective on businesses (industries, hotels, resorts, etc.), especially the small ones. This generally means that incremental changes may be handled well by financial institutions, but more fundamental changes (involving processes or structure of production, for example) may not be handled well. Consequently, the financial institutions themselves can impose their short-term perspectives on new or small establishments, which will find difficulties to fund their own growth.

This sort of financial environment is hardly conducive to the rational planning of the long-term future of the industrial base. Short-term decision making is crowding out long-term issues, and leaving businesses weaker in the long term. Hence, within Caribbean economies, we need to establish institutional structures to plan for the future. Just as there are systemic arguments for relying on the creative dynamics of the market forces to play a centrally important role in Caribbean economies, there are parallel arguments for imposing on these market forces coherent strategies, within which they are allowed to operate (Cowling, 1990, pp. 11-12, 13-14).[10]

For local production to achieve its full potential, it is imperative that the state should stay focused and draw up thorough strategies for implementation. Initially it is important to divide consideration of the key issues related to the structure of Caribbean industries into three sections: (1) issues influenced by government policy and general policy issues; (2) issues influenced by specific industries or specific sectors; and, (3) market-driven issues. On this account, we limit strategic intervention to those parts of Caribbean economies where government intervention is going to have its most significant potential impact on their overall dynamism and intensive economic growth. Indeed, strategic industrial policy targets and centres around strategic sectors, which can be expected to fuel future economic growth. By recognising differentiation of propulsive sectors and industries, policy can address the problems that are rooted in the development of these sectors and industries, and thus become effective.

In some sectors (such as, tourism, entertainment, agro-processing, food and beverage, etc.), the region already has a strong basis on which to build. These sectors require significant investment expenditure, rejuvenation and repositioning, and have to address a number of serious economic, social and environmental issues simultaneously; but all of these problems are - in principle - solvable. Provided that the immediate problems are solved, the targeted sectors are clearly capable of considerable further growth (Clayton, 2001, p.7). In fact, the mutually beneficial relationship between tourism and agro-industry can provide the foundation which alternative endogenous development strategies can build on. With a rigorous priorities formation, scarce resources will increasingly be allocated efficiently, productivity and profitability will increase, and the propulsive and dynamic sectors will become increasingly attractive to the private sector.

In addition, the growth process is expected to lead to a widening of the local markets,[11] which in turn will require and/or bring about better transportation and communications systems. Hence, after resources have been developed and/or put to use, changes in technology will broaden the Caribbean production base, will provide sufficient stimulus to the mobilisation of resources of all kinds and/or the inducement to invest, will bring about a net addition to the effective use of local resources and, therefore, to the overall growth of the region.

The proposed approach takes into account the inter-relations among a number of 'stylised facts' such as domestic resources, capital, social structure, the level of technology and skills, scale and transformation. Such a pragmatic approach can successfully contribute to long-term supply-side initiatives aimed at creating or promoting particular dynamic sectors and prioritised activities, and create external economies and economies of scale, conditions and opportunities, conducive to faster growth of existing and incoming enterprises (a 'big push'). Economies of scale and learning will bring about multiple effects on, and changes in, the structure of local economies. The object, of course, would be to increase value-added to the local sectors and strengthen intersectoral linkages (e.g., tourism and commodity production sectors), which would then be capable of spilling their expansionary forces into other sectors and activities: the support and development of indigenous resources, firms and industries; the maximum utilisation of planned investments (mainly in R&D and skills); the exploitation of external economies (thereby dealing with issues of scale and scope); the removal of bottlenecks on the demand side which are imposed by the narrow size of the local markets and their poor manufacturing base; an improvement in the range of services likely to be available to people and to industry (transportation, information); the application of productivity-enhancing production methods and techniques so as to raise efficiency and competitiveness; the diversification, restructuring, transformation and strategic repositioning of local economic activities; and the capacity to correct the region's tendency towards external disequilibrium as well as high dependency on foreign economic activity, and withstand the effects of future structural changes and cyclical downswings.

Production and Operations Quality

In this age of rapid technological changes, a quality emphasis should encompass the entire organisation of production of Caribbean economies, from suppliers to customers, including: equipment layout; purchasing and installation of proper machinery and equipment; layout strategy (capacity needs, inventory requirements, etc.); facility location and expansion; supporting facilities and utilities; sanitary arrangements and utility specifications; refrigeration specifications; maintenance training; products technology training; implementation of strict quality control programmes; and just-in-time decisions and scheduling.

For both Caribbean businesses and Caribbean national economies to compete effectively in the global economy, products and services must meet global quality and price expectations. As the countries (and the whole Caribbean region) face crucial challenges, especially in light of strong international competition, it is essential to ensure that quality standards and value for money are improved. Inferior products will harm the firms' revenues and profitability, and will further deteriorate the balance of payments of Caribbean economies (Heizer and Render, 1996, pp.79-80).

Politico-institutional Changes

Analysing the institutional conditions in today's Caribbean reveals substantial failures in the region, which has largely suffered from impeding prevailing institutions as well as a lack of institutional arrangements. Caribbean governance structures lack the ability to prevent arbitrary political action, and rely heavily on clientelism and favouritism.

Furthermore, policies of the weak or soft Caribbean states (in Myrdal's sense: what characterises a 'weak' state is not the extent of intervention but its quality) are captured by vested interests, dominated by too many rent-seeking activities of lobbying groups, and can hardly implement governance structures that decisively promote economic reforms (Myrdal, 1968; Ahrens, 1997, p.119). Consequently, it is unlikely that significant state intervention would be warranted in the Caribbean given the inadequate capacity and competence of government institutions; the institutional deficiencies and impediments to economic development in the region.

For this reason, the pursuit of thorough Developmental State strategies and policies requires a careful moulding of appropriate institutions, mechanisms and instruments which are necessary for the formulation and implementation of selective interventions in certain key sectors (like tourism, food processing, agro-industrial sectors, etc.) of Caribbean economies. By establishing the appropriate institutional network, strategies and policies can be designed and incentives created to channel resources and decision-makers' commitment into those local productive activities that are compatible with sustained economic development, and prompt private firms and industries to carry out long-term investments (Ahrens, 1997, p.118).

Thus, Developmental State action needs to be accompanied by institutional reforms, which not only lay the foundation of effective execution and enforcement of production-oriented policies but also create the suitable environment for local socio-economic development.

Other Important Issues

The 'new' tourism has already begun taking on a different shape - responding to, and internalising a number of signals (social, economic, cultural, technological, ecological and institutional) that emanate from the global environment. Flexible specialisation as a core element of the 'new tourism best practice' is driven by new information technologies as well as new managerial and organisational principles of creativity, scope economies, product differentiation and niche markets (Poon, 1993, p.274).

Thus, much more attention has to be placed on these important issues, as the new tourism is a highly complex and volatile industry. Likewise, as new tourism depends upon environmental quality, the issue of environmental protection has to be accorded a greater priority by policy makers in order to cope with a product that has already begun to deteriorate. In fact, although the Caribbean environment is the islands' basic tourism resource, there appears to be a huge gap between this recognition and putting effective controls in place. Therefore, a much closer link is required between tourism policy and environmental control and preservation.

In addition, good air access to Caribbean islands from all the main generating markets is very important. As the Caribbean is highly dependent and vulnerable to changes in the structure of air services, the region is facing the prospect of becoming a 'service taker' in its main market regions.

Yet, the growing influence of the major Computer Reservation Systems (CRS) in the USA, Canada and Europe is a further source of concern to the Caribbean. The only solution for the region's carriers may be to form cooperative alliances in the key areas of marketing and scheduling with some of the major carriers in order to avoid being entirely left out (given that cost-effective and efficient marketing and distribution are crucial to the success of tourism promotion).

Indeed, the building of strategic alliances and partnerships within and outside of the tourism industry is expected to enhance the competitiveness of the sector (Poon, 1993, p.273). This action can:

- assist towards establishing a Caribbean-wide air transport policy and promote regional cooperation in air services including marketing agreements;
- improve airport infrastructure;
- monitor Computer Reservation Systems developments closely and ensure that the region in general is not disadvantaged in this area;

- strengthen the capital and management bases of the airlines;
- monitor and forecast air transport developments in so far as they affect the Caribbean.

With cooperative arrangements and regional approaches to tourism, Caribbean territories can share the huge expenses of building marketing intelligence systems, information technology networks as well as the promotion and public relations campaigns. Likewise, to develop any viable food production programme, a joint CARICOM (Caribbean Community) approach should be undertaken. Most individual Caribbean islands cannot grow most of the basic foodstuffs, but collectively this goal could be achieved in order to meet the demands of the region. It is indeed these cooperative arrangements and united effort that can considerably increase the strength of the bargaining power of the entire region (Poon, 1993, p.276).

Conclusion

Capitalist growth has always been growth with increasing disequilibrium, constant technological revolutions and growing concentration and centralisation of capital. These development trends of capitalist production are closely linked to production for profit and competition. Uneven development is fundamental and inevitable condition of the capitalist mode of production. Yet, the unevenness of development and growth in all capitalist economies over time is matched by an unevenness between different geographical areas, regions and nations, as market forces tend to promote the concentration of growth in some areas at the expense of others.

The recent globalisation as the new face of imperialism has continued to take advantage of the less-developed countries, by appropriating the lion's share of their resources and granting them the 'widow's mite' in return. The resultant unequal exchange - coupled with the emerging role of regionalisation as an unevenly developing, heterogeneous and multi-dimensional phenomenon in a globalising world - has served to accentuate and augment the vicious web of dependency and underdevelopment in the Third World. In this global era, however, - contrary to the current orthodoxy - the solution may be to bring the 'nation state back to business'.

Notes

1. Recently, the USA and other leading capitalist countries appear to emphasise more the virtues of the 'Western liberal humanitarian democracy' based on consensus, instead of the frequent use of military power, for three main reasons: (i) it creates socio-political instability which may discourage foreign investment; (ii) it creates strong anti-Western, anti-American, anti-imperialistic feelings; and, (iii) it strengthens left-wing political parties and/or revolutionary groups.
2. The concept 'imperialism' is both relevant and scientific for analysing the relations of domination of some nations by others.
3. Further political and diplomatic manipulation for further exploitation.

4. Employing a neo-Marxist analytical framework over that of globalisation not only provides a better understanding but also points towards social forces of resistance and opposition that through political action may bring about necessary change. The main aim should be to demonstrate, by means of quite different analyses and thorough concrete alternatives, a wide opposition to the dominant ideology of neo-liberalism and the dictatorship of capitalism over global society.
5. Eugene Black, an expert on foreign aid and a former President and Chairman of the World Bank.
6. For further discussion see: Thomas, 2000, pp.8-22; Girvan, 2000, pp.65-87.
7. Also, Cowling (1990, p.15) identifies a third central tendency within modern market economies: 'centripetalism'. These fundamental tendencies (i.e., transnationalism, short-termism and centripetalism) are all interrelated, and all related to an underlying concentration of power, and hence decision making, in modern capitalist economies (Cowling, 1990, p.12). But these tendencies, structural dependence and foreign domination on the other hand, can be the basis for recommending a framework of, and establishing a role for, national strategic planning in Caribbean countries (within which to approach and position the transnational corporations and the powerful foreign interests).
8. Recent multi-dimensional global changes have arguably cast doubts on the ability of national governments to pursue independent and effective economic policies.
9. One may recall the post-Keynesian analysis of growth and income distribution.
10. There is an on-going debate on the relevance of the nation state in this global era, given the very real constraints that the global political economy imposes. However, even under the current conditions of globalisation and liberalisation, and the pressures from international organisations such as the WTO and the IMF, Caribbean governments still have room for Developmental State policies (Chang, 1998; Karagiannis, 2002). Also, research suggests that nations which do best in the international arena are those which can manage change and use their national institutional arrangements to protect their national economies from international vagaries and disorder (Tyson, 1992; Chang, 1994; Singh, 1995, 1998; Boyer and Drache, 1996; Karagiannis, 2002; - among others).
11. Besides, stopover visitors expand the domestic markets in the region.

References

Amin, S. (1974), *Accumulation on a World Scale*, Vols. I&II, Monthly Review Press, London.
_____ (1997), *Capitalism in the Age of Globalisation*, Zed Books, London.
Arestis, P. and Sawyer, M.C. (eds) (1998), *The Political Economy of Economic Policies*, Macmillan, London.
Baker, D., Epstein, G. and Pollin, R. (eds) (1998), *Globalisation and Progressive Economic Policy*, Cambridge University Press, Cambridge.
Baran, P.A. (1957), *The Political Economy of Growth*, Monthly Review Press, New York.
Baran, P.A. and Sweezy, P.M. (1966), 'Notes on the theory of Imperialism', *New Left Review*, March.
Benn, D. and Hall, K. (eds) (2000), *Globalisation: A Calculus of Inequality*, Ian Randle Publishers, Kingston.
Boyer, R. and Drache, D. (eds) (1996), *States against Markets: The Limits of Globalisation*, Routledge, London.

Cowling, K. (1990), 'The Strategic Approach to Economic and Industrial Policy', in K. Cowling and R. Sugden (eds), *A New Economic Policy for Britain: Essays on the Development of Industry*, Manchester University Press, Manchester, pp.6-34.

Emmanuel, A. (1972), *Unequal Exchange: A Study of the Imperialism of Trade*, New Left Books, London.

Frank, A.G. (1971), *Capitalism and Underdevelopment in Latin America*, Monthly Review Press, New York.

Girvan, N. (2000), 'Globalisation and Counter-Globalisation: The Caribbean in the Context of the South', in D. Benn and K. Hall (eds), *Globalisation: A Calculus of Inequality*, Ian Randle Publishers, Kingston, pp.65-87.

Kaldor, N. (1978), *Further Essays on Economic Theory*, Duckworth, London.

Krugman, P. (ed.) (1986), *Strategic Trade Policy and the New International Economics*, MIT Press, Cambridge (Mass).

_____ (1991), *Geography and Trade*, MIT Press, Cambridge (Mass).

Lopez, J. (1998), 'Growth Resumption and Long-run Growth in Latin American Economies: A Modest Proposal', *International Papers in Political Economy*, Vol. 5:1.

Myrdal, G. (1957), *Economic Theory and Underdeveloped Regions*, Duckworth, London.

OECD (1987), *Structural Adjustment and Economic Performance*, OECD, Paris.

Petras, J. and Veltmeyer, H. (2001), *Globalisation Unmasked: The New Face of Imperialism*, Zed Books, London.

Romer, P.M (1986), 'Increasing Returns and Long-run Growth', *Journal of Political Economy*, Vol. 94:5, pp.1002-37.

_____ (1990), 'Endogenous Technological Change', *Journal of Political Economy*, Vol. 98, pp.71-102.

_____ (1994), 'The Origins of Endogenous Growth', *The Journal of Economic Perspectives*, Vol. 8:1, pp.3-22.

Sawyer, M.C. (1989), *The Challenge of Radical Political Economy*, Harvester Wheatsheaf, Hemel Hempstead.

_____ (1992), 'Reflections on the Nature and Role of Industrial Policy', *Metroeconomica*, Vol. 43, pp.51-73.

Solow, R. (1991), 'Growth Theory', in D. Greenaway, M. Bleaney and I. Stewart (eds), *Companion to Contemporary Economic Thought*, Routledge, London.

_____ (1994), 'Perspectives on Growth Theory', *The Journal of Economic Perspectives*, Vol. 8:1, pp.45-54.

Thomas, C.Y. (1974), *Dependence and Transformation*, Monthly Review Press, New York and London.

_____ (2000), 'Globalisation as Paradigm Shift: Response from the South', in D. Benn and K. Hall (eds), *Globalisation: A Calculus of Inequality*, Ian Randle Publishers, Kingston, pp.8-22.

Tobin, J. (1996), 'Prologue', in M.U. Haq, I. Kaul and I. Grunberg (eds), *The Tobin Tax: Coping with Financial Volatility*, Oxford University Press, New York and Oxford.

United Nations Development Programme (UNDP) (1992), *Human Development Report 1992*, Oxford University Press, New York and Oxford.

_____ (1996), *Human Development Report 1996*, Oxford University Press, New York and Oxford.

_____ (1997), *Human Development Report 1997*, Oxford University Press, New York and Oxford.

Chapter 2

Are There Any Limits to 'Globalisation'? International Trade, Capital Flows and Borders[1]

Grahame F. Thompson

Introduction

In this chapter, I raise some issues about the nature of economic borders and their continued pertinence in the context of the debate about 'globalisation'. In large part this has to do with borders around national economies. It is concerned with both the conceptual implications of the way economics has set about thinking the nature of borders and the effects of such national borders on the economic interactions that take place across and around those borders. In looking at these issues I ask the question: 'Are there any limits to globalisation?' The strong globalisation thesis would seem to imply an ever expanding universe of economic interdependency and integration between national economies, so that the pertinence of national borders for economic activity disappears, but why should this be the case?

Clearly, for economics national borders set up the issue of 'international trade' as a subcategory of the general analysis of trade. Indeed, international trade is itself part of the whole question of cross-border economic interactions involving capital flows, technological flows, migration, environmental pollution, etc, i.e., anything that involves a potential cross-border economic interaction.

All these issues are a major concern of political geography and international relations where there is a massive literature on the constructions and consequences of frontiers and borders.[2] The main focus of this literature is on the formation and dissolution of borders, on cross-border activities and what this does to the notion of 'territoriality', and on the regulation and management of this kind of activity. It is useful for thinking about the consequences of regulating and managing the activity of cross-border (economic) interactions. While these emphases are understandable and important from the point of view of geography and of international relations, the remarks below concentrate upon something that is relatively neglected by these approaches (though not totally ignored by them, of course). What is asked is the status of national borders in economic analysis and the way in which economic activity itself 'deals' with borders. This is then related to the way borders (or their supposed dissolution) is linked to globalisation. Hence, while the IR literature and political geography are more concerned with the *de-jure* consequences of economic borders, here we are more interested in their *de-facto* consequences. How do they affect what private agents do and how the market reacts to them? Therefore, we are asking how economic activity 'governs itself' in respect to borders rather than how it is governed by other agencies (Thompson, 2001). Of course, the *de-facto* and the *de-jure* are not unconnected.[3] They feed off one another and are interconnected. But the point here is to lay the stress on the *de-facto* in the first instance.

Borders and Globalisation

The stimulus for these remarks is an ongoing interest in 'globalisation' (Hirst and Thompson, 1999). It is well known that the strong globalisation thesis postulates that national borders are increasingly irrelevant for economic activity since trade interdependency and investment integration sweep the globe. Although not all supporters of this approach would go along with Kenichi Ohmae's rather extreme presentation of the case (Ohmae, 1990, 1995) he does have the virtue of putting the issue starkly and saying what he thinks the nature of the new global 'borderless' economic system would look like. And this prefigures much of what more cautious observers would be forced to argue as the ultimate outcome of any commitment to a strong globalisation position.

Ohmae argues that this new global economy is an 'inter-linked' one in which 'stateless' corporations are now the prime movers, centred on North America, Europe and Japan. He also contends that macroeconomic and industrial policy intervention by national governments can only distort and impede the rational process of resource allocation by corporate decisions and consumer choices, which are now made on a global scale. The emergence of 'electronic highways' enables anyone to, in principle, plug into the global market place. Hence, what all corporate players need to do in order to prosper is to shake off their nationally-orientated bureaucratic style of management, and the state intervention that goes along with it, and enter the new world of open global marketing and production networks. The vision is clearly one of a large inter-linked network of producers and consumers plugged into an efficiently operating 'level playing field' of open and competitive international and globalised economic relationships. International markets provide coordinative and governance mechanisms in and of themselves: national strategies and policy intervention are likely merely to distort them. The era of effective national economies, and state policies corresponding to them, is over. The market will, and should, decide.

The fact that the international economy looks nothing like that sketched by Ohmae, and does not seem to be converging towards it, should not divert us from the power of the imagery he offers. In fact, of course, his imagery is a familiar one. It is that of a market system of the ideal type (neoclassical perfect competition). In principle, the conception of a market is constructed by economics as unconstrained by space (and time, in many respects). There are no necessary 'borders' around the notion of a market in a spatial sense. Nor is there a natural 'duration' for market exchange, since it exists out of historical time; it is 'timeless'.

In effect what has just been said implies that there are no transaction costs associated with market exchange. Where there are no costs associated with the pursuit of the gains from trade, international trade (or any other trade) is only limited by the extent of the division of labour (usually expressed as 'the extent of the market'). However, with extensive property rights and transaction costs, 'the extent of the market' (and thus a 'boundary' around the market) can be established by calculating the (marginal) transaction costs and benefits of market exchange as opposed to hierarchical organisation.[4] The 'externalities' of market exchange, measured in terms of transaction costs, can be 'internalised' via the activity being brought within the confines of the firm or other hierarchical form of organisation. In this way, 'social costs' and 'private costs' are combined and reduced to the latter. In fact, anywhere where social cost and private costs diverge, an externality is created; and externalities imply a limit or boundary within market exchange - they set up a transaction cost. Thus, in this way, property rights, transaction costs and externalities do in effect put potential boundaries round the market, and create the conditions for limits on the extent of market exchange. The consequences of this are taken up later in the chapter. But, these limits are not territorial limits in a spatial sense; in the sense that the market is necessarily 'confined' by them to a particular location or national territory (at least not in the first instance - see below). The boundary is drawn in the first instance organisationally or institutionally, which need not coincide with a definite geographical territory.

Measuring the Extent of Trade Globalisation

The motivation for the following empirical analysis is provided by the evidence presented in Table 2.1. If we look at merchandise trade flows between the main economic blocs expressed as a proportion of the originating country/bloc GDP then, for the most part, very low percentages of GDP seem to have been traded by the late 1990s.

Only Western Europe appears anywhere close to being an integrated trading zone with 18 per cent of its combined GDP traded between the countries of Western Europe. The only other relationship that appears significant is that between the East Asian traders and North America, where the former exported just under 11 per cent of their GDP to North America, mostly to the USA (the results for intra-East Asian trade are very rough estimates and we should not be at all confident about these).

Of course, there are a number of objections that could be mounted to this way of measuring the extent of trade 'globalisation'. The first of these objections is that it concentrates upon merchandise trade only, which is made up of agricultural, mineral and manufacturing trade. This ignores service trade which, it is often claimed, represents a new and dynamic element in the overall globalisation of trade. But this is not altogether the case. While service trade has undoubtedly grown over the last thirty years in absolute terms, as a proportion of overall world trade it has remained markedly stable at about 20 per cent (19.6 per cent in 1975, 20.5 per cent in 1998). Thus, by concentrating just on merchandise trade we are still capturing a roughly stable 80 per cent of all world trade.

Table 2.1   Merchandise trade flows as a percentage of originating Triad bloc/ country GDP (1998)

	To	North America	Western (a) Europe	Japan (J)	East Asian (b) Traders	J + E.A.T.
From						
North America		3.8	2.0	0.7	1.1	1.8
Western Europe (a)		2.3	18.0	0.4	1.0	1.4
Japan (J)		3.3	2.0	-	3.0	3.0
East Asian Traders (b)		10.7	6.9	4.1	(11.6)	(15.7)
J + E.A.T.		14.0	8.9	4.1	(14.6)	(18.7)

Notes:
(a) Western Europe = EU + Switzerland, Turkey, Norway, Malta, Liechtenstein and the states of the former Yugoslavia.
(b) East Asian Traders (EAT): China, Hong Kong, Taiwan, Korea, Malaysia, Thailand and Singapore.
() Figures in brackets are very rough estimates.
Sources: 'WTO Annual Report 2000, Volume II International Trade Statistics', derived from various tables; World Bank, 'World Economic Indicators 2000', Table 4.2; 'Taiwan Statistical Data Book 2000'.

A more important objection is that the data in Table 2.1 does not compare like with like. Merchandise trade is expressed as a proportion of total GDP, which is made up of a number of components other than merchandise output, including service output and the government sector. Service output and the government sector have been expanding at the expense of the merchandise trade and are now a bigger contributor to overall GDP than is the traditional merchandise sector. The data in Table 2.1 need adjusting to take this into account (see also Irwin, 1996).

The results of such an adjustment are shown in the next table - Table 2.2. In this case, merchandise trade is compared with just the merchandise component of GDP as measured by the value added in agriculture, mineral extraction (including petroleum) and manufacturing. Again, the outstanding result relates to Western Europe, where a staggering 80 per cent of merchandise output is traded amongst the European nations. Clearly, as far as merchandise trade is concerned, Western

Europe does represent a highly integrated trading zone. But once again, with the possible exception of the relationship between the East Asian traders and North America, and to a lesser extent intra-North America (USA and Canada), the proportions are still relatively low despite the fact that we are dealing with the most mature part of international trade (and several years after NAFTA was established).

A further objection to these figures is that they need to be cast in a 'real value' and PPP context. This would allow for the effects of exchange rate variations that might produce a distorted picture for any particular year's figures. Other than the fact that comprehensive PPP data is not available for the kinds of adjustments needed to recast Table 2.2 data in these terms, such an adjustment is more relevant for comparisons over time than it is for a cross-sectional analysis conducted at a particular point in time (see Hirst and Thompson, 2000, where a constant price comparisons over time along these lines is conducted).

The final objection considered here relates to the relationship between these trade figures and international investment. One of the clear trends since the 1970s, and particularly over the last twenty years, has been the growth of FDI. To a large extent, FDI substitutes for international trade as businesses look for competitive advantage by supplying foreign markets from output platforms located in the foreign economy. Thus, to some extent, trade and FDI are substitutes. What is needed, therefore, is a way of taking account of the 'lost' trade that might have taken place had such FDI not developed. The counter-factual is the trade that FDI displaced.

This is very difficult to do for the range of countries and blocs shown in the Tables so far. It requires a detailed analysis of what firms have been doing and the data cannot be generated from ordinary FDI or Balance of Payments returns. Only the USA and Japan provide anywhere near the kind of data required, which is based upon surveys of the business activities of their own MNCs and of those foreign MNCs located on their domestic territories. What I do here is take the USA as a mini case-study since it has by far the most comprehensive data which is the most easily accessible (see Mataloni, 2000; and Zeile, 2000). First this requires the rendering of the kind of analysis undertaken so far for North America into one based solely on the USA and then a series of further delicate adjustments to make the data as compatible as possible with the counter-factual.

Let us take total US GDP figures first, and compare them to US merchandise exports to the various country groupings used so far. Thus, here, we are doing an analysis for the USA similar to that contained in Table 2.1. This is shown as the first line in Table 2.3. The second line in the Table then adjusts for the extent of the relevant activity of US MNCs in the host country groupings. Here, we first add to merchandise trade between the USA and the countries the gross 'value added' of the merchandise output of US companies operating in Canada, Western Europe, etc. separately, and then add back the total value added of US MNCs to the 'domestic' GDP of the USA. So, the presumption here is that if US MNCs were not operating abroad, they would have supplied the foreign markets with the same output from the domestic US economy, which would have been an addition to domestic US GDP. These new totals are then expressed as percentages as before. Thus, these adjustments complete a comparable analysis to that shown in Table 2.1.

Table 2.2   Estimate of merchandise trade flows as a percentage of originating Triad bloc/country merchandise GDP (1998)

	To	North America	Western Europe (a)	Japan (J)	East Asian Traders (b)	J + E.A.T.
From						
North America		3.8	2.0	0.7	1.1	1.8
Western Europe (a)		2.3	18.0	0.4	1.0	1.4
Japan (J)		3.3	2.0	-	3.0	3.0
East Asian Traders (b)		10.7	6.9	4.1	(11.6)	(15.7)
J + E.A.T.		14.0	8.9	4.1	(14.6)	(18.7)

Notes:
(a) Western Europe = EU + Switzerland, Turkey. Norway, Malta, Liechtenstein and the states of the former Yugoslavia.
(b) East Asian Traders (EAT): China, Hong Kong, Taiwan, Korea, Malaysia, Thailand and Singapore.
() Figures in brackets are very rough estimates.
Sources: Compiled from WTO, 'Annual Report 2000, Volume II, International Trade Statistics', various tables; World Bank, 'World Development Indicators 2000'; 'Taiwan Statistical Data Book 2000'; UN, 'Statistical Yearbook 1999'; OECD, 'National Accounts 1999'.

The third line in Table 2.3 begins to do for the US case what the Table 2.2 analysis did above, that is concentrate solely on the merchandise sector in respect to both trade and GDP. Line three shows the position in respect to the merchandise sector for the USA, then line 4 adjusts for the relevant operations of US MNCs in respect to just their merchandise output and trade, again as before. Adding back the 'lost' merchandise GDP now located abroad gives a basis for making the relevant ratio calculations.

Table 2.3 US GDP, merchandise GDP and trade with initial 'one way' MNC adjustment

Trade to	Canada	Western Europe	Japan	E.A.T.s	J + E.A.T.s
1] Total GDP unadjusted	1.9	2.0	0.7	1.1	1.8
2] Total GDP with MNC adjustment	2.2	4.2	0.8	1.3	2.1
3] Merchandise GDP unadjusted	8.7	9.2	3.3	5.2	8.5
4] Merchandise GDP with MNC adjustment	9.3	17.9	3.3	5.5	8.8

The results contained in Table 2.3 we can call a set of 'one way' adjustments. However, they are not the ends of the matter. Not only are US MNCs operating and producing abroad, but foreign MNCs are also operating on US territory and supplying the domestic US market from there. This can also be considered as a substitute for trade with the USA, but more importantly from the point of view of US GDP it in effect acts as a 'contribution' to domestic US GDP. If foreign companies were not located on US territory and supplying the domestic US market from there we are presuming that they would export to the USA instead, which would thus form part of foreign countries GDP and exports. So, the counter-factual this time must take away this part of US GDP, and repeat the calculations on this basis but with the foreign trade totals similarly adjusted. The results of these calculations are shown in Table 2.4, again first for recalculated 'total GDP' (line 1) and then for just recalculated 'merchandise GDP' (line 2). These we can call a set of 'two way' adjustments, and this is about as far as we can go given the limitations of the data and the kinds of sensible counter-factual that it is possible to construct.

It should be clear that while what has just been done for the US case is in principle possible for the other countries and groupings contained in the earlier Tables, this would be a formidable and complicated exercise which might quickly begin to lose relevance and credibility. How far can we presume, for instance, that FDI based output is a prefect substitute for trade? And gathering sensible data on the EATs in respect to the extent of the MNCs operations is more or less impossible.

Table 2.4   US GDP, merchandise GDP and trade with final 'two way' MNC adjustment

Trade to	Canada	Western Europe	Japan	E.A.T.s	J + E.A.T.s
1] 'Total U.S. GDP' with domestic adjustments	2.4	4.4	0.8	1.4	2.2
2] 'Merchandise U.S. GDP' with domestic adjustments	10.9	20.5	3.4	6.4	9.8

But what this analysis does is to point up that, even after all these adjustments, there remains a surprisingly low level of trade integration both in the case of the main blocs and in respect to the USA on its own. Clearly, the introduction of the merchandise GDP adjustment does alter the picture considerably, particularly in the case of trade between the USA and Western Europe.

Borders and Barriers

The appearance of clear national borders on a global scale in the latter part of the 19th century and early years of the 20th century - and the rise of the discourses and practices of national economic management - raised the prospects of these being used as instruments of economic regulation and governance, hence the emphasis on tariffs and quotas (or capital controls). But note how these are viewed as an impediment and an obstacle to trade. National borders and their tariffs and quotas distort the normal or natural pattern of economic relationships. The market should not be 'bounded' by any of these restrictions on its embrace. At a fundamental level, even the existence of national borders as such represent an impediment to the 'natural' development of market forces (since these borders inevitably pose some obstacle to an interaction); so, the advent of modern globalisation and a 'borderless world' is a triumph from the point of view of those supporting the position most clearly announced by the likes of Ohmae. It is almost despite national borders that trade across such frontiers takes place. The problem is to overcome these 'barriers' to trade.[5]

How is international trade analysed in economics? Despite the seeming sophistication of much international trade theory, when it comes to the empirics the approach here is still fairly simple. At heart it relies on operationalising a 'gravity' model.[6] This is so whether a factor endowment approach or a relative price approach is used to theoretically model trade. Empirically, trade is thought to be positively related to the 'size' of the communities between which it takes place and negatively related to the distance between them. This can be written as an equation, and then tested against the evidence of actual flows (Figure 2.1 below).

Note here how this model pertains to any trade flow between any community or nodal points. It is general to 'trade' as such, whether this is domestic or international. As we will see, this poses problems for the specification of what is distinctive about international trade.

But, as usual, there are other problems as well. Generating a testable model relies upon a number of 'short cuts'. The distance (D) between nodal points is not difficult, once those points have been chosen. For international trade, these points are usually taken as some representative city or population agglomeration within the country. As well as the populations of countries, some measure of their wealth (like GDP per head - GDP/P) is often also included.

Then there follow a series of dummy or 'control' variables designed to capture other relationships between countries that might stimulate trade between them. These can include such aspects as whether countries share a common border (BDR), whether they share a common language (LAN), whether they have had some colonial connections (COL), whether they belong to a common trade bloc (BLOC - e.g., EU, ASEAN, NAFTA, etc.), what the position is in respect to common jurisdictional standards and the legal enforceability of contracts between them (CORPT), and so on.

The variable D is the most consistent and significant explanatory variable of international trade (see Learner and Storper, 2000). But an interesting feature of recent trade empirics is the central importance that has emerged for the 'cultural' determinants of trade specified by the dummy or control variables just mentioned. As will be seen, once the contributions of, say, migration (which can be proxied by variables such as BDR, LAN and COL), and different legal cultures (CORPT) have been accounted for in regression analyses, the specific contribution of the growth of GDP as such as a determinant of trade growth is severely limited, and indeed becomes less than 1 in many cases. The significance of this is stressed below.

Figure 2.1 Gravity model equation for trade

$$Tij = a + b\left(\frac{GDPi}{Pi}\right) + c\left(\frac{GDPj}{Pj}\right) - d\left(Dij\right)$$

$$+ e\left(BDRij\right) + f\left(LANij\right) + g\left(COLij\right)$$

$$+ h\left(BLOCij\right) + k\left(CORPTij\right) + u$$

Another important approach to the way trade is considered in respect to borders is illustrated by the schema of different types of trade shown in Figure 2.2.

Figure 2.2 Types of trade

1. THOSE GOODS EXCHANGED ON 'ORGANISED MARKETS' (e.g., minerals, raw material, primary agricultural products)

2. THOSE GOODS EXCHANGED ACCORDING TO 'REFERENCE PRICES' (e.g., processed raw materials, chemicals, basic standardised components)

3. THOSE DIFFERENTIATED GOODS AND SERVICES EXCHANGED ON THE BASIS OF 'NETWORKS' (e.g., complex manufactured goods and services)

Note: This schema is based upon Rauch (1999).

International trade can be divided into three categories. The first is that traded on organised exchanges like minerals and agricultural products (primary products), where price is established according to classic market mechanisms. Here one might think of markets like the Chicago grain markets, the London metal exchanges, the Rotterdam spot market for oil. The second category is intermediate goods that are traded according to 'reference prices' quoted in specialist publications and the like (such as chemicals, processed raw materials, etc.). For the prices of these goods you would consult a reference manual or trade price book. These are readily available in an openly published form. And the third type of trade is differentiated manufactured goods and services where there is no organised market or quoted reference prices. Here we do not find a uniform standard price but rather more of 'one-off' pricing, differentiated according to complex networks of supply.

Unlocking the complex determinants of trade with respect to each of these categories is not easy (see Rauch, 1999). Although the first, and to a lesser extent the second, of these categories display a high international trade to production ratio so that a high proportion of their output is exported, these are declining in importance as components of total international trade. These categories of trade are also less sensitive to the 'cultural variables' mentioned above in the context of the gravity model, so they are more closely correlated with the growth of wealth and income. But what has expanded rapidly is the third category, particularly complex manufactured goods. And this has a relatively low production to trade ratio, when all the other variables that determine trade have been accounted for. The key here is these 'cultural' influences, which act at the expense of income growth as such. There is a lot of production but relatively lower levels of it are exported abroad as a pure consequence of income growth rather than as a consequence of other variables like distance, migration and legal differences, etc.

Thus, we have a situation where those categories of trade with high income elasticity related production propensity to export are declining in significance, while that category with a lower income elasticity related production propensity for export is increasing in importance. Perhaps this is at least one of the reasons for the relative lack of international trade, as opposed to domestic trade within a country.

And the reasons for these different propensities are interesting and important. Where there is an organised market for trade, as in the case of the first category, the organisation of the exchange is relatively easy and cheap. Transaction costs are low. But with sophisticated manufactured goods, there are no organised markets to facilitate exchanges. Rather, they are traded in the context of often 'one-off', lengthy, and complex networks of supply and distribution. Hence, manufactures have to set up webs of distribution systems, which are often singular and unique for each category of good. They require the seeking out of trading partners and the securing of a network of participants. But above all, these systems are costly to set-up and maintain - transaction costs are high. This may account for the lack of trading in these goods across frontiers relative to their trading at home, and put a limit or constraint on the extent of their expansion. It is just too costly, for instance, for US manufacturers to secure distribution systems for their goods in Japan, so there are low levels of US exports to Japan, as shown in Tables 2.1-2.4 above.

Comparing markets and networks in this way is instructive at a number of levels. It could mean there might be an optimal extent to globalisation - that there will not be a continual growth of economic interdependency and integration between countries as implied by the strong globalization thesis - but rather there may be legitimate limits to globalisation. And further, these limits may be fast approaching for the advanced countries in particular. This we look at now in greater detail.

To get back to the specific effect of national borders on international trade and the globalisation debate, there has recently been something of a test case analysis of this involving the border between the USA and Canada. If globalisation has emerged, then surely this border would have been one of the first to lose its pertinence as far as trade, investment and migration is concerned. But it has not. The careful analyses by McCallum (1995), Engel and Rogers (1996), and Helliwell (1998) demonstrate the continued central importance of this border as an 'obstacle' to trade (and other flows) between the USA and Canada even as tariffs and quotas have been eliminated, NAFTA established, and other barriers removed. So, these analyses are confirmed by the empirical presentation and adjustments conducted above in Tables 2.3 and 2.4 for the case of US and Canadian trade. What these analyses do is begin to confront the mysteries of the 'missing trade' at the international level (Trefler, 1995). Far from there being an 'excess' of international trade there is not enough of it, and this goes for capital flows as well which is discussed below.

The great advantage of these approaches is that they are able to compare Canada-USA cross-border trade flows with inter-province trade flows within Canada and inter-state trade flows within the USA. For the first time this has enabled a proper comparison to be made of the specific effect of an international border on trade. Wei (1996), Helliwell (1998), and Parsley and Wei (1999) extend this type of analysis to other OECD and developing countries as well.

What most analyses of the growth of international trade do is to look only at international trade without comparing it with what is going on in the home territory at the same time. International trade is expanding but so too is domestic trade, and it looks as though domestic trade is expanding at a much more rapid rate than is its international equivalent (after accounting for the other control variables), even as NAFTA has been established between the USA and Canada.[7] McCallum and Helliwell's analysis confirms that the intensity of trade between the USA and Canada had stabilised (and perhaps even lessened in the first instance), compared to the growth of their respective inter-domestic trade levels, after the establishment of NAFTA rather than increased. Thus, it may be that agreements like NAFTA actually stimulate domestic trade in the first instance rather than international trade, reinforcing the effects of borders rather than displacing them (almost the exact opposite of the strong globalisation thesis). A policy designed to increase the potential for international trade actually stabilises or decreases this and encourages domestic trade instead.[8] We might need to be a little more cautious here, however, since these analyses were conducted for the very early years of NAFTA. Recent evidence suggests that cross-border US-Canada trade has escalated; Canada's total trade with the USA soared from 31 per cent of its GDP in 1990 to 58 per cent in 1999, for instance (Wolf, 2000) - though this does not of itself refute the previous analyses.

Engel and Rodgers (1996) found that there was no clear convergence of price dispersion across locations involving the Canada-USA border (thereby going against the 'law of one price'), while McCallum and Helliwell found that there was up to twenty times more inter-provincial trade (Canada) and inter-state trade (USA), compared to cross-border trade, than would have been expected from gravity model specifications. Therefore, the border continues to be a remarkable 'barrier' to trade in and of itself, even after taking account of all the usual variables that might determine trade. In a provocative conclusion, Helliwell suggests, as a result, that the gravity model predicts trade relations well but not international trade relations. Trade theory is alive and well but not necessarily international trade theory. What is more there is evidence that even the state boundaries within the USA act as a 'barrier to trade', so the view that it is tariffs and quotas or other at-border international impediments to trade that represent the obstacles to international integration is further put into question (Wolf, 1997). Furthermore, differences in cultural and legal systems between these two countries - which might be thought to inhibit trade, as suggested above - also appear small in this particular case.

What is more these results are confirmed in the case of the other OECD countries analysed by Wei (1996) and Helliwell (1998) - though admittedly on the basis of less appropriate and reliable data. Here the effect of borders is less pronounced, however, reducing international trade by about three times compared to what trade theory would predict. But the case of US and Japanese trade is particularly interesting. Parsley and Wei (1999) confirm that international borders matter a great deal in this case; in terms of price dispersion between the two countries, crossing the US-Japanese border is equivalent to adding between 2.5 and 13 million miles to the cross-country volatility of relative prices. Again, this is confirmed by our analysis above as it dealt with US and Japanese trade. According to the analysis of Parsley and Wei, only if distance and shipping costs could be eliminated, exchange rate variation curtailed, and relative variability of wage rates eliminated, would the affect of borders be undermined. But these are either what this particular border involves (a four thousand mile sea or air journey, for instance) or precisely the consequences of the border (differences in wages and exchange rate variability), so the argument seems rather tautological.

In addition, there is good evidence that migration is a significant stimulus to trade (Casella and Rauch, 1997; Rauch, 1999). It is very significant, for instance, in the case of imports into the USA. Migration sets up networks of relationships across borders, making it easier to establish a low transaction cost mechanism for the conduct of international trade as indicated above. So, the lack of extensive migration between the USA and Canada may actually be part of the explanation for the relative underdevelopment of trade between the two countries. Clearly, this is likely to be part of an explanation, but it does not fully meet the McCallum/ Helliwell points about the efficient and optimal levels of border effects. As long as countries maintain their commitment to regulate their populations in some sense (which is almost a defining feature of the notion of geographical 'territoriality'), then this situation will continue to hold. In particular, in so far as states continue to clamp down on migration this will inhibit the growth of international trade.

It seems that this particular point is crucial in the context of the jurisdictional consequences of borders; the fact that any movement across a national frontier involves the movement from one legal, regulatory and cultural jurisdiction to another. These jurisdictions proscribe, adjudicate and enforce a wide range of norms, rules, habits, networks, and the like that involve much more than just the 'obstacles' to trade found at the point of the frontier itself. An interesting suggestion here is that it may be the state of the legal and administrative certainty associated with the enforcement of contracts (with respect to both trade and capital flows) that is the key to the OECD bias in international economic transactions. When Anderson and Marcouiller (1999), for instance, introduced measures to represent this in their international trade equations (a 'corruption indicator' and a 'legal enforceability' variable), they found that these variables accounted for such a significant proportion of the growth in international trade that the impact of income growth *per se* was less than 1.

Thus, the implication here is that GDP growth has a less than proportionate impact on international trade growth; the bulk of the growth in international trade over the post-Second World War period being accounted for by the 'one-off' impact of legal enforceability. This thereby points to a potential optimal level of international trade as this one-off boost to trade eventually exhausts itself. Clearly, what this point raises is the 'transactions costs' associated with the enforcement of contracts. As these might be expected to be easier to enforce within a specific jurisdictional community, as opposed to as between such communities, there could be a direct mapping of organisational and institutional features on to territories - of which the nation state remains the most obvious. Consequently, as long as there are different jurisdictional communities there will remain at least this particular 'obstacle' to trade. The question becomes, then, an empirical one: the precise kinds of transaction and enforcement costs associated with different kinds of economic activity, and how these vary territorially.

Therefore, we seem to have a robust general result emerging here, the wider consequences and implications of which are taken up in a moment. But first, an obvious question is whether there is any general evidence emerging that trade globalisation is slowing? Here the evidence remains somewhat ambiguous, as is illustrated by data plotted in Figures 2.3 and 2.4.

Figure 2.3 plots an index of examples of the growth for two of the polar types of trade discussed in the context of Figure 2.2, namely agricultural exports as an example of category 1 ('market exchange'), and manufacturing exports as an example of category 3 ('network exchange'). Also plotted is the overall growth of world GDP. Clearly, there is a downturn in the growth of both categories of trade in the second half of the 1990s (more extreme in the case of agricultural exports), so the graph begins to form a classic logistics curve. However, both categories of trade have expanded at a faster rate than world GDP growth, though this needs to be interpreted with caution in the light of the discussion above. These trade figures do not remove the other influences on trade growth discussed in the context of the gravity model. If they were expressed in this way, the implication is that these categories of trade would have expanded at a rate *less than* world GDP growth as such. Also, note that exports declined while real GDP did not. The data plotted in Figure 2.4 confirm the seeming logistic curve form observed in Figure 2.3.

Figure 2.3   World merchandise exports compared to world GDP (1990=100)

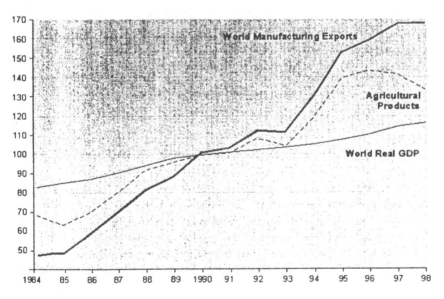

Source: Derived from WTO, 'Annual Report 2000', Vol. II, 'International Trade Statistics'.

Figure 2.4   World exports and imports of goods, 1978-1999 (US$ billions)

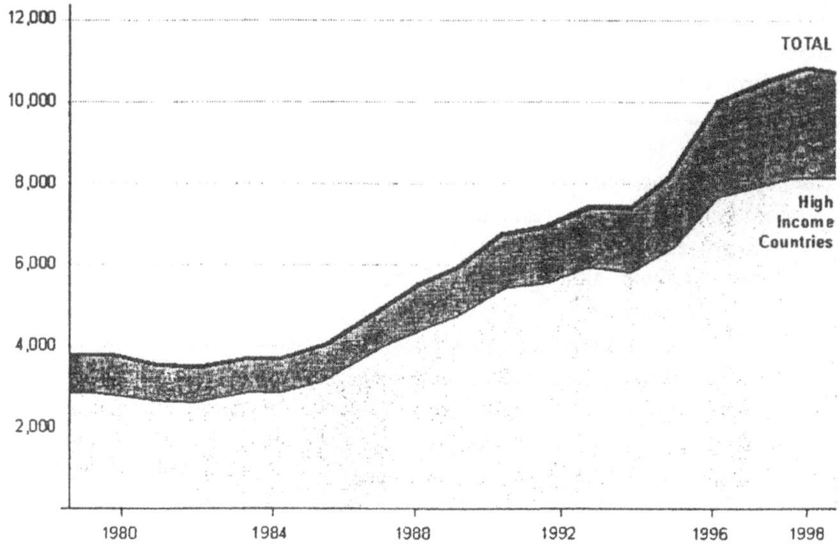

Source: Derived from IMF, OECD, UN and World Bank, '2000: A Better World for All', Paris (2000).

Figure 2.4 presents the growth in world trade in a slightly different way, expressing it in money terms. The rise in the value of international trade through the 1980s and early 1990s is evident but the growth seems to have tailed off in the late 1990s. Of course, we also need to be cautious here. The recent tailing off of the growth in world trade could be the result of 'cyclical' factors rather than 'structural' ones; the results of the East Asian financial crisis for instance, though the downturn looks to have begun well before the onset of this. In addition, as noted above, there has been little indication of a downturn in the growth of world GDP.

National Borders and Capital Markets

Is there a truly global capital market? The answer to this still has to be 'no' despite the popular belief to the contrary, fuelled as this is by the machinations of the press, business interests and the political class. Elsewhere I have indicated to the continued national specificity of capital markets in great empirical detail (Hirst and Thompson, 1999, chapter 2), and this analysis is not repeated here. Rather, the discussion draws attention to the more conventional literature that addresses the issue of international capital mobility.

As part of the mystery surrounding the missing international trade referred to earlier, there is an equally puzzling mystery about the missing international capital flows. Standard financial economic modelling frameworks (such as the 'efficient market' or 'risk premium' methods) when applied to an international environment do not perform well in predicting the levels of cross-border capital flows (King *et al.*, 1994; Gordon and Bovenberg, 1996; Bayoumi, 1999; Lewis, 1999). But there remains a massive 'home bias' in the asset and liability structure of financial institutions and household portfolios. The question is how to explain this lack of international portfolio diversification, the continued real interest rate differentials across countries and the high correlation between domestic savings and investment expenditure.

Broadly speaking, although a lot of this remains a mystery even after careful analysis, it is clear that:[9] (1) 'risks' are assessed and priced quite differently in different national markets leading to a great deal of residual 'idiosyncratic' risk, and thus excess volatility in the system as a whole (King *et al.*, 1994); (2) relatedly, it is 'asymmetric information' amongst players rather than government policy, say in the form of different corporate income tax regimes, that accounts for immobility (Gordon and Bovenberg, 1996); (3) as yet still unmeasured hedge demands and unidentified costs may generate the home biases observed in equity portfolios (Lewis, 1999); and, finally, (4) while short-term trades may be mobile, long-term trades remain low because of the residual threat of capital controls, which are dissolving so that integration will grow in the future (Bayoumi, 1999). Basically, all these analyses speak to the lack of an explanation rather than a clear positive picture.

Interestingly, only in the case of the European Union has there been some analysis that could bolster the 'optimal level' of integration argument considered above in the case of trade. What are the consequences of the formation of an EU monetary union on intra-EU real capital flows? Here issues of FDI arise. As exchange rate 'stability' (indeed 'fixity') is imposed across the EU, intra-European FDI flows may themselves stabilise or decrease even, since European producers could then export from their home base with confidence across Europe without hedging their intra-EU activities with FDI (de Menil, 1999). Transaction costs and political risks are reduced.

Also, Rauch (1999) speculates that portfolio-type 'merger and acquisition' (M&A) FDI and 'green field' FDI share many of the characteristics of the first and last trade categories as mentioned above. M&A FDI is organised though well established and low transaction cost stock markets, whereas green field FDI requires all the costly establishment of new sites, networks of suppliers and distribution systems, etc. and is thus subject to similar 'constraining' limits on its expansion in the long term as is category 3 trade. At present of course, it is the high overseas orientation of M&A FDI that is dominant and eclipses the less elastic and more networked 'green field' FDI form, but these trends and emphases could change in the future.

Rather like trade statistics, current indications of global capital flows present a mixed picture from the viewpoint of a possible emergent change in the globalising trend of international capital movements. The boom in FDI continued in 1999 (then in its seventh year) with record inflows of US$ 865bn worldwide (UNCTAD,

2000). Of this total, US$ 718bn was cross-border M&A activity (83% of total FDI activity). This was essentially driven by M&A activity between the Triad bloc, which accounted for some US$ 596bn (this time 83 per cent of all M&A activity). And here Western Europe was the world's leading region for cross-border M&A in 1999 representing 73% of the total (OECD, 2000b, p.30). So, as yet at least, the boom in intra-European FDI has not abated. And total foreign production and sales continue to increase at a faster rate than total world output.

But although overall FDI flows to the developing countries increased in 1999 (after a lapse in 1998), there was a continued downturn in *total* financial flows to the developing countries as commercial bank loans, portfolio flows and official assistance fell away. Whether this was a temporary and short-term reaction to the financial turmoil of the late 1990s (Russia, Brazil, East Asia) or a longer-term change remains to be seen.

However, there are some interesting potentially longer-term trends associated with international financial activity which it is worth commenting on. One preliminary difficulty here is that many of these trends involve cross-border financial *service* activity rather than financial investment and capital flows proper (OECD, 2000a). Thus, strictly speaking, this should be categorised as service trade rather than investment. Also, these are often intimately related, as in the case of cross-border investment banking services (such as underwriting fees and trading commissions) and M&A activity. But it is difficult to directly observe financial service trade that has, as a consequence, to be inferred from either balance of payments data, the balance sheets of financial institutions or capital stock and flow movements. So, here, I rather run these together.

For instance, it is not clear whether the international wholesale commercial banking in the 1990s increased significantly over that of the 1980s, other than for basically cyclical reasons (OECD, 2000a, p.29). The slowdown in the cross-border inter-bank activity within Europe is clearly indicated by the data in Figure 2.5.

As Figure 2.6 shows, the turnover in financial derivative instruments was on a long-term decline in Asian markets, and the growth in North America and Europe during the latter half of the 1990s was reversed in late 1998 and during 1999. Furthermore, as Table 2.5 shows, while international bond and equity markets were very buoyant during much of the 1990s, and revived again in late 1999 and early 2000 after a difficult period in 1998 and early 1999, the spectacular growth rates of the recent past (expressed as a proportion of GDP) slowed or were reversed (BIS, 2000; OECD, 2000c).

Finally, looking at the overall development in equity financial market integration, Figure 2.7 plots the changes in the percentage of foreign stocks in equity portfolios for a number of the most advanced countries between 1987 and 1996. Interestingly, while there was some upward growth for the USA and Canada over the period, this actually levelled out in the early 1990s. For the UK and Germany, the percentage seems to have hovered around the 20 per cent mark over the entire period. Again, for a supposedly rapidly integrating international financial system these changes look modest, with rather stable (or slightly declining) ratios during the mid-1990s (except for Japan).

Figure 2.5   Cross-border European inter-bank activity, 1990-1999   (amounts outstanding at end-quarter, in US$ bn)

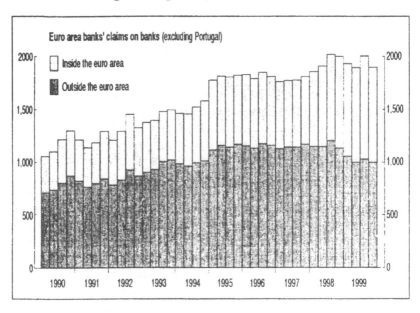

Figure 2.6   Turnover of exchange traded derivative instruments (options and futures, US$ trn).

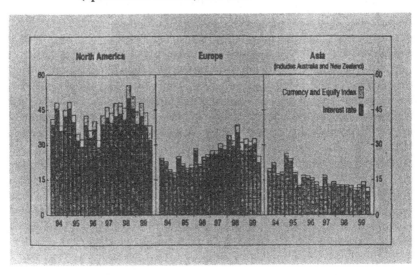

Source: BIS, 'Annual Report and Accounts 2000', Graph VI.9, p.115, Basle (2000).

Table 2.5   Cross-border transactions in bonds and equities[1] (% of GDP)

	1975–79	1980–89	1990–94	1995	1996	1997	1998	1999 p
United States								
Bonds	4.0	36.5	94.0	110.2	129.0	163.6	166.3	125.8
Equities	1.9	6.7	14.7	22.4	27.2	44.3	56.5	53.1
Japan								
Bonds	2.2	63.3	74.5	55.2	66.1	78.3	72.4	56.0
Equities	0.6	9.7	9.8	9.6	13.4	17.1	18.2	29.1
Germany								
Bonds	5.3	25.0	87.3	148.8	171.0	211.6	259.1	250.9
Equities	1.6	7.3	15.2	18.5	24.8	44.7	69.8	83.4

Notes:
[1] Gross purchases and sales of securities between residents and non-residents.
p: provisional.
Source: BIS, 'Annual Report and Accounts 2000', Table V.2, Basle (2000).

What this brief overview of the recent trends in international financial activity demonstrates is that it is difficult to tell how much of the downturn in activity in the later part of the 1990s was the result of purely short-term cyclical features or the beginnings of a more longer-term change that could see some slowing in the growth of 'financial globalisation'. So much here depends upon what happens in the next few years to the American economy; a slowdown could increase the trends towards domestic retrenchment and re-adjustment.

On the other hand, if the dollar collapses against the Euro this could stimulate further cross-Atlantic capital flows as US fund managers looked for more lucrative investments in the EU. In addition, the OECD's relatively successful onslaught against off-shore financial centres could also reduce the extent of international financial lending as banks retreated from these territories and re-established now equally attractive 'domestic' business. The general point to note, however, is that there is no necessary reason why cross-border financial activity should continue to grow at the rates it did over the 1980s and much of the 1990s; cyclical and structural features might quite easily merge to set a different trend in the 2000s.

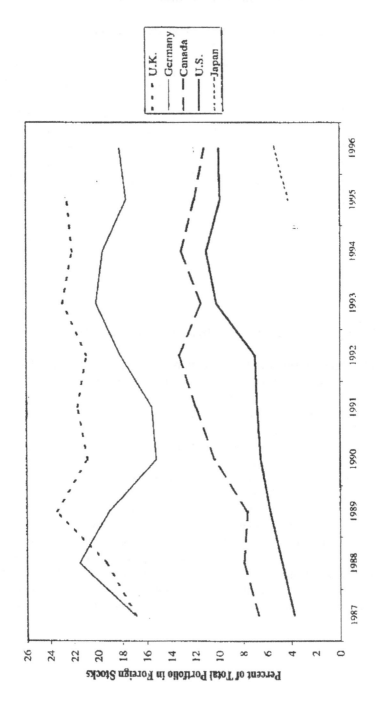

Figure 2.7 Home bias in equity portfolios, 1987-1996

Conclusion

The types of analysis of international trade and investment flows provided in this paper serve to undermine expectations about the necessary continued expansion of interdependency, integration, and international economic interactions as a result of 'globalisation'. Thus far from 'globalisation' leading to the further 'extension of the market' and ever more and more integration (a truly 'borderless' world), there may be legitimate limits to such integration. Borders may be economically 'efficient'. There may be limits to the international division of labour, rather than its unlimited extension as implied by a conception relying on a purely ideal market approach.

And in the context of 'taking economic borders seriously', the question to ask is why borders continue to operate in this way. Given that national borders are not going to go away quickly we are left to ponder their 'determining' influences on trade, real capital flows and other cross-border interactions like migration. The analysis above provides some hints at this. Broadly speaking, these proceed along the following lines, which overlap to a large degree.

First, as stressed by Krugman (1993) in a slightly different context, state policies continue to have an impact. However much these government policies have been adapted to the new realities of the internationalisation of economic activity, they still continue to place 'obstacles' on the full development of 'cross-border' economic interactions. Such is the situation with labour flows in the US-Canada case; there being no completely open migration between the two countries, which could have an ongoing impact on trade flows.

Secondly, there are some 'hysteresis' effects i.e., time path dependencies based upon prior decisions and events that lock economic relationships into an enduring pattern with which it is difficult to break (such as the residual worry about the imposition of capital control mentioned above). No doubt this is true to a certain extent, but an appeal to hysteresis almost avoids an explanation. The issue is to explain the good reasons now for those patterns and relationships as they endure.

Thirdly, and potentially more profitably, there is an appeal to a set of 'cultural' characteristics that set different populations apart, and which hence reinforce the jurisdictional points made above. These can lead to sometimes subtle differences in the demand patterns, technological characteristics, quality expectations, choice variables, etc. of goods and services even amongst what might otherwise seem relatively 'homogeneous' populations in terms of tastes, like those existing either side of the 49th parallel (let alone in somewhere like Europe). If 'globalisation' implies an increased local cultural differentiation rather than its increased homogenisation, which is a perfectly reasonable implication to be drawn for the wide globalisation debate, then paradoxically this differentiation could act to undermine the very economic globalisation that helped to stimulate it in the first place.

Fourthly, we would need to look closely at the supply side of the equation. This pertains to the characteristic patterns of production, domestic divisions of labour, sectoral and branch specialisation, company organisation, etc. Here we might appeal to the notion of the typical and often informal networks of production, sometimes organised in the form of very localised industrial districts and regional economies (*Journal of International Economics*, 1999).

Finally, there are issues of socialisation and civic participation too; what is sometimes called 'social capital'. Again, these can set up particular kinds of 'social networks' that operate to maintain differentials and demarcations between populations in terms of their attitudes, economic participation and tastes.

What this all amounts to is to stress the continuing diversity, and its possible extension, during a period of 'globalisation', which might inhibit the development of international economic interdependence above some (no doubt flexible) minimum level. Continuing market segmentation internationally could prevail.

In terms of the strong globalisation thesis, though, the general point is that this analysis confirms the likely limit to the extent of the growth of international inter-dependency and integration. And nor should this matter much. Too great a fuss is made in the conventional literature about the undoubted benefits of completely 'open' economies, when in fact there is growing evidence that the relationship between openness and economic growth is doubtful to say the least (Rodriguez and Rodrik, 1999; Rodrik, 1999 - but Edwards, 1997 offers a somewhat different view).

Notes

1. This paper is based on remarks originally made at the 'Workshop on the Persistence of Boundaries', University of Surrey, England, 15-16 May 2000; and in my Inaugural Lecture at the Open University, 28 October 2000: 'The Globalisation Debate: Where are We?'. I thank Simon Bromley, Will Brown, Alan Hudson, Noel Parker and Paul Hirst for very helpful discussions and comments on these matters. Since preparing these remarks, Dani Rodrik has raised similar issues (Rodrik, 2000).

2. For recent and representative examples of this literature see Anderson, 1996; Rosenau, 1997; Newman, 1999; and the references therein, and almost any issue of *Society and Space* or *Progress in Human Geography* which seem to have become almost the house journals for this kind of approach.

3. I thank Simon Bromley for reminding me of this point.

4. 'In a zero transaction cost world, infinite exchange would allow perfectly efficient allocation. In a positive transaction cost world –the world as it is- a decision maker might accept some transaction costs in order to enhance gains from trade, or accept reduced gains from trade in order to reduce transaction costs even more. The actual decision depends on the magnitude of each' (Trachtman, 1997, pp.501-2).

5. Krugman (1993, pp.70-72), in what is for other reasons an interesting and worthwhile contribution, also adopts this position as part of his modelling strategy.

6. See Raunch, 1999; for an interesting recent deployment of the gravity model approach.

7. This problem of comparing like with like, in terms of what is going on between nations as well as within them, is tackled in terms of MNC operations in Hirst and Thompson, 1999, chapter 3; and in terms of the long history of international trade and capital flows in Hirst and Thompson, 2000.

8. These points should not be confused with the usual questions economists ask of the formation of trading blocs; whether they are trade creating or trade diverting. Trade

creation and trade diversion refer to the effects of the newly combined economic bloc in either stimulating combined trade from, or diverting combined trade away from, the new configurated entity. In the case being discussed here it is a matter of the effects as between the constituent parts themselves (see further comment on this in relation to the formation of the EU.)

9.   For instance, King *et al.* conclude that 'only a small proportion of the covariances between national stock markets and their time-variation can be accounted for by "observable" economic variables' (1994, p.901).

References

Anderson, J.E and Marcouiller, D. (1999), 'Trade, Insecurity, and Home Bias: An Empirical Investigation', *NEBR Working Paper No. 7000*, Cambridge (Mass).

Anderson, M. (1996), *Frontiers: Territory and State Formation in the Modern World*, Polity Press, Cambridge.

Baldwin, R.E. and Martin, P. (1999), 'Two Waves of Globalisation: Superficial Similarities, Fundamental Differences', in H. Siebert (ed.), *Globalization and Labour*, Mohr Siebeck, Tubingen.

Bayoumi, T. (1999), 'Is There a World Capital Market?', in H. Siebert (ed.), *Globalization and Labour*, Mohr Siebeck, Tubingen.

BIS (2000), *Bank for International Settlements: 7th Annual Report*, June, Basle.

Bordo, M.D., Eichengreen, B. and Irwin, D.A. (1999), 'Is Globalisation Today Really Different than Globalisation a Hundred Years Ago?', *Brookings Trade Forum 1999*, Cambridge (Mass).

Casella, A. and Rauch, J.E. (1997), 'Anonymous Market and Group Ties in International Trade', *NBER Working Paper No.6186*, Cambridge (Mass).

de Menil, G. (1999), 'Real Capital Market Integration in the EU: How Far has it Gone? What will the Effect of the Euro Be?', *Economic Policy*, No. 28, April, pp.167-201.

Edwards, S. (1997), 'Openness, Productivity and Growth: What Do We Really Know?', *NBER Working Paper No. 5978*, Cambridge (Mass).

Engel, C. and Rogers, J.H. (1996), 'How Wide is the Border?', *The American Economic Review*, Vol. 86(5), pp.1112-25.

Gordon, R.H. and Bovenberg, A.L. (1996), 'Why is Capital So Immobile? Possible Explanations and Implications for Capital Income Taxation', *The American Economic Review*, Vol. 86(2), pp.1057-75.

Helliwell, J.F. (1998), *How Much Do National Borders Matter?*, Brookings Institution, Washington DC.

Hirst, P.Q. and Thompson, G.F. (1999), *Globalisation in Question: The International Economy and the Possibilities of Governance*, 2nd edition, Polity Press, Cambridge.

_____ (2000), 'Globalisation in One Country: The Peculiarities of the British', *Economy and Society*, Vol. 29(3), August.

Irwin, D.A. (1996), 'The United States in a New Global Economy? A Century's Perspective', *The American Economic Review*, Vol. 86(2), pp.41-6.

Journal of International Economics (1999), Symposium on 'Business and Social Networks in International Trade', Vol. 46, pp.3-150.

King, M., Sentana, E. and Wadhwani, S. (1994), 'Volatility and Links between National Stock Markets', *Econometrica*, Vol. 62(4), July, pp.901-33.

Krugman, P. (1991), *Geography and Trade*, MIT Press, Cambridge (Mass).

Learner, E.E. and Storper, M. (2000), 'The Economic Geography of the Internet Age', forthcoming in *Journal of International Business Studies.*

Lewis, K.K. (1999), 'Trying to Explain Home Bias in Equities and Consumption', *Journal of Economic Literature,* Vol. .XXXVII, June, pp.571-608.

Mataloni, R.J. (2000), 'US Multinational Companies: Operations in 1998', *Survey of Current Business,* Vol. 80(7), July, pp.26-45.

McCallum, J. (1995), 'National Borders Matter: Canada-US Regional Trade Patterns', *The American Economic Review,* Vol. 85(3), pp.615-23.

Newman, D. (ed.) (1999), *Boundaries, Territory and Postmodernity,* Frank Cass, London.

OECD (2000a), 'Cross-Border Trade in Financial Services: Economics and Regulation', *Financial Market Trends,* No. 75, March, OECD, Paris.

_____ (2000b) 'Recent Trends in Foreign Direct Investment', *Financial Market Trends,* No. 76, June, OECD, Paris.

_____ (2000c) 'Highlights of Recent Trends in Financial Markets', *Financial Market Trends,* No. 77, October, OECD, Paris.

Ohmae, K. (1990), *The Borderless World,* Collins, London and New York.

_____ (1995), *The End of the Nation State, The Rise of Regional Economies,* Free Press, London.

Parsley, D.C. and Wei, S-J. (1999), 'Border, Border, Wide and Far, How I Wonder What You Are', *World Bank Policy Working Paper No. 2217,* World Bank, Washington DC.

Rauch, J.E. (1999), 'Networks versus Markets in International Trade', *Journal of International Economics,* Vol. 48, pp.7-35.

Rodriguez, F. and Rodrik, D. (1999), 'Trade Policy and Economic Growth: A Skeptic's Guide to the Evidence', *NBER Working Paper No.7081,* Cambridge (Mass).

Rodrik, D. (1999), 'The New Global Economy and Developing Countries: Making Openness Work', *Policy Essay No. 24,* ODC, Washington DC.

_____ (2000), 'How Far Will International Economic Integration Go?', *Journal of Economic Perspectives,* Vol. 14(1), pp.177-86.

Rosenau, J. (1997), *Along the Domestic-Foreign Frontier: Exploring Governance in a Turbulent World,* Cambridge University Press, Cambridge.

Thompson, G.F. (2001), 'Introducing Economic Governance', in G.F. Thompson (ed.), *Governing the European Economy,* Sage, London.

Trachtman, J.P. (1996), 'The Theory of the Firm and the Theory of the International Economic Organisation: Towards Comparative Institutional Analysis', *Northwestern Journal of International Law and Business,* Vol. 17, pp.470-555.

_____ (1997), 'Externalities and Extraterritoriality: The Law and Economics Perspective on Jurisdiction', in L. Bhandari and A. Sykes (eds), *Economic Dimensions in International Law: Comparative and Empirical Perspectives,* Cambridge University Press, Cambridge.

Trefler, D. (1995), 'The Case of Missing Trade and Other Mysteries', *The American Economic Review,* Vol. 85(5), pp.1029-46.

UNCTAD (2000), *World Investment Report 2000: Cross-border Mergers and Acquisitions and Development,* United Nations, New York and Geneva.

Wei, S-J. (1996), 'Intra-National versus International Trade: How Stubborn Are Nations in Global Integration?', *NBER Working Paper No. 5531,* Cambridge (Mass).

Wolf, H.C. (1997), 'Patterns of Intra and Inter-State Trade', *NBER Working Paper No. 5939,* Cambridge (Mass).

Wolf, M. (2000), 'The Chancellor at the Controls', *Financial Times,* 14 June, p.23.

Zeile, W.J. (2000), 'US Affiliates of Foreign Companies: Operations in 1998', *Survey of Current Business,* Vol. 80(8), August, pp.141-58.

Chapter 3

The Political Economy of International Integration: Small States in the Caribbean and the Free Trade Area of the Americas (FTAA)[1]

Robert Read

Introduction

Small states are an increasing feature of the contemporary international economic environment as a direct consequence of both decolonisation and, more recently, the disintegration of larger nation states into smaller independent ones. Paradoxically, this growth has been paralleled by the growing economic and political power of an increasing number of trade blocs, or regional trade agreements (RTAs), as the globalisation process has intensified. These developments represent a severe threat to the economic and political sovereignty of nation states, particularly developing countries and small states because of their marginality. In the face of these challenges, many small states however have demonstrated considerable resilience and enjoyed some significant success in achieving sustained economic growth and high per capita incomes. This growth success has stimulated a body of literature focusing on the key determinants of the economic performance of small states in the context of their size, vulnerability and the effects of globalisation (Armstrong and Read, 1998a, 2001a; Read, 2001).

This chapter is concerned with the implications for the small states in the Caribbean of the proposals for a Free Trade Area of the Americas (FTAA) made at the 1994 Miami Summit. This issue is analysed in the context of the participation of small states in RTAs in terms of the likely costs and benefits of membership. The discussion is intended to demonstrate that, in spite of the inferences of the orthodox theory of international economic integration, small states can be expected to be substantial economic losers from membership of such RTAs. This is because of their potential loss of autonomy over trade policy, the decline in trade tax revenue as well as their marginalisation and peripheralisation within an RTA. The political consequences of eschewing membership of an RTA such as the FTAA however, may also be substantial given the decline in the power of the nation state and the growth of regional trade blocs in an international economy characterised by globalisation. Small states, such as those in the Caribbean, therefore face a critical dilemma which has important implications for their sovereignty and their future economic growth.

The first section of this chapter provides a brief summary of the principal economic constraints imposed on small states by their size and the implications for their growth and development. Section 2 outlines the orthodox theory of economic integration and the principal economic and political costs and benefits that arise from participation in RTAs. This is followed by an analysis of the theory of economic integration as it pertains to small states as well as a discussion of the implications of the critical economic constraints identified in Section 1. Section 3 also considers briefly the past participation and experience of small states in RTAs. The final section assesses the likely effects of the participation of small Caribbean states in the FTAA and the key policy choices that they face.

The Economic Implications of Small Size

The analysis of the implications of the FTAA for small states in the Caribbean is based upon the insights of the specific literature on the economics of small states. This section draws upon these findings to outline the analytical methodology and summarise the economic constraints on small states as well as their implications for policy making, and growth and development.

Small Size: The Analytical Methodology

Orthodox economic theory makes great use of the small open economy paradigm to analyse a range of international trade and macroeconomic issues. This paradigm however, is based upon an economy being a 'price taker' in that it has little or no influence over the prices of its imports and exports in international markets. The approach has widespread applicability since very few countries actually possess significant market power in international markets but it is generally concerned with the analysis of relatively large Western industrialised economies. The generality of the small open economy paradigm therefore offers very few useful insights into the specific issues concerning truly small states.

Most analytical studies of small states instead make use of population as the principal indicator of size. While there is little consensus as to the critical population threshold, this approach means that small size can be conceptualised in terms of the impact of economies of scale on the intensity and range of feasible domestic economic activities. The economies of small states can thus be viewed as sub-optimal to the extent that they are unable to reach a critical mass in a wide range of domestic activities. The greater focus of this analytical methodology generates useful policy insights arising from the explicit interaction between small size, domestic economic activity and international trade, regardless of any specific size threshold.

Economic Constraints on Small States

The sub-optimality approach to the analysis of small states reveals a number of critical economic constraints imposed by small size which have important policy implications. A full discussion of these constraints can be found elsewhere (see, for example, Robinson, 1960; Demas, 1965; Selwyn, 1975a; Shand, 1980; *World Development*, 1980, 1993; Jalan, 1982; Dommen and Hein, 1985; Ashoff, 1989; Armstrong *et al.*, 1998). The principal constraints in the context of economic integration are summarised below.

Market size and specialisation in small states: A small home market and domestic supply constraints mean that scale economies preclude small states from achieving a critical mass in output of many goods and services so raising their unit costs of domestic production. This constraint greatly inhibits the development of large-scale manufacturing (Thomas, 1982) as well as indigenous R&D (Selwyn, 1975b; Briguglio, 1995). Small size thus constrains the range and extent of domestic economic activity. Further, the number of feasible incumbent firms in the small domestic market is also low such that small states are subject to the adverse competitive effects of internal and external monopoly.

The constraint on feasible domestic economic activities means that the structure of output and exports in small states is highly specialised and relatively undiversified. This results in a limited number of dominant economic activities and excessive dependence upon a few exports and export markets, so exposing the economy to greater risk of exogenous shocks. The impact of such shocks is likely to be large because any deterioration in their external terms of trade cannot be fully compensated for by an increase in export volumes. Although the general solution to export concentration and instability problems is diversification, its scope is limited in small states.

Openness and trade policy in small states: Small states are necessarily highly dependent upon imports because of their limited scope for sourcing a wide range of goods and services locally. This results in a significant asymmetry between the patterns of production and consumption (Kuznets, 1960) such that there are few opportunities for autonomous self-sustaining internal economic growth. Small states are therefore compelled to have a high degree of structural openness (a high share of trade in GDP/GNP) and be closely integrated with the international economy (Marcy, 1960; Scitovsky, 1960; Triffin, 1960). According to the orthodox theory, protectionist trade policy stance promoting widespread domestic import-substitution would thus impose severe adverse domestic price, income and competitive effects and is unlikely to be a feasible development strategy. This high degree of integration with the international economy however, makes small states highly susceptible to protectionist moves by their principal trading partners.

Furthermore, the high level of structural openness in small states has important macroeconomic policy implications in terms of their balance of payments, international monetisation, the exchange rate and domestic monetary autonomy (see, for example, Ally, 1975; Khatkhate and Short, 1980; Helleiner, 1982). Many small states therefore link their exchange rate to a hard currency or have joined a hard currency area to provide insulation against external volatility (Read, 1995; Armstrong and Read, 1998a, 1999; Chadha, 1998).

Policy implications for growth and development in small states: The economic constraints on small states have important implications for their strategies of growth and development because the scope and structure of domestic activity and their policy autonomy is greatly restricted. Small states can therefore be expected to experience significantly greater challenges in both generating and sustaining economic growth relative to larger states which are not subject to these constraints.

Structural transition and comparative advantage in small states: Economic growth and development is generally associated with industrialisation based upon the expansion of large-scale labour and technology-intensive manufacturing via the transfer of labour from subsistence agriculture (Lewis, 1955; Chenery and Taylor, 1968; Chenery and Syrquin, 1975; Chenery et al., 1986). This standard path of development however, is not open to most small states (Demas, 1965) because of their labour supply constraint and the infeasibility of growth based upon large-scale labour-intensive manufacturing. Instead, their structural openness requires their output and exports to be based upon inherent comparative advantage in higher value-added niche manufacturing and service activities (as well as natural resources). These niche activities utilise human capital intensively and have few associated scale economies (Bhaduri et al., 1982).

The empirical evidence suggests that the growth and development of many small states is associated with this pattern of sectoral specialisation. Average per capita income levels and growth rates vary between different structural types of small states with specialisation in service activities being associated with a strong performance (UNCTAD, 1997). Statistical analyses of this relationship find that growth in small states is significantly and positively associated with a rich natural resource base and a strong service sector, notably in financial services and tourism, and negatively associated with agriculture (Armstrong et al., 1998; Armstrong and Read, 1995, 2000, 2001b). These empirical results on the sectoral sources of growth in small states provide strong support for *a priori* reasoning concerning their comparative advantage and the critical role of international trade.

The vulnerability of small states: The general growth impact of the constraints on small states imposed by their size can be viewed in terms of the degree of risk embodied in their narrow specialisation and their greater exposure to exogenous shocks compared with larger states. This is generally referred to as 'vulnerability' and encompasses the exposure to economic shocks as well as the impact of strategic and environmental events over which they have little control. These effects are compounded in the case of small island states because of their topography and remoteness (Holmes, 1976; Commonwealth Consultative Group, 1985; Briguglio, 1995). The greater exposure of an economy to exogenous shocks gives rise to an increased risk of short-run volatility around the underlying trend rate of growth, i.e., there is a higher risk premium associated with their growth (Auffret and Mora Baez, 2000; Easterly and Kraay, 2000). For relatively wealthy small states, growth will therefore have a higher resource cost but for many small developing states, the scarcity of resources to smooth these fluctuations may result in a relatively lower long-run trend rate of growth. Small states therefore incur greater risks and higher costs than larger states in achieving growth and development (UNCTAD, 1988).

The growing literature on the vulnerability on small states deals with its sources, quantification (using vulnerability indices) and impact. The objective of much of this work is to demonstrate that simple per capita income measures do not fully reflect the structural and institutional constraints on the growth of small states. While the least developed countries and other small developing economies are clearly the most vulnerable however, the empirical analysis of the impact of vulnerability remains problematic for a variety of methodological and statistical reasons (Read, 2000).

New Growth Theory and Critical Sources of Growth in Small States

The understanding of the growth process in small states is illuminated by insights drawn from new growth theory. This is an extension of neoclassical growth models incorporating additional structural and conditioning variables, on theoretical grounds, to explain relative rates of growth between countries. The endogenous growth literature identifies three important conditioning variables of particular relevance to small states, namely openness to trade, human capital accumulation and the existence of convergence 'clubs'.

New growth theory argues that openness has beneficial effects on domestic competitiveness because imports have a contestable impact upon domestic prices and may also embody high levels of technology. Openness to trade in small states is size-induced rather than a revealed policy choice, requiring them to pursue policies promoting export-led growth. International trade is therefore the principal engine of economic growth for small states since it increases the extent of their domestic market and has significant multiplier effects (Ashoff, 1989). The benefits arising from increased specialisation through trade however, cannot completely offset the greater risks associated with the lower degree of domestic diversification of output and exports such that some trade-off is required.

The importance attached to human capital formation in new growth theory arises from its enhancement of labour productivity via investment in education, training and learning-by-doing without being subject to diminishing returns. The accumulation of human capital as a critical source of comparative advantage and growth in small states has already been highlighted. Of particular importance to small states, given increasing returns in R&D and innovation, is the interaction between openness and human capital since the absorptive technological capacity of an economy is dependent upon its stock of human capital.

The existence of convergence 'clubs' suggests that proximity and interaction with relatively high growth countries and regions may have additional beneficial growth effects. For small states, this suggests that their regional location may have an important influence on their growth performance.

Several additional factors are identified in the literature as critical determinants of growth of small states of which the most important is economic policy autonomy. This encompasses the determination of monetary, fiscal, trade and exchange rate policies as well as control over the domestic regulatory environment. In small states however, it is evident that the scope to use this economic policy autonomy is greatly limited by their small size. Further, the empirical evidence suggests that more successful small states are highly selective in their use of the policies available, often eschewing the domestic control of inflation, interest rates, money supply and exchange rates through effective membership of a hard currency area ('pseudo' monetary union) (Armstrong and Read, 1999). Any discussion of the economic policy autonomy of small states must also consider the international political economy dimension, given their scope for opportunistic free-riding and rent-seeking in the national self-interest.

Preferential Trade and Regional Trade Agreements (RTAs)

The economic analysis of free trade areas and customs unions, i.e., regional trade agreements (RTAs), is an extension of the theory of preferential trade. In an RTA, the trade preference is a zero-rated tariff that is applied generally to all mutual trade between the partner countries such that it results in a free trade area. Additional undertakings by member states within an RTA however, may lead to varying degrees of depth of integration and differing institutional configurations. The Free Trade Area of the Americas (FTAA) is envisaged to be, for the time being, purely a free trade area and therefore a continental extension of the present North American Free Trade Area (NAFTA), comprising Canada, Mexico and the USA. In contrast, the European Union (EU) is an RTA involving deep integration encompassing economic, monetary and possibly political union. This section provides an overview of the orthodox theory of economic integration as it relates to free trade areas, the principal effects of regional integration and critical factors which determine the magnitude of these integration effects.

The Economic Theory of Preferential Trade and RTAs

The orthodox economic theory of preferential trade initially viewed any move towards regional integration between countries as being an unequivocal Pareto improvement in global welfare given that it involved some reduction in trade barriers. This view underlay the original 1947 GATT - Article XXIV encouraging the creation of RTAs with the caveat that average post-integration tariffs of member countries should be no higher than the average pre-integration tariffs.

Viner (1950) demonstrates that the formation of an RTA is not necessarily Pareto welfare improving however, because it comprises elements of both internal free trade for members and external protectionism against third countries. As such, RTAs are therefore a 'second best' outcome of moves towards international trade liberalisation; that is, they may increase both aggregate global welfare and that of member countries but at the expense of non-members. The Vinerian analysis is an exercise in comparative statics and focuses on the relative magnitudes of the beneficial efficiency effects of free trade within an RTA, trade creation, and the adverse efficiency effects of external discriminatory protectionism, trade diversion. So long as trade creation outweighs trade diversion, the formation of an RTA raises global welfare. Subsequent developments in the theory of preferential trade have modified and extended Viner's analysis but his general conclusions remain pertinent (reviewed in depth in Panagariya, 2000). Given that countries can be expected to participate in RTAs only if they expect to benefit from membership in some way, the self-interest of member states ensures that RTAs raise global welfare in accordance with the requirements of GATT.

The Principal Static Effects of a Free Trade Area (FTA)

The Vinerian approach to the analysis of economic integration provides a means to identify the principal static economic effects arising from the formation of an RTA. These are once-and-for-all beneficial effects which are only fully realised if economic agents respond to the opportunities made available by integration.

The increased size of the internal or 'home' market of an FTA means that local firms can improve their efficiency through enjoying greater economies of scale and therefore lower unit costs in R&D, production and distribution. Internal free trade improves the internal allocation of economic resources so that the location of production and the pattern of trade more closely reflect comparative advantage. This leads to the spatial rationalisation of economic activity and the international division of labour within the FTA. In an FTA, the free internal movement of capital and labour is generally restricted; if not, the FTA is technically speaking a common market. Free trade within an FTA however, would be expected to bring about some degree of factor price equalisation (of capital and labour), particularly if its policies towards foreign direct investment (FDI) are relatively liberal. The market power of individual firms in national markets is reduced in an RTA, so eroding the position of monopolies and oligopolies and leading to greater competition. The increased intensity of competition also raises capacity utilisation, reduces X-inefficiency within firms and industries and encourages innovation. An RTA therefore creates downward pressure on prices with substantial potential benefits for consumers subject to there being an effective RTA-wide competition policy to limit the scope for abuse by dominant firms. An FTA may also increase the international economic and political power of the member countries to the extent that they act in concert. This can have a positive terms of trade effect, by reducing import prices (monopsony power) and by increasing export prices (monopoly power), as well as providing greater bargaining power in international policy-making at the UN and WTO.

The Principal Dynamic Effects of Economic Integration

The most substantial effects of the formation of RTAs relate to the important dynamic or long-run effects of economic integration. These are over-and-above the purely static effects and incorporate the full impact of free trade on the structure of production and the pattern of trade within an RTA through the response of firms and individuals.

The formation of an RTA assures free access for firms and products to markets in other member countries and therefore reduces the level of commercial risk. This reduction in risk also generates increased economic activity through greater volumes of trade. Increased growth and incomes as a result of an RTA will lead to some increase in imports, external trade creation, with beneficial effects for third country exporters. In addition, a larger home market coupled with efficiency improvements may enable some firms to increase their exports as they become increasingly competitive internationally, trade suppression. The absolute volume of FDI flows in an RTA, by both home and foreign firms, can be expected to increase so as to take advantage of a larger, richer and more dynamic internal market. Some foreign firms may adopt a defensive investment strategy to guarantee their market access and offset the risk of external protectionism. There may however, be some initial rationalisation of FDI within an RTA as firms consolidate their economic activities.

Adjustment and the Distribution of the Benefits and Costs of Economic Integration

Much of the success of an FTA clearly relies upon the internal rationalisation of production structures and trade patterns. This rationalisation has important implications with respect to the location of any adjustment as well as the spatial distribution of the benefits and costs of integration. Orthodox theory tends to side-step these issues by assuming that adjustment is instantaneous, and therefore costless, and that any benefits and costs are spread relatively equitably.

The adjustment costs of economic integration in an FTA arise in the form of unemployment and lost output when inefficient firms and industries close down as a consequence of the rationalisation of production and increased competition. Trade creation therefore gives rise to efficiency gains but at some (temporary) cost. Adjustment costs will persist so long as the capital and, in particular, the labour remain unemployed; in the latter case, supply-side policies may be needed to address problems of skills mismatch. Trade diversion avoids such costs but at the expense of efficiency gains and long-run growth.

Economic integration of any type is therefore likely to generate conflicting spatial effects because of the uneven regional distribution of benefits and costs, corresponding to Myrdal's spread and backwash effects or Hirschman's trickle-down and polarisation effects (Myrdal, 1957; Hirschman, 1958). Adjustment costs in particular are likely to be unevenly distributed owing to regional specialisation in economic activity and consequently may exacerbate centre-periphery problems. This suggests that, although all member states might be expected to gain from integration, they will not all benefit to the same extent.

Factors Determining the Magnitude of the Effects of Integration

The relative magnitude of the effects of economic integration outlined above can be seen to vary according to the degree of 'fit' between individual prospective member states. It is therefore possible to establish several conditions for selecting appropriate partner countries in an FTA so as to maximise the likely gains from integration and minimise the likely losses.

The gains from forming an FTA arise directly as a consequence of the interaction between trade and production such that the absence of trade precludes any effects at all. The extent of trade between countries is partly determined by their geographical proximity because of the impact of transport costs, hence regional trade agreements. The greater the intensity of trade between members of an FTA, the greater the potential to generate substantial efficiency gains through the spatial rationalisation of production. These efficiency gains are likely to be enhanced by increasing the number of member states since there is a greater likelihood that low-cost internationally competitive suppliers of a wide range of goods and services are included.

This analysis can be refined further to consider the production structures and consumption patterns of member states. The greater the extent of similarity between them, the greater the gains from integration since a greater degree of overlap in production, income levels and consumer tastes provides greater scope for efficiency gains through specialisation, economies of scale and trade. Similar supply side and demand structures promote intra-industry trade, i.e., in similar but differentiated products, while complementary structures promote inter-industry trade. Integration between complementary economies leaves the greater part of internal economic activity unaffected and so limits the potential for any efficiency gains. A further condition relates to the magnitude of members' trade barriers prior to integration and the subsequent external trade stance of the FTA. Members of an FTA however, are under no obligation to harmonise their external trade policy but if this varies significantly between them then enforceable Rules of Origin will be required for goods to prevent trade deflection. The greater the initial magnitude of trade protection, the greater will be the efficiency gains arising from a more liberal external trade policy stance of the members of an FTA.

Although this approach provides useful insights concerning the economic and geographic characteristics of potential members of an FTA, it is also necessary to consider the dynamic perspective. Economic integration involving relatively developed countries will itself tend to promote more rapid convergence of growth and incomes between member states in the form of a convergence 'club'. This has been the experience in the EU to-date and is expected to recur after Eastern Enlargement in spite of concern regarding structural divergence (Gabrisch and Werner, 1999).

The Implications of Economic Integration for Small States

The participation of small states in RTAs is an economic issue which has received relatively little attention in the theoretical literature. This is primarily because small states are regarded as being of relatively little importance and that the general conclusions concerning the benefits of economic integration apply, in spite of some dissension, in a straightforward manner. Nevertheless, the implications of economic integration need to be addressed in the context of globalisation coupled with the growing economic and political power of regional trade blocs in the international economy threaten to further marginalise small states, particularly developing ones. This section outlines the conclusions of orthodox integration theory concerning small states and then considers the impact of an FTA between partners of dissimilar size with specific reference to small states. This is followed by a brief discussion of the empirical evidence on small states participation in RTAs and its contribution to their growth performance.

Small States and the Orthodox Theory of Economic Integration

The orthodox theory of preferential trade, and therefore of RTAs, considers the implications for small states only very briefly. The general view is that the benefits accruing to them are nearly always positive; many texts tend to repeat the cliché that 'small states are the biggest beneficiaries of economic integration schemes'. The justification for this conclusion is that integration widens the extent of the market of small states and so enables them exploit previously constrained economies of scale at low risk. This gives rise to the potential for complete specialisation and thus greater proportionate gains than for larger states (Graham, 1923; Balassa, 1962, 1967). These gains are made possible by guaranteed access to the markets of larger partners which could not have been achieved through bilateral trade negotiations because of the disparity in bargaining power (Balassa, 1962).

The conclusion of orthodox theory is both logical and appealing, particularly in the light of the implications of the constraints on small states imposed by the small size of their domestic market. If these conclusions are correct, small states can be expected to be keen participants in regional integration schemes since membership would appear to be an important factor in their continued economic survival. The anecdotal evidence on small states' membership of RTAs provided below taken together with the empirical evidence on the determinants of growth in small states suggests that this is not, in fact, the case.

Asymmetric Economic Integration: Implications of Small State Participation in RTAs

Despite the favourable conclusion of the orthodox theory of economic integration however, it is necessary to look more closely at the implications of membership of RTAs for small states so as to take into account their particular economic structures and constraints. The most appropriate means to do this is to examine the issue from the perspective of asymmetric integration; that is, economic integration between partners of unequal size. But this analysis leads to rather different conclusions concerning the relative costs and benefits of membership of RTAs by small states.

Asymmetric Economic Integration, Regional Protectionism and Autonomous Trade Policy

The favourable conclusions of the orthodox theory of economic integration are predicated on two critical implicit assumptions: that integration takes place in an international economic environment characterised by pre-existing protectionism, and that the alternative to an RTA of bilateral trade agreements with large trading partners is infeasible or embodies unacceptably high risk. From Section 1, the pre-integration degree of trade protection by small state states would be expected to be relatively low such that their membership of an RTA would generate few of the trade gains anticipated by orthodox theorists. Further, the strongly positive effects of the lowering of partners' trade barriers depend critically on the initial existence of such barriers. The logical basis for this assumption has been greatly weakened by substantial across-the-board tariff reductions in most countries under successive GATT/WTO Rounds of trade liberalisation.

The reduction in the general level of international trade protection has two important implications in this context. Firstly, the marginal gains to most countries from further trade liberalisation are falling, depending upon import elasticities and the pattern of product protection, such that the benefits from economic integration are also falling. Secondly, small states are not necessarily dependent upon participation in RTAs to ensure access to partners' markets, regardless of their unequal bargaining power. Instead, they have been able to increase the extent of their market to obtain broadly similar benefits through normal bilateral (or multilateral) trading links. The only exception to this conclusion is where an RTA involves a large potential trade partner which is not a member of the WTO and which makes no bilateral trade concessions to any small states. This suggests that the orthodox case for small states participating in RTAs is severely undermined by the current liberal global trading environment.

The structural openness to trade of small states is identified in Section 1 as being both one of their principal economic constraints and a potentially critical contributory factor in their growth performance. This openness may mean that membership of an RTA may actually be unattractive because it greatly limits the potential for gains from integration. The implications of structural openness are independent of the general state of trade liberalisation in the global economy although the growth performance of most small states has certainly benefited greatly from the liberal international trading environment (Armstrong and Read, 1998a). The significant effect of structural openness in limiting the gains for small states from economic integration is generally ignored in most applications of orthodox theory.

The structural openness of small states also has important ramifications with respect to the post-integration trade policy stance of an RTA. The GATT/WTO Rules require that 'duties and other regulations...shall not on the whole be higher than or more restrictive than...prior to the formation' (GATT 1947, Article XXIV, paragraphs 5a & 5b), now evaluated in terms of the general incidence of weighted average tariff rates and customs duties (GATT 1994, Article XXIV, paragraph 5). The permitted post-integration trade policy stance of an RTA incorporating one or more small states is therefore potentially much more restrictive than their pre-integration openness because of the effect of the weighted impact of larger more protective partner countries (Read, 1998). Asymmetric integration may therefore greatly reduce the openness of a small state with respect to third countries and so reduce the extent of their market (Rothschild, 1944, 1963). This conclusion implies that asymmetric integration will generate relatively small trade creation effects through internal free trade and relatively large adverse trade diversion effects through the reorientation of imports towards less competitive internal suppliers.

In an FTA however, there is no obligation for participants to agree a unified external tariff structure such that each member states can retain their existing external trade policy subject to Rules of Origin. In this case, small states could expect to experience some trade creation and diversion effects because most do not operate completely free trade policies. The trade creation effects of an FTA, arising from the blanket removal of protection between member states, improve the access of both exports to partners' markets and previously restricted imports from partners and will be greatest for those goods with tariff peaks. The trade diversion effects will also be strongest for goods with local tariff peaks although their impact can be assuaged through autonomous trade policy adjustment.

A further issue relates to the impact upon income from international trade taxes, such as tariffs, licences and other quantitative restrictions, which are an important source of income for many developing countries regardless of size. An RTA may have important adverse trade tax revenue effects for its members as a result of the elimination of protection on internal trade. If the share of partners' trade in imports is large, this may result in the substantial loss of revenue from trade taxes (Bhagwati and Panagariya, 1996). This effect is likely to be amplified in the case of small states in cases such as the FTAA where they enter into an RTA with one or more large neighbouring states upon which they are dependent for a significant proportion of their total imports.

Asymmetric Economic Integration and the Spatial Distribution of the Benefits and Costs

The spatial distribution of the benefits and costs of economic integration, both between and within member states, is not fully considered in the standard theory although it is a critical factor in determining the overall gains from membership of an RTA. The primary distributive issue concerns the spatial burden of post-integration adjustment costs which, in turn, are affected by the pattern and structure of the regional specialisation in economic activity in member states. A further issue for small states in particular is the impact of the agglomeration effects of integration and the propensity of an RTA to exacerbate regional core-periphery problems.

Clearly, the magnitude of the adjustment costs is determined by the extent to which domestic economic activity is rendered uncompetitive by the liberalisation of protective trade barriers against imports from partner countries after integration. This is dependent upon pre-integration patterns of trade protection which, in the case of small states, is likely to be relatively low with possible tariff peaks. From Section 1, the narrow range of domestic output of tradeable goods and services in small states will tend to be internationally competitive because of the contestable impact of trade (Armstrong and Read, 1998b). Their sectoral specialisation will thus adhere closely to their underlying comparative advantage, primarily in human capital-intensive activities and niche manufacturing which are not dependent upon scale economies (Armstrong and Read, 1998a). This suggests that small states are unlikely to experience significant adjustment costs as a result of participating in an RTA. Neither however, can they be expected to benefit greatly from trade creation in the form of increased exports to partners' markets, in the absence of significant tariff peaks in specific goods, nor trade suppression. This view concerning low adjustment costs is based on the evidence that most small states specialise primarily in the production of services rather than goods. Membership of an FTA restricted to goods can thus be expected to have little impact on domestic economic activity. The impact of any adverse effects however, possibly from competition or regulatory changes, would be disproportionately large in small states given their narrow specialisation in both output and exports.

The spatial dynamics of RTAs suggest that the long-run beneficial impact on small member states will tend to be limited, if not detrimental. Indeed, economic integration favours the agglomeration of economic activity in larger and more prosperous central regions at the expense of poorer peripheral ones (Rothschild, 1944), giving rise to increasing polarisation. Virtuous circles of growth emerge in the wealthier central regions which attract the bulk of new flows of investment and skilled labour while the poorer peripheral regions experience a vicious spiral of decline. These polarisation effects are likely to be exacerbated if critical domestic policy autonomy is ceded as a condition of membership (Hirschman, 1958).

The spatial impact of economic integration can therefore be expected to be particularly adverse in the case of small peripheral member states. The adverse impact of these agglomerative effects would need to be addressed by an active

RTA-wide regional policy, not yet envisioned in the FTAA. Although membership of an FTA does not require national regional policy control to be relinquished, the impact of agglomeration may necessitate increased fiscal expenditure. While economic policy autonomy is an important contributory factor to the growth success of small states, their fiscal flexibility is limited by tight budget constraints, particularly for members of hard currency areas, as well as the inflationary impact of expenditure increases.

Asymmetric Integration: Political Economy Issues

A full assessment of the likely benefits and costs of economic integration needs to consider the international political economy dimension along with the possible consequences of remaining outside. This is particularly important in the context of small states because of their economic and strategic vulnerability. In spite of the apparent adverse imbalance between the economic benefits and costs outlined above, membership of an RTA may be attractive to small states if it significantly reduces their inherent vulnerability and therefore improves their long-term growth prospects. Several issues of particular relevance in this context are contained in the literature on the political economy of small states (Kakazu, 1994; Armstrong and Read, 1999).

Defence is a critical strategic problem for small states because of their size given the extremely onerous cost of creating a credible deterrent in spite of it being a public good (Kuznets, 1960). To this end, many small states eschew significant military expenditure in favour of free-riding on the defence umbrella of strategic alliances and the UN to deter strategic encroachment. This is a logical policy strategy with beneficial implications for domestic spending on other public goods, such as education and health (Armstrong and Read, 1999). Membership of an RTA involving large neighbouring states may therefore create explicit or implicit mutual defence obligations which reduce the strategic vulnerability of small states.

The acute dependence of small states on international trade suggests that they are likely to be significant beneficiaries of multilateral trade liberalisation. The core GATT/WTO principles of multilateralism and reciprocity have resulted in substantial positive externalities for small states being generated by successive Rounds of trade liberalisation. Such gains are unlikely to have arisen through bilateral negotiations with large countries. A key objective of international trade reform however, particularly since the creation of the WTO in 1994, is the creation of a level international playing-field. The increasing dominance of multilateralism over bilateralism is likely to increase the vulnerability of small states since their traditional niche markets are eroded (Armstrong and Read, 1998a). The only bilateral 'refuge' within the changing international economic order may therefore be membership of an RTA which provides some protection against the forces of globalisation by preserving (marginal) preferential access to partners' markets.

Domestic policy sovereignty plays a critical role in the growth of small states, and membership of an RTA has further implications over and above the loss of autonomy over domestic trade policy. Many small states have established distinct regulatory structures to support a range of domestic economic activities, notably strategic tax regimes favouring their niche offshore service activities in finance, insurance, etc. The international competitiveness of these sectors is based, at least partly, upon the existence of these distinct regulatory regimes. Membership of an RTA exposes small states to greater external pressure for regulatory harmonisation, a critical feature of the recent OECD/EU initiative against 'unfair' tax competition. Membership of an RTA may thus include additional obligations which undermine critical areas of domestic policy autonomy in small states.

Asymmetric Integration: Conclusions

It is evident that asymmetric integration by small states may only be of limited benefit such that most small states are thus unlikely candidates for participation in RTA schemes. The principal drawback of any RTA for small states relates to their ceding of autonomous control over their domestic trade policy which is likely to have adverse implications for their openness to trade and welfare. Further, the gains from integration identified by orthodox economic theory are predicated upon pre-existing protectionism such that RTA membership is the only means by which small states could gain access to the markets of other countries. In addition, joining an RTA may give rise to significant trade tax revenue losses, exacerbated in the case of many small states by their dependence upon a limited number of trade partners - the most likely other candidates for RTA membership. The critical issue for small states is therefore the extent to which an RTA can generate efficiency gains, reduce uncertainty through closer trade links, and increase economic interdependence as opposed to the loss of both policy sovereignty and trade tax revenue.

Asymmetric Economic Integration: RTAs versus Bilateral Trade Agreements

At this point, it is useful to consider the conjecture of orthodox theory that bilateral trade agreements are not a feasible strategic alternative to RTAs for small states in spite of the conclusions of the preceding discussion. If the gains ascribed to small states from RTA membership are as substantial as is suggested by orthodox theory then, on the basis of revealed preference, the expectation must be that small states will be enthusiastic participants in existing RTAs.

The evidence of small state participation in RTAs is surprisingly sparse and certainly not as prevalent as might have been expected. Luxembourg is the only case of asymmetric integration by a small state with larger ones, and its relatively central location within the EU means that it benefits from polarisation while minimising any backwash from agglomeration. Several small states however are expected to accede to the EU in the next decade, including Cyprus, Estonia, Latvia, Malta and Slovenia. The other small states in Western Europe, whether sovereign states or associated territories of full EU members, all possess very strong bilateral trade links with the EU but continue to remain outside (Armstrong and Read,

1995). Greenland became part of the EU upon Denmark's accession in 1973 but chose to withdraw in 1986 following a referendum.

The pattern is similar outside Western Europe. Only Singapore and Brunei in APEC, the anglophone small Caribbean states in CARICOM and CARIFTA and Botswana, Lesotho and Swaziland in SADC are currently members of functioning RTAs. Singapore gained independence initially as part of the conglomerated Malay Federation but withdrew rapidly after policy differences over industrialisation and trade issues with the central Government in Kuala Lumpur. The nascent West Indian Federation was a cluster of the larger British colonies in the Caribbean but collapsed soon after because its component countries preferred to pursue their own national policy objectives.

In contrast however, many small states have been highly successful in securing asymmetric (non-reciprocal) bilateral trade concessions with larger neighbouring states, including RTAs. This finding is somewhat surprising given the relatively weak bargaining power of small states with respect to their larger trading partners. The EU is notable for having granted many such bilateral concessions to small non-Member states, generally in the form of non-reciprocal free access to the EU market along with derogations for some sensitive exports (Armstrong and Read, 1995). These bilateral arrangements are in place for many small states in Western Europe as well as for many developing countries, primarily through the Lomé Convention. Most developing countries enjoy preferential access to the markets of the major industrialised countries under the GATT/WTO Generalised System of Preferences (GSP) and specific bilateral concessions to regional groupings. These latter agreements include, in addition to Lomé, the Caribbean Basin Initiative (CBI) and CARIBCAN for states in the Caribbean, with the USA and Canada, and SPARTECA for the Pacific islands, with Australia and New Zealand.

The main explanations for the current dominance of bilateral trade agreements over RTAs for small states are two-fold. The major industrialised economies, notably the EU, have been very willing to grant bilateral trade concessions to small states because of their negligible importance. The value of such concessions to the small recipients is significant in terms of assured market access and reduced risk associated with niche export strategies, while the cost to the large donor countries or trade blocs may be negligible. Until recently, the international economic order was content to permit bilateralism of this type in spite of it being contrary to the GATT regulatory framework. The creation of the WTO in 1994 however, has made informal bilateral trade arrangements increasingly susceptible to the current axiomatic commitment to multilateralism and non-discrimination, particularly between developing countries. Indeed, the more rigorous enforcement of the WTO rules through a more effective disputes system means that many of these bilateral agreements are no longer sustainable. The termination of these marginal yet critically important arrangements will deprive small states of some market niches and increase their exposure to the multiple effects of globalisation and a liberal international trading environment.

The anecdotal empirical evidence tends to support the earlier conclusions that small states are likely to prefer bilateral trade arrangements over membership of

RTAs. The future of WTO-incompatible bilateral agreements however, is severely limited. A notable casualty has been the Lomé Convention between the EU and the ACP (Asian, Caribbean and Pacific) states which has been superseded by the Cotonou Agreement. This involves the creation of Regional Economic Partnership Agreements (REPAs), incorporating FTAs, between the EU and regional groupings of ACP countries and replaces the non-reciprocal EU trade preferences of Lomé. The change in the enforcement of the rules of international trade under the WTO therefore has important implications for the trade strategies of small states generally. Further, the Cotonou Agreement can be seen to be a parallel (but earlier) development to that of the FTAA in terms of involving many of the small states in the Caribbean in an asymmetric FTA with larger industrialised states.

The FTAA and Small States in the Caribbean

The theoretical discussion of economic integration and its implications for small states provides a number of useful insights into the implications of the FTAA for the Caribbean. This section considers the prospects for the Caribbean in the context of the orthodox theory of integration and the special case of small states. It also considers the likely effects of the FTAA in the light of recent empirical work on the impact of the Cotonou Agreement and issues for the Caribbean arising from the on-going process of globalisation.

The Implications of Orthodox Theory of Integration for the Caribbean

The general conclusion of the orthodox theory of economic integration with regard to the impact of the FTAA on the Caribbean region is straightforward to the extent that any RTA involving small states is regarded as being highly beneficial. This accords with the oft-repeated assertion that small states are the greatest gainers from integration schemes and thus the discussion of the extension of the FTAA to include the Caribbean warrants very little debate. This unequivocally positive view however, does not stand up well to closer analytical or empirical scrutiny in that it is founded upon the erroneous assumption that small states have no viable alternatives to integration.

Economic Integration: The Special Case of Small States and Implications for the Caribbean

The proposed FTAA involves economic integration between the small states of the Caribbean and its larger neighbours, notably the USA, in an FTA and therefore represents a case of asymmetric integration. The potential impact of the FTAA requires careful consideration of both the magnitude and distribution of any potential gains, particularly in the light of the failure of orthodox integration theory to take into account the economic structures and constraints faced by small states.

The theoretical and empirical literatures on small states emphasise the critical role of trade in their growth and the structural openness of their economies. Any gains to the Caribbean small states from liberalising their trade with partners in the FTAA, except for the specific cases of tariff peaks, will in fact be very small. Further, because the integration is strongly asymmetric integration, many of the beneficial effects which do arise are likely to be distributed unequally between the member states, to the general detriment of the smallest ones. Economic activity will tend to agglomerate in the larger more prosperous member states, i.e., the USA in particular, at the expense of the smaller peripheral members of the FTAA, leading to increased adverse polarisation. However, the potential reversal of such polarisation effects by an active regional policy is not as yet envisaged within the FTAA. Further, the potential impact of the loss of trade tax revenue also needs to be considered.

This is not to say that the Caribbean region will definitely lose out from their membership of the FTAA but rather that the argument is nowhere as near clear-cut as has been suggested by the superficial conclusions of orthodox integration theory. There are additional factors, especially relating to defence and strategic issues, which may make the FTAA attractive to many small states in the Caribbean regardless of the possible negative economic effects of their membership. In this light, the example of small states in Western Europe is instructive since most have retained their policy sovereignty and continue to stay outside the EU while, at the same time, securing beneficial bilateral trade agreements.

The Impact of the FTAA: Empirical Inferences from the Cotonou Agreement

There is currently little in the way of an empirical literature on the effects of the FTAA, particularly with respect to its impact on the Caribbean. There are however, useful analytical parallels between the implications of the FTAA and that of the Cotonou Agreement mentioned above. The Cotonou Agreement, signed in 2000 and covering the period 2001 to 2020, has replaced the preferential trade structure of Lomé with a 'hub and spoke' system of interlocking FTAs as part of several REPAs between various ACP countries, including the Caribbean and the EU. The only real difference between the Cotonou Agreement and the FTAA is that the former incorporates an FTA between the Caribbean and the EU as opposed to the USA. In the absence of empirical analysis of the proposed FTAA, useful insights can be derived from the results of research on the impact of Cotonou on the Caribbean small states.

The most notable empirical work in this context focuses on the impact of Cotonou on revenue from trade taxes in selected small Caribbean economies (McKay *et al.*, 2001). The study uses import shares and forecast tariff reductions within an AIDS model to estimate the potential revenue impact of an FTA between Jamaica, Trinidad & Tobago, and the Organisation of Eastern Caribbean States (OECS) and the EU. The data indicate that several Caribbean states have a high level of fiscal dependence on trade taxes for tax revenue and current expenditure, specifically The Bahamas, Dominica, Grenada, St. Kitts, St. Lucia and St. Vincent, i.e., most of the smallest states. Further, the results suggest that all of the Caribbean states will lose tax revenue under the FTA and the smaller states in particular. For Jamaica, this represents an average of 3.5 per cent (1997-2000), Trinidad & Tobago 3.7 per cent and the OECS 15.0 per cent (McKay *et al.*, 2001). This is equivalent to about 0.2 per cent of GDP in 1999 for Jamaica and Trinidad & Tobago and 1.2 per cent for the OECS (own calculations). While these effects are not large neither are they particularly small, and McKay *et al.* suggest that some form of redistribution may be required within the REPA between the EU and CARICOM to alleviate the impact of such shortfalls in revenues.

In the absence of data on the relative import shares of the EU and US/NAFTA in the Caribbean countries, any conclusions concerning the impact of the FTAA on trade taxes can only be very tentative. Nevertheless, if the respective import shares are in any way of a similar magnitude, then the long-term impact of the FTAA on tax revenues will be significant with knock-on effects on government expenditure and, to some extent, GDP in the Caribbean. These effects will be particularly acute for those smaller states with a high fiscal dependence upon trade taxes, such as the OECS.

It is important to note that the effects of a reduction in trade taxes in the Caribbean are in addition to the agglomeration and polarisation effects discussed earlier. While the loss of some import-dependent activities to more central regions of the FTAA may offset some of the negative trade tax effects, Caribbean states may find themselves caught in a vicious downward spiral of diminishing economic activity and fiscal revenue.

Globalisation and the FTAA: Issues for Small States in the Caribbean

It is useful to conclude this chapter with some general comments regarding the implications of the FTAA for the Caribbean in the context of the globalisation process based upon insights from the empirical analysis of growth in small states.

Regional issues: The small Caribbean states are fortunate, in many ways, to be located adjacent to both North America and Latin America. The former is a large and generally buoyant prosperous region with the USA and Canada (High Income countries) together with Mexico, while the latter is a large region, primarily comprising Upper-Middle and Lower-Middle Income countries with high growth potential. The FTAA therefore represents an important opportunity for greater economic cohesion in the entire region with potential spill-over benefits for the Caribbean (Nicholls *et al.*, 2000). The failure of the Caribbean Basin Initiative (CBI) of the late 1980s however, suggests a note of caution.

Patterns of trade: The trade patterns of many small states in the Caribbean are still strongly oriented towards the EU, and their (former) metropolitan countries in particular. This is not particularly disadvantageous given the significant reduction in transport costs over recent decades. However, the prospect of substantial growth opportunities in the North American and Latin American regions should not be ignored, and would also facilitate some diversification of export markets.

Sectoral issues: Globalisation means that small states with their high degree of trade-dependence need to be especially vigilant concerning changes in the world trade regimes of specific sectors as well as the need for domestic adjustment and restructuring. Many small states in the Caribbean specialise primarily in business services - notably in offshore finance and insurance - tourism and agriculture. There are potential problems relating to all three sectors, mainly because many small states in the region specialise in identical or similar niches. This gives rise to a 'fallacy of composition' problem whereby they compete directly with each other for a limited regional market with a downward effect on local value-added. The offshore finance sector is currently subject to strong pressure from the OECD and EU concerning the status of 'tax havens' and the control of money laundering. International trade in agriculture remains highly protected in spite of liberalisation. However, agricultural trade reform may have unexpectedly negative consequences, notably the outcome of the recent WTO dispute in bananas.

Economic sovereignty issues: Many of the small states in the Caribbean have been relatively successful in achieving growth and high living standards but there still remains a need to improve the effectiveness of economic policy making. The widespread use of hard currencies or a regional currency has limited the need for an active domestic macroeconomic policy (Anthony and Hughes-Hallett, 2000), and has provided the foundations for a dynamic export-oriented business services sector. This hard currency link has, at times, tended to undermine the potential for regional trade links, particularly with Latin America, because of exchange rate instability in times of regional macroeconomic problems.

Note

1. This chapter draws upon a number of ideas originally contained in a paper presented by the author at the 2nd Annual Conference of the Centre for Research in International Economics (CRIE) at Middlesex University, 9 July 1998. This chapter makes use of the generic term regional trade agreement (RTA), which applies to all economic integration schemes, and also the term free trade agreement (FTA), which applies specifically to the FTAA under consideration. The two terms are not used interchangeably but rather to distinguish general from specific points.

References

Ally, A. (1975), 'The Potential for Autonomous Monetary Policy in Small Developing Countries', in P. Selwyn (ed.), *Development Policy in Small Countries*, Croom Helm, Beckenham, pp.115-33.

Anthony, M. and Hughes-Hallett, A.H. (2000), 'Is the Case for Economic and Monetary Union in the Caribbean Realistic?', *World Economy*, Vol. 23(1), pp.119-44.

Armstrong, H.W., Jouan de Kervenoael, R., Li, X. and Read, R. (1998), 'A Comparison of the Economic Performance of Different Micro-states and between Micro-states and Larger Countries', *World Development*, Vol. 26(4), pp.539-56.

Armstrong, H.W. and Read, R. (1995), 'Western European Micro-states and EU Autonomous Regions: The Advantages of Size and Sovereignty', *World Development*, Vol. 23(8), pp.1229-45.

_____ (1998a), 'Trade and Growth in Small States: The Impact of Global Trade Liberalisation', *World Economy*, Vol. 21(4), pp.563-85.

_____ (1998b), 'Trade, Competition and Market Structure in Small States: The Role of Contestability', *Bank of Valletta Review*, No. 18 (December), pp.1-18.

_____ (1999), 'The International Political Economy of Micro-states: An Overview of the Issues', paper presented at the IESG International Political Economy Conference, University of Warwick, 15-16 April 1999. Revised version appeared as 'The Importance of Being Unimportant: The Political Economy of Trade and Growth in Small States', in S.M. Murshed (ed.), *Issues in Positive Political Economy*, Routledge, London, 2002.

_____ (2000), 'Comparing the Economic Performance of Dependent Territories and Sovereign Micro-states', *Economic Development and Cultural Change*, Vol. 48(2), pp.285-306.

_____ (2001a), 'The Determinants of Growth in Small States', *The Round Table*, forthcoming.

_____ (2001b), 'Explaining Differences in the Economic Performance of Micro-states in Africa and Asia', in P. Lawrence and C. Thirtle (eds), *Africa and Asia in Comparative Development*, Palgrave, Basingstoke, pp.128-57.

Ashoff, G. (1989), 'Economic and Industrial Development Options for Small Third World Countries, *Occasional Paper* No. 91, German Development Institute, Berlin.

Auffret, P. and Mora Baez, J. (2000), 'Absence of Optimal Risk Sharing: Large Costs for Developing Economies, Huge Costs for Small States', paper presented to the ISISA Islands of the World VI Conference, Portree, Isle of Skye, 16-20 October.

Balassa, B. (1962), *Theory of Economic Integration*, Johns Hopkins University Press, Baltimore.

_____ (1967), 'Trade Creation and Trade Diversion in the European Common Market', *Economic Journal*, Vol. 77(3), pp.1-21.

Bhaduri, A., Mukherji, A. and Sengupta, R. (1982), 'Problems of Long-term Growth in Small Economies: A Theoretical Analysis', in B. Jalan (ed.), *Problems and Policies in Small Economies*, Croom Helm for the Commonwealth Secretariat, Beckenham, pp.49-68.

Bhagwati, J. and Panagariya, A. (1996), 'Preferential Trading Areas and Multilateralism: Strangers, Friends or Foes?', in J. Bhagwati and A. Panagariya (eds), *The Economics of Preferential Trade Agreements*, AEI Press, Washington DC, pp.1-78.

Briguglio, L. (1995), 'Small Island Developing States and their Economic Vulnerabilities', *World Development*, Vol. 23(10), pp.1615-32.

Chadha, J (1998), 'Some Observations on Small-state Choice of Exchange Rate Regime', revised version of a paper presented at the UK IESG Conference, Small States in the International Economy, University of Birmingham, 16-17 April.

Chenery, H.B., Robinson, S. and Syrquin, M. (1986), *Industrialisation and Growth: A Comparative Study*, Oxford University Press, Oxford.

Chenery, H.B. and Syrquin, M. (1975), *Patterns of Development: 1950-1970*, Oxford University Press, Oxford.

Chenery, H.B. and Taylor, L. (1968), 'Development Patterns: Among Countries and Over Time', *Review of Economics and Statistics*, Vol. 50(4), pp.391-416.

Commonwealth Consultative Group (1985), *Vulnerability: Small States in the Global Society*, Commonwealth Secretariat, London.

Demas, W.G. (1965), *The Economics of Development in Small Countries: With Special Reference to the Caribbean*, McGill University Press, Montreal.

Dommen, E.C. and Hein, P.L. (eds) (1985), *States, Microstates and Islands*, Croom Helm, London.

Easterly, W. and Kraay, A. (2000), 'Small States, Small Problems? Income Growth and Volatility in Small States', *World Development*, Vol. 28(11) pp.2013-27.

Gabrisch, H. and Werner K. (1999), 'Structural Convergence through Industrial Policy?', in J.M. van Brabant (ed.), *Remaking Europe: The European Union and the Transition Economies*, Rowman & Littlefield, Lanham, pp.139-61.

GATT (1947), *General Agreement on Tariffs and Trade 1947*, GATT Secretariat, Geneva.

GATT (1994), *General Agreement on Tariffs and Trade 1994*, GATT/WTO, Geneva.

Graham, F. (1923), 'The Theory of International Values Re-examined', *Quarterly Journal of Economics*, Vol. 37, reprinted in H. Ellis and L.S. Meltzer (eds), (1961), *Readings in the Theory of International Economics*.

Helleiner, G.K. (1982), 'Balance of Payments Problems and Macroeconomic Policy', in B. Jalan (ed.), *Problems and Policies in Small Economies*, Croom Helm for the Commonwealth Secretariat, Beckenham, pp.165-84.

Hirschmann, A.O. (1958), The Strategy of Economic Development, Yale University Press, New Haven.

Holmes, F. (1976), 'Development Problems of Small Countries', in L.V. Castle and F. Holmes (eds), *Co-operation and Development in the Asia Pacific Region: Relations Between Large and Small Countries*, Japan Research Centre, Tokyo, pp.43-66.

Jalan, B. (ed.) (1982), *Problems and Policies in Small Economies*, Croom Helm for the Commonwealth Secretariat, Beckenham.

Kakazu, H. (1994), *Sustainable Development of Small Island Economies*, Westview Press, New York.

Khatkhate, D.R. and Short, B.K. (1980), 'Monetary and Central Banking Problems of Mini-states', *World Development*, Vol. 8(12), pp.1017-26.

Kuznets, S. (1960), 'The Economic Growth of Small Nations', in E.A.G. Robinson (ed.), *The Economic Consequences of the Size of Nations*, Macmillan, London, pp.14-32.

Lewis, W.A. (1955), *The Theory of Growth and Development*, Allen & Unwin, London.

McKay, A., Milner, C. and Morrissey, O. (2001), 'Evaluating the Fiscal Impact of a Regional Economic Partnership Agreement (REPA) between the European Union and CARICOM', mimeo.

Marcy, G. (1960), 'How Far Can Foreign Trade and Customs Agreements Confer upon Small Nations the Advantages of Larger Nations?', in E.A.G. Robinson (ed.), *The Economic Consequences of the Size of Nations*, Macmillan, London, pp.265-81.

Myrdal, G. (1957), *Economic Theory and Underdeveloped Regions*, Duckworth, London.

Nicholls, S., Birchwood, A., Colthrust, P. and Boodoo, E. (2000), 'The State of and Prospects for the Deepening and Widening of Caribbean Integration', *World Economy*, Vol. 23(9), pp.1161-94.

Panagariya, A. (2000), 'Preferential Trade Liberalization: The Traditional Theory and New Developments', *Journal of Economic Literature*, Vol. XXXVIII (2), pp.287-331.

Read, R. (1995), 'Microstates and Currency Systems: A Review of the Issues and Evidence', paper presented to the IESG Easter Mini-Conference, University of Manchester, 20-21 April, mimeo.

_____ (1998), 'The Asymmetric Effects of Economic Integration: Small States and the Formation of Regional Trade Blocs', paper presented at the 2nd Annual Conference of the Centre for Research in International Economics (CRIE) at Middlesex University, 9 July 1998.

_____ (2000), 'The Characteristics, Vulnerability and Growth Performance of Small Economies', Briefing Paper for the WTO Seminar on Small Economies, 21 October, WTO, Palais des Nations, Geneva.

_____ (2001), 'Growth, Economic Development and Structural Transition in Small Vulnerable States', in S.M. Murshed (ed.), *Globalisation and the Obstacles to the Successful Integration of Small Vulnerable Economies*, Routledge, London.

Robinson, E.A.G. (ed.) (1960), *The Economic Consequences of the Size of Nations*, Macmillan, London.

Rothschild, K.W. (1944), 'The Small Nation and World Trade', *Economic Journal*, Vol. LIV, April, pp.26-40.

_____ (1963), 'Kleinstaat und Integration', *Weltwirtschaftliches Archiv*, Vol. 90, pp.239-75.

Scitovsky, T. (1960), 'International Trade and Economic Integration as a Means of Overcoming the Disadvantages of a Small Nation', in E.A.G. Robinson (ed.), *The Economic Consequences of the Size of Nations*, Macmillan, London, pp.282-90.

Selwyn, P (ed.) (1975a), *Development Policy in Small Countries*, Croom Helm, Beckenham.

_____ (1975b), 'Industrial Development in Peripheral Small Countries', in P. Selwyn (ed.), *Development Policy in Small Countries*, Croom Helm, Beckenham, pp.77-104.

Shand, R.T. (ed.) (1998), *The Island States of the Pacific and Indian Oceans: Anatomy of Development*, Development Studies Centre Monograph No. 23, Australian National University, Canberra.

Thomas, I. (1982), 'The Industrialisation Experience of Small Economies', in B. Jalan (ed.), *Problems and Policies in Small Economies*, Croom Helm for the Commonwealth Secretariat, Beckenham, pp.103-24.

Triffin, R. (1960), 'The Size of Nation and its Vulnerability to Economic Nationalism', in E.A.G. Robinson (ed.), *The Economic Consequences of the Size of Nations*, Macmillan, London, pp.247-64.

UNCTAD (1988), *Specific Problems of Island Developing Countries*, UNCTAD, Geneva.

_____ (1997), *The Vulnerability of Small Island Developing States in the Context of Globalization: Common Issues and Remedies*, UNCTAD, Geneva.

Viner, J. (1950), *The Customs Union Issue*, Carnegie Endowment for International Peace, New York.

World Development (1980), Vol. 8(12), special issue.

World Development (1993), Vol. 21(2), special issue.

Chapter 4

Globalisation, Technology, Trade and Development[1]

Anthony Clayton

Technology and Development

We are living in an era of unprecedented technological change. Technology is, in turn, one of the most fundamental drivers of social and economic development. Each radical innovation, incremental improvement and/or new deployment of technology both enables and spurs further phases of economic and technological change, in a positive reciprocating dynamic. Some estimates clearly indicate that innovation *per se* now accounts for more than half of economic growth in the advanced industrial/post-industrial economies, with much of the remainder derived from incremental technological and managerial improvements that raise per capita productivity and thereby increase both output and real income. There are a number of rapidly maturing technologies in the pipeline, and new composite materials, biotechnologies, informatics, microfabrication techniques and nanotechnologies will soon allow a wide range of radically new solutions and opportunities.

Globalisation and Development

The pace of technological change is likely to be further accelerated by the process of globalisation; the progressive removal of barriers to international trade, as the general effect of market liberalisation is to promote greater specialisation and efficiency, increase competition, reduce costs, accelerate the dissemination of ideas and technologies and thereby spur innovation. This combination stimulates growth and development, partly by increasing the size and efficiency of markets, partly by encouraging the development of new products and services, and partly by forcing the pace of restructuring and the redeployment of labour and materials into more productive uses (although this last aspect can present some serious practical and political difficulties, particularly for weaker nations with a slender economic base and little capacity to manage the transition).

It is important to note therefore that we are still at an early stage in the process of international market liberalisation. At present, only 20 per cent of world output is *contestable,* which means open to both international acquisition and global competition in the supply of goods or services. If the transitional logistical and political difficulties can be resolved, however, that segment appears set for rapid growth. Micklethwait (1999), analysing reports by McKinsey, recently predicted that by 2030 some 80 per cent of world output would be contestable.

The accelerating pace of both technological progress and market liberalisation indicate that we are moving into an era of particularly rapid changes, where corporations and countries alike have to learn to operate in an increasingly fluid, dynamic and borderless world economy, and where a stream of new technologies will constantly transform the array of business constraints and opportunities.

The Nature of Development

Development is a highly complex and only partially understood process. It reflects, in essence, a series of economic changes and complex transformations, each with a technological underpinning. Indeed, the primary driver of change is innovation, which creates new services, products and markets, and thereby generates additional wealth. This, in conjunction with the associated redistribution of resources and power, fosters social and political change, which in turn shapes the next phase of technological innovation and economic development. As Schumpeter (1950) noted, this process entails a powerful intertwined cycle of constant creation and destruction, as new ideas and technologies create new opportunities, demands and markets, but simultaneously render old technologies obsolete and the associated skills redundant. Consequently, the economic 'status quo' and the associated political arrangements are constantly disrupted by innovations that fundamentally restructure the competitive environment.

Two of the other drivers involved in this process are particularly important. The first is profits; the return on new investments is relatively high when countries are industrialising and capital is scarce, which serves to promote saving and attract investment capital from abroad, and the combination of big, profitable projects and inflows of capital promotes rapid development and economic growth. The high growth rates allow levels of development to converge over time, thereby narrowing the gap between poor and rich nations.

The second factor is the rate of technological development, dissemination and uptake. The rate of innovation has been accelerating since the start of the first industrial revolution, as many new technologies themselves stimulate or enable further scientific and technological advances. This ensures that the process broadens and gathers momentum, with increasingly rapid progress being made on an expanding front. More recently, the rate of uptake has also started accelerating, because the technical developments that increase manufacturing productivity now disseminate very rapidly across borders. There is some variation by sector; but improvements in computer design, for example, can now be copied and cloned in a matter of weeks. As a result, the mature industrial economies have been unable to maintain their advantage in manufacturing, and this role is being increasingly taken by countries such as South Korea, Taiwan and China, which have industrialised, diversified and developed a sustained dynamic for further economic growth. China's development has been particularly rapid; over the last two decades, China has moved from being a poor developing country to become the world's fourth largest industrial manufacturer and the largest exporter to the USA. If the current rate of growth and corporate outsourcing continues, China will shortly overtake Germany and Japan to become the world's second largest industrial power.

The importance of both factors highlights the critical importance of trade in promoting flows of ideas, technologies and capital, and thereby in underpinning development. Besides, policies, politics, governance, institutions and development assistance mechanisms are, of course, vitally important, as they can either facilitate or impede the process of development, but they do not drive it.

Development transforms human potential and the quality of life. The 2001 *Human Development Report* (UNDP, 2001) noted the astonishing progress made in recent years.[2] In 1975, the majority of countries were defined as 'low and medium' development. By 2001, the majority of countries were defined as 'medium and high' development. Therefore, the majority of the world's population is no longer subject to the worst effects of poverty.

Indeed, this is largely the result of a remarkable acceleration of the rate of technological advance and global economic growth, which has transformed the development prospects of many countries. Brown *et al.* (1997) noted that Gross World Product was $4.9 trillion in 1950, which equated to $1,925 per capita (in 1995 dollars). By 1995, Gross World Product was $26.9 trillion, which equated to $4,733 per capita, indicating an exponential rate of growth (Brown *et al.*, 1998).[3] Vaitheeswaran (2002) notes that current World Bank projections, assuming that this rate of acceleration will continue, indicate that Gross World Product will be approaching $140 trillion by 2050.

This process of development and growth and the associated five-fold increase in aggregate wealth over the last 50 years has brought widespread benefits. World averages for health, nutritional and educational status have improved markedly, infant mortality and poverty indices have fallen significantly, and life expectancy has increased from 47 years in 1950 to 66.4 years today, a 41 per cent gain over the period.

The South-South Divide

The rich nations have prospered greatly, as North America, Europe and Japan still contribute about two-thirds of this expanded Gross World Product. Some people believe that the rich nations have got richer at the expense of the poor nations, but this is belied by the fact that many of the benefits of this accelerating process of global economic development and growth have accrued to previously poor nations. Since 1970, average incomes in the developing world have increased from $1,300 to $2,500, adult literacy has increased from 47 per cent to 73 per cent, and life expectancy has extended by about eight years (UNDP, 2001). The World Bank's current Gross World Product forecasts (2001) also indicate that this dissemination of benefits will also accelerate, so that today's low to middle-income countries will contribute about 45 per cent of the greatly expanded Gross World Product by 2050 (i.e., over $60 trillion, over 50 per cent more than today's total Gross World Product).

However, about one-third of the population of the planet live in countries or regions that have still not yet managed to establish a process of durable economic development, are still locked into low or negative development pathways and, as a result, are being left further and further behind. Some countries have fallen back in both relative and absolute terms. About ten countries in Africa, for example, now have lower standards of living than they did in 1960.

This widening 'south-south' divide indicates clearly that some developing countries are capitalising on opportunities and adapting successfully to the new global environment; others are not. The urgent question now is to understand what makes that difference; why some countries are succeeding, while others appear to be locked into patterns of underdevelopment.

The true significance of this fundamental divide can be seen in the markedly different responses to the same factors in the changing external environment. The same process of trade liberalisation that has underpinned much of the current era of economic development and growth and opened new development opportunities for the newly industrialising countries has also exposed several structural economic weaknesses in some of the under-developing countries, and thereby undermined their development prospects. Some of the newly industrialising countries have moved rapidly from exporting commodities into manufactures, and more recently into services, whereas the under-developing countries have tended to remain primarily dependent on commodity exports, and have therefore become trapped by falling commodity prices that have eroded their sources of the foreign exchange needed to support development and diversification.

This suggests that the process of market liberalisation is not formulaic, but interacts with internal factors (such as, for example, political systems, cultural behaviours and beliefs, market structures and other economic and institutional arrangements that can either facilitate or obstruct change), and that this complex interplay then determines whether the process operates to a country's advantage or accelerates its decline. At a minimum, it is clearly important for countries to have the human capacity and other resources required to accommodate change and manage the process of transition to a more open, competitive trading environment.

At present, the situation of many of the under-developing countries is not promising, since many of them are now contending with an exceptionally difficult set of complex and interacting problems. They have to determine their areas of comparative advantage and restructure their local economies accordingly, improve general productivity in order to increase the output of wealth, increase business efficiency in order to make domestic firms competitive, stimulate new business development and create job opportunities in order to meet the needs and aspirations of growing populations, and increase the efficiency of energy and resource-use in order to reduce the rate of environmental depletion - and all against a background of declining aid, growing public health problems and a degrading environmental resource base.

In such difficult circumstances, many people are understandably reluctant to contemplate yet further change. At times of great uncertainty, in particular, there is a common human tendency to hold fast to residual beliefs, and a reluctance to relinquish familiar theories and institutional arrangements. Unfortunately, it has also become clear that some traditional models of development have failed, while others are still current but have become increasingly contentious. For example:

- The oil crisis and recession of the 1970s precipitated the collapse of the notion of developmentalism - the idea that every nation could catch up economically if the state took appropriate action - as many of the countries pursuing these policies saw their investments fail, debts and financial dependency increase, credibility erode and average living standards decline. But this combination frequently led to internal disorder, which further discouraged foreign direct investment (FDI).

- State-led development *per se* is no longer very credible, basically because civil servants and politicians have typically been less skilled at understanding markets and managing developments than industrialists,[4] while politically-directed investment has frequently been influenced by political rather than business criteria,[5] and this combination has resulted in a history of poor performance, clientelism and corruption.[6]

- The 'Fordist' belief during the 1970s and 1980s that heavy industry was the key to economic growth, in conjunction with a common donor preference for large projects, resulted in the provision of large-scale plant and infrastructure; but this frequently failed to demonstrate the projected economic multiplier effect. Besides, in some cases, undermined by inadequate market and technical analysis, the failure of these projects left little apart from a significantly increased debt burden.

- The even more pervasive and long-term belief that capital would unlock development by raising disposable incomes and encouraging investment led to an emphasis over some four decades on bilateral and multilateral government budgetary assistance to remedy shortages of development capital. But the argument for this approach has been weakened by the growth of FDI, as global flows of private investment capital now dwarf flows of aid and development assistance. More fundamentally, the World Bank's finding that countries with bad policies and poor governance can absorb large amounts of donor capital over decades to no effect has undermined the earlier emphasis on the role of capital *per se* in enabling development (World Bank, 1998).

- Recent research indicates that technical capacity is a critically important factor in development, and that managerial capacity is the key to successful transfer of both technology and technical capacity (Sachs, 2000; Xiaobai Shen, 2001). These findings, in conjunction with the two points above, suggest that the role of FDI in transferring managerial and technical capacity may have greater long-term developmental significance than the provision of capital or physical

plant *per se*.[7] This, in turn, suggests that good ideas, worthwhile projects and good management can attract capital, but the converse is not necessarily true.
- Furthermore, the effectiveness of traditional aid delivery mechanisms has been questioned. As Easterley (2002) points out:

> (Foreign aid) allows rich country politicians to feel that they are doing all in their power to help the world's poor, supports rich nations' foreign policy goals, preserves a panoply of large national and international institutions, and provides resources to poor country politicians with which to buy political support. In short, foreign aid works for everyone except for those whom it was intended to help, with results such as the aid agencies' calculation that it takes $3,521 in aid to raise a poor person's income by $3.65 a year.

- The failings of the traditional aid formula have led various governments and NGOs to re-focus on the role of trade as an engine of development. However, a complete replacement with a 'trade not aid' formula would risk bypassing the countries that are still too constrained by logistical, governance or other deficits to be able to trade normally or effectively.
- On a similar point, the recent re-emphasis of the role of international trade has highlighted the importance of competitiveness, but this has in turn led to some misunderstanding as to the role of the state in this regard, because states do not compete (indeed, individual firms compete but nations trade on the basis of comparative advantage). This common misunderstanding has led some to believe that trade negotiations should be 'win-lose' games;[8] a particularly unfortunate outcome that has resulted in several mishandled negotiations.
- There have also been several shifts in donor focus even under the general heading of trade-enabled development, so that development assistance has switched from helping countries to remove the physical and institutional constraints on world trade (e.g., by building access roads) to analysing the characteristics of export markets (e.g., by market-scoping studies) to market access issues (e.g., by negotiating for the removal of tariff and non-tariff barriers to particular markets). Of course, all of these issues are important, but shifts like this in donor focus can cause certain policies of the recipient government to become 'donor-driven' and thereby gradually erode the sense of local ownership and control.
- Preferential trade arrangements have a particularly poor record. For example, the preferential arrangements that the EU accords the ACP nations were intended to help the latter to increase their share of the European market, diversify their economies and establish a positive dynamic for growth. However, an EU review in 1997 of the preferential arrangements noted that the ACP share of the EU market had declined from 6.7 per cent in 1976 to just 3 per cent in 1998, that just 10 products still accounted for 60 per cent of total ACP exports to the EU, and that per capita GDP in sub-Saharan countries covered by the trade terms grew by just 0.4 per cent per annum over the period 1960-1992, compared with 2.3 per cent for the developing countries as a

whole. Therefore, the preferential trade terms had failed to achieve any of their primary objectives. An even more serious indictment was the possibility that the preferential trade terms had had the unintended effect of encouraging countries to persist in economic activities in areas in which they had no 'real' competitive advantage, discouraged diversification and allowed over-manning, thereby postponing the inevitable accommodation to market reality to the point where the adjustment would inevitably be more painful.

* Finally, the IMF's 'Washington Consensus' model, which emphasises a small set of simple and apparently universal principles of good macroeconomic management, has been widely critiqued because of its perceived inflexibility and failure to acknowledge the significance of variants in socio-cultural values, institutional arrangements and governance. It became apparent during the 1980s and 1990s, for example, that similar programmes of economic reform in different countries facing apparently similar economic problems can result in significantly different outcomes, highlighting the important role that internal factors can play in shaping national outcomes.

This patchy, costly history of theories, models and attempts at development as well as the apparent intransigence of the barriers to development in the non-developing countries have left a legacy of donor fatigue and cynicism, both amongst donors and recipients. As Easterley (2002) also points out:

> If all foreign aid given since 1950 had been invested in US Treasury Bills, the cumulative assets of poor countries by 2001 would have amounted to $2.3 trillion. The World Bank's administrative expenses went from $81 million in 1959-60 to $1.5 billion in 1993-94 (in constant 1993 dollars), while its staff went from 657 to 7,106 (Kapur *et al.*, 1997). Meanwhile, the typical poor country has stagnated over the last two decades, and in many aid-intensive African countries for even longer. There have been individual success stories and progress on other indicators like infant mortality and school enrollment. But the goal of increased living standards and reduced poverty in the typical poor country was not attained. The decline in the 1990s reflects some aid weariness amidst the feeling that foreign aid created something much less than $2.3 trillion in productive assets.

This history also partly explains why the Johannesburg 2002 Summit made most progress on basic health and infrastructure issues, like water supply and sewerage, and on 'common' issues, such as fisheries management. These are clearly essential goals in themselves, but the relatively limited set of agreements also represents a partial retreat from earlier, more ambitious development aims.

However, the extent of the theoretical and ideological change over the last four decades, and the growing contrast between development failures and successes, does at least support the general conclusion that an approach that works well for one country will not necessarily work equally well for all. Development cannot be reduced to a simple formula; if it could, all countries would be prosperous. But as indicated earlier, countries have diverse histories, climates, natural endowments, demographics, institutions, cultures, problems, opportunities and constraints, and all these factors clearly have an important role in shaping events and influencing outcomes.

The Logic of Liberalisation

The logic underpinning the current process of market liberalisation and the rapid and dynamic changes currently reshaping the external environment is the *principle of comparative advantage*. This is the primary reason and motivation for world trade which, in turn, - as noted earlier - forms one of the principal conduits for the dissemination of new ideas and technological change, promotes specialisation and accelerates the formation of capital. The principle of comparative advantage, first stated by David Ricardo (1772-1823), is widely known but perhaps slightly less widely understood, as it can appear quite counter-intuitive. It is therefore worth giving a simple example.

Suppose that a poor county, with little in the way of advanced infrastructure or skills, has to compete in the same global economy as a rich, powerful country. The rich country has a large, predominantly service-based economy, but also has extensive manufacturing and other industrial operations and a modern, mechanised primary sector with efficient production of energy and agricultural products. The poor country has a slender range of service activities, provides mostly basic manufactures, and exports mostly primary products produced with relatively cheap labour. The rich country is more efficient, mechanised, profitable and competitive than the poor country in every sector. It would therefore appear that the poorer country has little basis on which to compete, and therefore no way of improving its position and prospering.

This is, however, wrong. The reason lies in the 'principle' of comparative advantage. Essentially, this explains why the total combined wealth of the rich and poor country is greatest when each does what they do most profitably. Consider the following simplified illustration.

Every Country Has to Specialise

No country has unlimited human, financial and natural resources. All countries therefore have to make some decisions as to how best to deploy their limited resources in order to generate wealth (this is true whether the allocation decisions are taken by a central planner or via decentralised market operations). If the resources are deployed inefficiently, then that country will produce less wealth and be poorer than it need be.

This is easier to understand by imagining a situation where a country's labour and capital are being used as intensively as possible. In that situation, it would be impossible to put labour and capital to any new or additional activity without taking them away from somewhere else. This is referred to as being at the 'production possibility frontier' (Samuelson, 1980). If the labour and capital in the economy were fully employed in this way, then it would be impossible to divert resources from steel fabrication into electronic goods, for example, without some reduction in the output of steel. However, this would be a sensible thing to do if the increased output of electronic goods was worth more than the lost output of steel. Of course, if too many resources were switched out of steel into electronics, there might be a glut of electronic devices and a shortage of steel, so the price of electronic goods would fall and the price of steel would start to rise. Eventually it would make sense to switch resources out of electronics and back into making steel. In practice, of course, the aim is to find the point of balance at which resources are allocated to best effect. Therefore, resources should be progressively diverted from steel into electronics until the point at which the additional output of electronics would be worth less than the lost output of steel.

Resources are allocated optimally at those points at which no further switching of resources could result in a net increase in value. This is often referred to as being at the margin, the point at which the switch of the last (or marginal) unit of resources results in a net loss of value or welfare. The maximum possible total value of goods and services will be produced, with maximum efficiency, when a society is at its production possibility frontier and resources are optimally allocated. If a country has too many people working in the wrong sector (still making steel, for example, and trying to sell into an over-supplied market with depressed prices) when they should be in another (for example, high-growth markets for consumer electronics) then resources are not being allocated efficiently, less wealth is being created, and society ends up poorer as a result.[9]

The Advantages of Specialisation

Assume that the rich country's most efficient, value-generating and profitable activity lies in the provision of financial services. Besides, the rich country has accumulated a wealth of talent in this area, and can offer a combination of diverse skills, deep liquidity and a wide range of sophisticated financial instruments. As a result, the rich country can provide financial services 100 times more efficiently than the poor country. The rich country also has an extensively industrialised farming industry, and can therefore provide agricultural products 10 times more efficiently than the poor country (for simplicity, assume that a 'unit' of service output is worth the same as a 'unit' of agricultural output).

The poor country has a small financial services sector, which is constrained by a shortage of human capital, liquidity and the necessary ICT infrastructure. The poor country also has a functional agricultural sector and an extensive ancillary rural economy, however, which still generates the majority of its exports, although the sector is performing below its potential as a result of lack of irrigation and mechanical cultivation, shortages of agrochemicals and limited extension services.

The circumstances of the rich country and the poor country are very different, but they still have to make essentially the same decision about how to best allocate their limited resources in order to produce the maximum possible total value of goods and services with the greatest efficiency.

The rich country observes that its financial services sector generates more wealth, and also notes its greater long-term potential (as agricultural output can obviously be expanded, but not indefinitely, whereas services can be expanded indefinitely). Now assume that if the rich country switched all its resources into producing services it could produce a maximum of 100 units of service output, and that if it switched all its resources into agriculture it could produce a maximum of 50 units of agricultural output.

The poor country has a similar choice. However, if it switched all its resources into producing services, it could produce a maximum of just 1 unit of service output (since it is only 1% as efficient as the rich country), while if it switched all its resources into agriculture it could produce 5 units of output (because its farms are 10% as efficient as the rich country's farms).

Now imagine that both countries decide to allocate 50% of their resources to services, and 50% to agriculture. This gives the following outcome:

	Service Output	Agricultural Output	Total Value
Rich country	50 units	25 units	75 units
Poor country	0.5 units	2.5 units	3 units
			78 units

Now imagine that the rich country decides to phase out its agriculture, and switch all its resources into services. The poor country focuses on its agriculture, and switches its slender resources out of services.

	Service Output	Agricultural Output	Total Value
Rich country	100 units	0 units	100 units
Poor country	0 units	5 units	5 units
			105 units

So, if both countries specialise in what they individually do best, the total output goes up from 78 to 105 units, which represents a gain of nearly 35% in additional production. Even more important (with regard to ensuring the necessary support for such a significant change) is that both countries benefit. By switching the remaining 50% of its resources out of agriculture into services, output in the rich country increases from 75 to 100 units (a gain of 33%), while by switching the remaining 50% of its resources out of services into agriculture, output in the poor country increases from 3 to 5 units (a gain of 66%).

Specialisation has another, related benefit; if everyone does what they do best, then all goods and services are produced with the greatest relative efficiency and so at lowest cost. This raises real wage rates everywhere (since everything becomes cheaper), which means that specialisation leads to greater wealth for everyone.

Free trade between these nations is then (a) essential and (b) of mutual benefit, as the price of goods and services will be reduced for all participants.[10]

This means that even if the rich country has a more efficient agricultural sector than the poor country, it can still make sense for the rich country to reduce the size of its agricultural sector, switch its resources into increased output of services instead, and make up the reduction in output of agricultural products by importing more of them from the poorer country. This allows the rich country to become more prosperous. However, the poor country makes an even greater gain, with a 66% increase in output as opposed to the rich country's 33%. Besides, the mutual specialisation allows the poor country to secure a durable revenue stream that, wisely invested, can transform its circumstances and prospects.

Complications...

Thus, specialisation and free trade really does work to everyone's advantage - but in practice, of course, these choices are much more difficult than indicated in the simplified example above. This is for various reasons. First, the example involves just two countries. The choices involved in specialisation are rather more complex when nearly two hundred countries are involved.

Second, the 'units' may not be entirely equivalent. It is quite true, of course, that $10,000 worth of output is worth $10,000 regardless of whether it is from agriculture, manufacturing or services, but there is a separate issue about the 'structure' of economic activity, because some sectors have more long-term growth potential than others. As argued in more detail below, $10,000 worth of sales of cattle may not indicate the same growth potential as $10,000 worth of sales from an embryonic nanotechnology firm, as the true significance of the latter may lie in its long-term potential to transform the productivity and efficiency of other sectors.

Another common problem is that skills are not equally allocated, and are not always transferable. Redundant miners are unlikely to find immediate employment as financial consultants or redundant sugar cane cutters are equally unlikely to find immediate employment in off-shore data-processing or call centres. Even though the total number of employment opportunities may rise, over time, the fact that new skills will typically be required indicates that many individuals will have great difficulty in bridging between one form of labour and another. This highlights the need for a comprehensive strategy for managing the process of transition.

This problem can be further compounded if countries that invest in education and training to foster the new skills required find their efforts undermined by an even more rapid haemorrhage of the newly-skilled people. As Clayton (2001) points out, there is little convincing evidence that the process of economic development can be supply-pushed by education. An oversupply of over-qualified graduates in a poor country can lead, instead, to a situation where many university graduates are unemployed or underemployed, and consequently disaffected, or emigrate in search of better opportunities overseas. This can make it appear that the poor country is supplying trained workers, at its expense, to contribute to the generation of wealth in rich countries, although it should also be noted that many diaspora communities actually contribute significantly to their countries of origin via remittances, investment, and the transmission of new ideas and technologies.

More fundamentally, the application of the principle of comparative advantage itself becomes more complex when both labour and capital are mobile, because both labour and capital will, in the absence of any barriers to their free movement, tend to migrate towards opportunities for jobs, advancement and profits (Ricardo, of course, developed his theory at a time when labour was relatively immobile). If there is a general trend away from depressed or less advanced regions towards more prosperous, more advanced or more rapidly developing regions, this could deprive the less advanced regions of the kind of skills on which their strategy for development may depend.

There is also an important political dimension to these issues. The policies that countries develop to address their problems are usually hemmed in with political constraints, cultural beliefs, path-dependencies and contingent inefficiencies. The industrial countries, for example, may be reluctant to cede particular sectors of industry regarded as strategic, or that continue to be major employers. These countries have been notably reluctant to open their markets for agricultural commodities, textiles and steel. Many countries are still particularly sensitive about agriculture, and the associated concerns about food security and the management of the landscape, which means that this sector in particular is often regarded as particularly deserving of protection.

Some of the developing countries have a different but functionally similar problem; historical colonialism may have had the effect of re-orienting subjected economies towards types of commodity production geared to the needs of the colonial power at the time - and, as the costs of reconstructing the economy around the production of other exports may be relatively high for a developing country, such contingent inefficiencies could persist for some time after decolonialisation (Smith, 1991).

To compound this problem, some developing nations have pursued policies that have effectively impeded the kind of structural changes required. Relatively closed markets, a reliance on preferential (and non-reciprocal) terms of trade, an emphasis on import substitution and the use of tariff barriers have protected particular industries and favoured domestic companies, but in some cases at the cost of insulating them from normal competitive pressure and thereby removing the main spur to change, innovation and development. As a result, some of these industries and companies have fallen further behind world standards, and thus become even less competitive. This problem has been further exacerbated in those cases where governments have resisted mechanisation and modernisation in industries that were major employers, in effect preferring to use them to absorb labour and thereby reduce unemployment.

The emphasis on import substitution in particular has been underpinned by dependency theory, the belief that the advanced economies (the 'metropoles') maintain their power by controlling flows of wealth, and maintain their wealth by abstracting it from the developing nations. This theory is no longer credible, as it cannot account for the fundamental divide between the developing nations that are rapidly becoming major global centres of manufacturing and commerce and the developing nations that are still locked in poverty and underdevelopment, but it still survives as the philosophical underpinning of various policy positions still held by a number of developing nations. Indeed, some countries still pursue forms of import substitution, the idea being to promote national independence, build economic strength, reduce outflows of capital, and resolve balance of payments problems by encouraging local manufacturers to supply domestic markets instead of foreign suppliers. The problem with this approach is that the local manufacturers usually have to be given preferential treatment in the form of grants or tax breaks,[11] or foreign manufacturers penalised (with additional tariff barriers or more onerous legal requirements) in order to enable the local manufacturers to compete. If the local manufacturers were genuinely competitive, of course, they would not require protection - but if they were genuinely competitive, then they would also be exporting more, the country would be less likely to have a balance of payments problem, and would be less likely to be pursuing import substitution.

Therefore, import substitution tends to be pursued by countries that are trying to prop up uncompetitive local manufacturers. This policy favours the local manufacturers, of course, but penalises both the local taxpayers (who pay more taxes or lose other services) and the local consumers (who pay more for products that are often inferior). It may also give the local manufacturers encouragement to compete directly in areas in which they actually have no advantage, which means that they can usually only stay in that market for as long as they can be protected and subsidised. By providing an incentive to remain in these areas, the policy may incur an even more fundamental long-term problem; that the local manufacturers are then actually less likely to move on, and specialise in the areas in which they could be competitive. In effect, they are bribed with subsidies from the taxpayers to become less competitive.

However, four reservations stand out here. The first is that import substitution is now more likely to be referred to as 'efficient' import substitution. This policy itself may be presented as patriotic and populist but, as import substitution usually leads to higher prices, the results of the policy are not always popular. The idea now, therefore, is to encourage import substitution only in selected areas (even so, this policy may manifest, in practice, the same problems as before). The second concerns the concept of the 'fledgling industry'; the idea being that some firms may need a period of protection in order to allow them to develop their product to the point where they can compete. This argument does have genuine merit, but only if the period of protection is time-limited or ends when the goal is achieved (or should have been achieved, or it becomes clear that the goal will never be achieved), a condition that is not always met. The third reservation concerns the related concept that certain sectors (such as advanced weapons manufacture) are vital to national security, must deal with highly classified information, and so must be closed off to foreign competition. This argument led to cost-plus bidding in closed markets in the USA, for example, which led in turn to some remarkably padded budgets. The fourth reservation is the most fundamental; that there are many different kinds of imports, with very diverse economic implications. Imports of computers are not equivalent, in this regard, to imports of luxury consumer goods; both represent an import bill but only the former can allow local businesses to migrate onto the web and develop a global presence.[12]

These economic policies have, unintentionally, led to a general lack of the kind of technological uptake that would support increased technological/business dynamism. As the remaining preferential terms of trade are gradually removed, of course, the hidden cost of the lost competitiveness is becoming painfully apparent.

The most fundamental point, however, is that the principle of comparative advantage only works, in practice, if economies actually restructure around the most valuable activities they can achieve. As Reich (1999) pointed out:

> Buried in the economic theory of comparative advantage is one stark political reality: trade benefits an economy only to the extent that it restructures the economy, making it more efficient. Trade reduces the demand for people and capital where they are less productive and increases the demand for them where they can be more productive. The bigger the gains from trade, the bigger the dislocation.

This process of restructuring is frequently badly managed however, and it can be distorted or prevented by social constraints, including political concerns about the transitional problems involved. These transitional problems can be very effective impediments to change, however desirable and necessary that change might be in the long term. People living at the margin of survival cannot survive drawn-out transitions, let alone invest in their future. People without the skills required in the emerging opportunities and markets may see the change as profoundly threatening, and elites may resist change in order to protect their interests and preserve their privileges.

Furthermore, it is important to note that it is particularly difficult for countries to restructure and reallocate resources to their areas of comparative advantage if the markets for the goods and services that they can produce most efficiently and profitably are closed off to them. For example, agriculture might represent the area of comparative advantage for a number of countries in Africa, but those countries in Africa will not be able to optimise their economies if the world's major markets in North America, Europe and Japan do not allow a significant increase in their imports of agricultural produce. This problem may be further compounded by four related market distortions:

- Many of the developing countries that have undertaken trade liberalisation and reduced their import tariffs have not - to-date - been granted reciprocal trade liberalisation and market access by the major markets. This means that these countries will benefit from some cheaper goods in some areas, but will be denied the opportunity to increase their exports in others. This will typically cause unnecessarily severe dislocation. In Haiti, for instance, trade liberalisation in the 1980s included reducing the tariff on imported rice from 50 per cent to 3 per cent, which benefited the urban population by reducing the cost of the staple foodstuff, but penalised the rural population that lost their main source of income. However, if Haiti's export markets had responded with reciprocal liberalisation, Haiti's rural population would have had a better chance of finding new export opportunities and livelihoods.

- The point above is fairly common knowledge. It is less widely known that the majority of developing countries maintain even higher tariff barriers than the advanced economies, averaging about 13 per cent as compared to the average 3 per cent of the advanced economies. Therefore, the trade barriers of the poor countries against each other actually represent an even more significant restraint on their own development.

- Some countries subsidise their exports. This may take the form of direct support, as with the EU export subsidy regime, or indirect support, as with the US Foreign Sales Tax, or even less obvious support, as with the irrigation subsidy provided via the US Army Corps of Engineers to sugar producers in Florida, but all equally represent a form of export subsidy. This distorts prices and markets, and may also represent unfair competition for other producers elsewhere who do not have access to the same subsidies. This can then prevent those other producers from increasing their exports into the markets supplied by the subsidised producers.

- The preferential terms of trade such as the sugar protocol and the banana regime operated by the EU also represent a perverse subsidy, as these may provide an incentive to countries to remain in export markets in which they are actually not competitive, and, equally, a disincentive to the reallocation of resources that would actually allow those countries to become more efficient, competitive and prosperous.

There Is a Need for Change...But What Change?

The need for structural change has been evident in many developing and industrial countries for some time. This suggests that what is needed is better management of change, and in some cases, to address the sensitive issue of the future of certain sacred cows (such as 'national champions' or other protected companies and industries). This is in turn part of a general problem with perverse subsidies, in addition to the use of various measures (including scarce public funds) to insulate some uncompetitive industries from market realities.[13]

The difficulty of the task is greatly magnified, however, by the fact that the process of development has itself become more complex since Ricardo. To be able to trade effectively and profitably today, a country must be able to identify and secure points of transient advantage in a rapidly changing world, and specialise accordingly. However, there are very complex choices involved in specialisation in an expanding international trading environment, partly because of the risks and uncertainties involved in dealing with a large and inherently dynamic and complex set of trading relationships with many different countries, each of whom will be innovating, developing, and changing their patterns of demand and consumer preferences accordingly.[14]

This argument explains why one of the most important strategies for development today, in an era of rapid technological innovation, market liberalisation and social change, is to encourage the development and growth of flexible, competitive firms that can both supply the domestic market efficiently and also expand into export markets, and thereby generate foreign exchange.

In addition, the management capacity transferred via FDI, joint ventures and acquisitions tends to be practical and focused on the specific issues and problems associated with the business sector. This can then transfer fairly readily or supply other satellite activities and, consequently, underpin the gradual development of a strong cluster, especially as a number of large corporations increasingly see the benefits of providing training and thereby supporting the development of a larger pool of more skilled suppliers (since this tends to improve the reliability and ensure the consistent quality of their supplies). Therefore, the more applied management skills transferred via FDI may have more chance of transferring successfully, being of more practical value in a development context, and underpinning a wider and more durable process of economic expansion.

Comparative and Competitive Advantage

Traditional macro-level models of comparative advantage required maximising the most valuable output, and depended primarily on the relative costs of labour, knowledge and materials, and thus were determined by various fairly tangible factors of production: skill, soil, climate, the costs of skilled and manual labour, materials and so on. Competitive advantage is a rather more subtle and complex concept, although the fundamental underlying principle is still that of comparative advantage. The reason for the new emphasis on competitive advantage can be seen in the following example. Many consumer products from competing manufacturers are effectively identical. But in a consumer-driven market, this factor is usually less important than image. Consider, for example, the 10-fold price difference between leading brands of training shoes and otherwise similar clones. This highlights the crucial importance of branding, and of building a strong image to establish a strong consumer demand for particular brands and product lines.

As this example suggests, the process of product identification, development and marketing has become fundamentally important with most consumer products. Markets must be identified and assessed, prototypes developed, consumer reaction gauged, prototypes sifted and modified, and so on, in an iterative process that eventually leads to the launch of a new (or modified) product. Thus, the key factor in securing and maintaining a competitive position in these new consumer markets is to develop strong relationships with customers, brokers, and suppliers, because product development and marketing is now a two-way, interactive process. The precise formulation of each product has to be determined in close collaboration with the technical and marketing divisions of client firms. The precise nature and even quality of the product is no longer the sole determinant of marketability. It is now essential to develop a market entry strategy, target a market share, secure a client base and distribution channels, determine the optimal product mix, and agree effective polices on branding, pricing and volume. In the majority of markets, many distributors operate just-in-time delivery systems, which means that quality control and product consistency are now of paramount importance, in addition to reliability with regard to delivery schedules.

Today's much more demanding markets therefore require a broad and diverse set of skills: knowledge, dynamism, innovative ability, as well as particular skills at marketing, branding and positioning. To develop a position of competitive advantage, in this much more complex and fluid terrain, requires a much larger complex of attributes. Flexibility is critically important, as is the ability to anticipate a change in the nature or structure of the market. Thus the new emphasis on finding points of competitive advantage requires a focus on human capital, the processes of technological dissemination and uptake, and on the building of the innovative and technological dynamism, decision-making capacity, the knowledge networks and business clusters needed to develop and disseminate information and capitalise on the rapidly transforming array of problems and opportunities in the global environment.

Knowledge and Change

Evidently, general understanding of some of the basic concepts and determinants of development has changed and evolved over the last three decades. For example, it is now widely agreed that skill and knowledge are critically important factors in economic development, but the underlying model of the nature of knowledge has changed and evolved. Dependency theory, for instance, saw knowledge as a fixed commodity, but it is now more generally understood as a dynamic configuration of infrastructure, information, management, technology and skill that has to be continuously updated and constantly restructured in order to keep pace with changing demand. It is now generally agreed that knowledge (in this broad sense) is a key factor in enabling and underpinning the process of development, and that good governance can help to accelerate and widen the process. The other factors of development (such as capital) will generally follow, as capital will be attracted by the opportunity to develop strong market positions and make good profits. This highlights the importance of developing skill-based activities across all major sectors in order to restructure and transform economies.

This also suggests that many of the weaker developing economies will actually have to undertake a further significant internal restructuring in order to create the conditions for the formation of the human capital required to underpin the generation of advanced knowledge and technical skill, and thereby develop a real, sustained dynamic base for further economic growth. As indicated earlier, many of these countries still rely largely on commodity exports for foreign revenue, and are therefore vulnerable to a range of exogenous factors that influence commodity prices. But with accelerating technological and geopolitical change, in addition to market liberalisation, commodity prices are likely to fall further, foreclosing various options for economic development. New opportunities will open, of course, but countries must be able to anticipate these openings if they are to deploy their scarce resources into the formation of the necessary skill base and infrastructure. There are difficult choices to be made, for example, as to where and when scarce resources should be devoted to introducing concepts such as cleaner technology to improve the efficiency and competitiveness of viable existing industries, and when they should be invested instead in the development of new industries as existing industries decline.

Such a process of restructuring is intrinsically long term, because it takes years to build the technical and managerial capacity, strong science base, infrastructure, techno-entrepreneurial dynamism, supportive government policies and the strong, functioning, trusted institutions needed to sustain a skilled workforce and the associated high rates of innovation. As indicated earlier, however, the under-developing countries are usually constrained by a general lack of capacity, in particular with regard to the knowledge and skill base needed to foster innovation and technological advance, upgrade the performance of the business sector and underpin any sustained improvement in the quality of governance. It is particularly important, therefore, that these countries allocate their slender human and financial resources to best effect. The cost of an unwise investment in a rich country is largely the opportunity cost of wealth foregone, but the cost of a bad investment in a poor country is usually prolonged misery and suffering.

Notes

1. Sections of this chapter are based on material from Clayton, A., Wehrmeyer, W. and Ngubane, B. (2003); and Clayton, A., Wehrmeyer, W. and Vento, E. (eds) (2003).
2. China now makes 50 per cent of the world's cameras, 30 per cent of all air conditioning units, 25 per cent of all washing machines and 20 per cent of all fridges (*Far Eastern Economic Review*, 2002).
3. World output grew by some $7 trillion between 1986 and 1996, which means that the output growth in that decade was substantially more than the total growth over the rest of human history.
4. When governments try to 'pick winners' and support particular firms or projects they are, in effect, trying to second-guess the market system. This approach depends on the assumption that a small number of politicians and officials have superior knowledge or in some way understand the market better than industrialists, investors and traders. This is not usually true, which is why this approach does not have a good track record.
5. There may be political pressure, for example, to locate plant within constituencies with high unemployment, or those represented by powerful politicians. The plant may hence not be built on the most efficient scale, or may be awkwardly located, which can result in lost economies of scale and increased transport costs. There may be similar pressure to resist shedding labour, since workers are also voters. This can result in resistance to modernisation and mechanisation, falling per capita productivity and unnecessary wage costs. Finally, firms with political access and privileges frequently exploit their position to secure government contracts and subsidies, while using their political contacts to close off their markets to rivals. All these factors, in conjunction, can steadily erode efficiency, profitability and competitiveness. The high costs and poor service that result

are usually then passed on to consumers, adding to their costs, reducing levels of disposable income and thereby reducing the rate of new business development.

6.   There is an important distinction between state-led and state-coordinated, because some state-coordinated initiatives have been very successful. For example, the Ministry of International Trade and Industry (MITI) played a key coordinating role in the post-war development of Japan, and the US Navy played a similarly important role in driving and coordinating the development of strategic GPS technology (*Economist Technology Quarterly*, 2002). There is, similarly, an important distinction between the failed model of state-led development and the widely accepted core role of the state in actively providing the conditions needed for business to flourish, which Keynesians would extend to include activist measures such as counter-cyclical economic stimulation to shorten the depth and duration of a recession.

7.   Therefore, the market-pulled economic development may provide a more durable and useful means of skill and technology transfer than the abstract 'capacity-building' projects currently fashionable with most of the major donors. In fact, donor-driven approaches to capacity building usually result in funding for new degree courses, support programmes in government ministries or new posts in NGOs. The problem with the first is that - in the absence of a strong market-pull factor - the students may graduate into unemployment; the problem with the second is that government policy can become donor-driven, constantly redrafted to reflect current donor priorities; while the problem with the third is that NGOs can become increasingly top-heavy, dependent on continued donor funding, and more remote and less effective as a result.

8.   This is, of course, incorrect, as the primary reason for trade is that both parties benefit; each party exchanges something of lesser value (to them) for something of greater value (to them). This means, in turn, that trade negotiations should be aimed not at win-lose outcomes, but at agreeing the regulatory and legal context (definitions, standards, mechanisms of contract enforcement and so on) needed to provide a durable platform for win-win exchanges.

9.   In practice, societies do not reach their production possibility frontier. This is so for several reasons, including social concerns (society may choose a sub-optimal allocation of resources in order to achieve certain changes in the distribution of income and wealth), imperfect competition and/or asymmetric information (as market operators sometimes have to compete on unequal terms for the available resources; so outcomes can depend, at least in part, on these inequalities), and imperfect information (people sometimes make mistakes and irrational decisions). In a situation where an economy is performing below its production possibility frontier i.e., below its full potential, growth in output can occur by taking up the slack, that is, by putting unemployed labour or capital to work. This does not necessarily entail any loss in output from other sectors of the economy (although in practice it can, because of the unequal distribution of assets such as skills and knowledge).

10.   It is important to note however, that trade in physical goods and commodities generates a demand for transport, and that free trade and the associated economic organisation of the trading nations has been made possible in part by readily available cheap energy for transport. This raises an important issue about the environmental cost of significant increases in the volume of trade, which in turn highlights the critically important role of energy-efficient transport infrastructure in enabling further specialisation.

11.   These routes differ, but effectively represent the same subsidy from the taxpayer.

12.   Thus, it may not necessarily make sense to be primarily concerned about the balance of payments *per se* as the *structure* of the import and export flows may be much more significant indicators of development.

13. For example, Jamaica's sugar production costs now average some two or three times the actual market price of the sugar. Industries cannot normally survive when the costs of production exceed the value of the product, at which point they become net destroyers of value. Jamaica's sugar industry has survived, however, at least to-date, because it is a major recipient of EU and domestic subsidy. As the subsidy also exceeds the value of the output, Jamaica's sugar industry has effectively become a mechanism for converting EU and domestic tax revenue into a number of largely low-waged, low-skill jobs in an industry that does not appear to have a future. Now that the preferential trade arrangements are to be phased out, Jamaica must either reduce production costs of these commodities to competitive levels, or accept the eventual loss of these markets to more efficient producers. Negotiations with regard to the remaining preferential trading arrangements with the EU may provide a short-term extension of market access but this will not provide a solution to the basic problem, which is that the sugar industry has gradually become less and less competitive as a result of having being shielded from market pressures that would have acted as a spur to modernise and improve efficiency.

14. Traditional forecasting and planning methods are no longer adequate tools for mapping business or national development strategies for coping with these transformations, as they have a limited ability to predict or survive 'discontinuities'; significant changes in the external or internal environment that force a fundamental reevaluation of strategy or goals. Major discontinuities (like the outbreak of war, the development of a radically new, disruptive technology, a political revolution or an economic collapse) can influence the interdependent relationships between the major economic, political, social and cultural factors that determine the dynamics of development. As the socioeconomic system itself changes, its behaviour in the past no longer forms an entirely reliable guide as its likely behaviour in future. This also means, of course, that conventional forecasting will tend to become less useful at times of particularly rapid change, when firms and/or countries must respond quickly and decisively to a rapidly transforming array of problems and opportunities in the external (international) environment, and serious discontinuities are relatively frequent. Even though there are important new strategic management tools, such as scenario planning, foresighting and backcasting, that can allow a company or a country to capture both the technological and economic changes in the external environment and the central importance of the social factors and dynamics in the internal environment, these tools are used predominantly by large corporations and the governments of industrial nations. There has been relatively little uptake of these tools by developing countries, which has left them significantly less well-equipped to manage the task and, consequently, at an even greater disadvantage. This particular skill gap therefore represents a particularly pressing challenge for the less-advanced transitional and developing nations, many of whom do not currently have the strong base of technical skills required to sustain large-scale external scoping and mapping studies and scenario planning exercises, and little tradition or experience in using these dynamic planning tools. Without specific remedial programmes, this is likely to further exacerbate the 'active-reactive' divide between the economically strong post-industrial and industrialising nations and the economically weak under-developing countries. The former can usually respond effectively to external events and have the capacity for proactive development, while the latter have less capacity to anticipate change and respond proactively, and are more driven by external events and impacts as a result.

References

Brown, L., Renner, M. and Flavin, C. (1997), *Vital Signs 1997-1998*. Earthscan, London.

Brown, L., Renner, M. and French, H., *State of the World 1998*, Earthscan, London.

Clayton, A. (2001), 'Developing a Bio-industry Cluster in Jamaica: A Step towards Building a Skill-based Economy', *Social and Economic Studies*, Vol. 50(2), pp.1-34.

Clayton, A., Wehrmeyer, W. and Ngubane, B. (2003), *Foresighting for Development*, Earthscan, London.

Clayton, A., Wehrmeyer, W. and Vento, E. (eds) (2003), *Foresighting and Innovative Approaches to Sustainable Development Planning*, Greenleaf Publishing, Sheffield.

Easterly, W. (2002), *The Cartel of Good Intentions: Bureaucracy versus Markets in Foreign Aid*, Center for Global Development, Washington.

Economist Technology Quarterly (2002a), 'Accuracy is Addictive', 14 March.

_____ (2002b), 19 September.

European Commission Directorate General 8 (Development) Review, (2002), 'The Cotonou Agreement', *http://europa.eu.int/comm/development/cotonou/lome_history_en.htm*.

Far Eastern Economic Review (2002), cited in *BBC Business News*, 11 November.

Micklethwait, J. and Wooldridge, A. (2000), *A Future Perfect: The Challenge and Hidden Promise of Globalisation*, William Heinemann, London.

Reich, R. (1999), 'Trading Insecurities', *Financial Times*, 20 May.

Sachs, J. (2000), 'A New Map of the World', *The Economist*, 22 June.

Samuelson, P. (1980), *Economics*, McGraw-Hill, New York.

Schumpeter, J.A. (1950), *Capitalism, Socialism and Democracy*, Harper & Row, New York.

Shen, Xiaobai (2001), 'China Reconstructs: The Transformation of Management in Two Telecommunications-technology Producers', in R Thorpe and S. Little (eds), *Global Change: The Impact of Asia in the 21st Century*, Palgrave, Basingstoke and New York.

Smith, P. (1991), 'Sustainable Development and Equity', in P. Smith and K. Warr (eds), *Global Environmental Issues*, Hodder and Stoughton, London.

United Nations Development Programme (UNDP) (2001), *Human Development Report 2001*, Oxford University Press, New York and Oxford.

Vaitheeswaran, Vijay (2002), 'The Great Race', *The Economist*, 4 July.

World Bank (1998), *Assessing Aid*, World Bank Policy Research Report, Oxford University Press, New York and Oxford.

PART II
POLICY ISSUES

Chapter 5

Monetary Policies for Small Island Economies

Carlos J. Rodriguez-Fuentes

Introduction

Orthodox monetary theory rules out the possibility for monetary policy to promote economic growth in very small open economies, such as island economies. The theoretical arguments for this explanation can be found in the global monetarism doctrine, which maintains that extreme (financial) openness and small size imply that small island economies face an horizontal money supply (due to the existence of perfect capital mobility). The conclusion that follows then is that small island economies would not have the possibility to implement their own monetary policy. It is in this sense that some economists point out that small island economies have no 'monetary identity' at all and that the best they can do in this regard is to follow the monetary conditions set up by the international financial markets.

Some economists go even further and point out that it would be impossible for monetary policy to promote growth because of the structural characteristics of small island economies: high dependence on imports to satisfy consumption and exports to generate revenues; low possibilities for developing local activities (apart from some services and agriculture); high dependence on international capital flows to maintain investment in local productive sectors, etc.

In this chapter we question the above argument and explore the possibilities of monetary policy in small island economies from a very different perspective. Our argument will be that the effectiveness of the monetary policy to promote growth will heavily depend on what is meant by monetary policy. For orthodox monetary economists, monetary policy means the control of the domestic money supply, which is exogenously determined by the central bank, according to the 'natural' rate of growth of the economy. Since growth in the long term is assumed to depend only on real factors such as population, raw materials or technical change, all that the central bank should do is to supply the 'right' quantity of money that long-run output demands ('transaction motive'). Monetary policy then is ineffective to promote growth since this depends on factors which have nothing to do with money. It is also worth pointing out that monetary policy has little to do with price stability (inflation) as extreme economic openness to trade makes small economies price takers in international markets (domestic prices are thus driven by external forces which have nothing to do with domestic monetary policy).

On the contrary, we will argue in the chapter that economic growth can also be influenced by monetary policy, although, as it will be shown, by monetary policy we have in mind a richer range of policies than simply money supply control. Another point which is raised in the chapter is that the possibilities of monetary policy depend on some institutional factors, like the stage of banking development, which make some monetary theories suitable for some stages but not for others. It is necessary then to take into account these institutional factors when analysing the role that monetary policy may have for the economic development of small island economies.

The chapter is organised as follows. Section 2 reviews the orthodox approach to the channels of transmission of monetary policy. Section 3 deals with the literature on monetary policy in small islands. As this literature applies either the monetarist or the Keynesian transmission mechanism, it concludes that monetary policy cannot help much to the development of such economies. By using a post-Keynesian approach, Section 4 explores the possibilities of monetary policies in small open economies. Although the conclusion is also that monetary policy cannot solve structural problems of small island economies, some possibilities for monetary policy to overcome such economic problems are explored. Section 5 draws some conclusions.

The Transmission Mechanism of Monetary Policy and Its Implications for Economic Growth

The discussion about the monetary policy effectiveness usually distinguishes two alternative transmission mechanisms. On the one hand, there is the monetarist mechanism which assumes a direct impact of money on income. On the other hand, there is the traditional Keynesian mechanism which assumes a rather indirect effect of monetary changes on income. However, these two different views share a common assumption: the existence of a real and a monetary side in the economy, the transmission mechanism being the link between the two sides. Although each view proposes a different mechanism for monetary policy, they are 'consistent with several specifications of the structural equations of ISLM' and, therefore, differences between them are concerned with some value parameters of a general model, but not with the model itself (Davidson, 1971; Chick, 1973, p.19). This explains why the debate between these two schools of economic thought has mainly taken place on an empirical ground, as some authors argue that 'the basic differences among economists are empirical, not theoretical' (Friedman, 1970, p.234), and that the only way to see which 'pudding' is best is by eating them (Friedman, 1956, p.17).

Another shared assumption by these two schools of economic thought is their lack of reference to institutional aspects when analysing the effectiveness of monetary policy. Therefore, the discussion about the transmission mechanism of monetary policy has ruled out the possibility that monetary policy may work differently under different institutional circumstances.

It is by assuming that: (1) the market economy is naturally stable and in an equilibrium state; and, (2) equilibrium output depends on real factors (labour and physical capital) that the monetarists arrive at the conclusion that money only causes disturbances (either inflation in the long term or business cycles in the short). But what is important to consider is that this statement is in itself a sort of 'unavoidable' conclusion that follows from the assumptions made by monetarists: money is considered only to be 'a machine for doing quickly and commodiously what would be done, though less quickly and commodiously, without it' (John Stuart Mill, as quoted in Friedman, 1969, p.105).

This point is very clear: money is only a 'technical input' and as such it should be supplied according to the real needs (i.e., transaction motive) given by real production (Dow, 1985, p.182). Since output is considered to depend on (physical) capital and labour, and those are relatively fixed within the short term, monetarists expect that any increase in expenditure only causes a temporary increase in output (a fluctuation over its long-run trend), which ends with higher inflation rates in the long term (and the same real income level). That is why some economists argue that when monetary policy is used to do 'what monetary policy cannot do', that is, to maintain interest rates and unemployment rates below their 'natural' levels (Friedman, 1969, p.99), it causes disturbances which impede sound economic growth. According to this view, what policy makers should do is 'to prevent money itself of being a major source of economic disturbance ... and provide a stable background for the economy' (Friedman, 1969, pp.105-106).

Contrary to monetarists, Keynesian economists think that for the economy to work at its full employment level some economic management is required. It is because of this that Keynesians have focussed their attention on the capacity of both fiscal and monetary policy to restore effective demand and thereby to achieve full employment (equilibrium). With regard to the monetary policy, the standard Keynesian monetary transmission mechanism is indirect since it is assumed that changes in the money supply can only affect income if both the demand for money and expenditure (consumption and investment functions) are sensitive to changes in interest rates.

It is the case that in small open economies the effectiveness of monetary policy also depends on the exchange rate effect and the degree of capital mobility. The existence of a fixed exchange rate and perfect capital mobility makes monetary policy totally ineffective to affect output since changes in the domestic money supply are unable to alter interest rates. But when the exchange rate is flexible or the capital mobility is less than perfect, then monetary policy effectiveness to affect income increases.

When the monetarist and Keynesian views about the transmission mechanism of monetary policy are applied to a small open economy, the conclusion is clear: monetary policy is ineffective to promote economic growth. To monetarists, this is so because economic growth only depends on real factors that have nothing to do with money. To Keynesians, the ineffectiveness of the monetary policy would be explained by some structural characteristics of small open economies. On the one hand, perfect capital mobility would make impossible for monetary policy to set interest rate at a different level from the international financial markets. On the other hand, a high propensity to import notably reduces the economic impact that any expenditure expansion may have on national income. As the next section will show, literature on monetary policy in small island economies also arrives at the same conclusions.

Monetary Policy in Small Island Economies: A Brief Review

Most literature on monetary policy in small island economies points out its ineffectiveness to promote economic growth (Ally, 1975; Caram, 1985; Carlene, 1986; Crusol, 1986; Worrel, 1991). It is mainly the structural characteristics of island economies that reduce the effectiveness of monetary policy since this has to deal with two objectives/fronts: 'first, to service the existing system of production and exchange and, secondly, to manage money and credit in such a way as to facilitate the process of structural transformation and economic integration' (Ally, 1975). This is what makes a difference when analysing the possibilities of monetary policy in small developing countries. Structural characteristics such as political and economic dependence on other countries; high economic openness, both commercially and financially; low economic diversification; high propensity to import; low levels of purchasing power; absence of developed capital markets and highly dependent monetary systems; underemployment of labour and high unemployment rates; uneven income distribution etc., make monetary management difficult and reduce 'standard-text-book' effectiveness of monetary policy.

The 'economic dualism', which normally characterises these economies, also modifies the effectiveness of monetary policy. This point has been made by Caram (1985) and Worrel (1991), among others. These two authors point out that the effectiveness of monetary policy may be overestimated if the distinction (as well as economic size and relevance) of the traded and non-traded sectors is not taken into consideration. Caram (1985), for example, considers that the printing of new money and its introduction into the economic system may have virtually no effect on domestic production/employment because of short-term inelasticity of local supply and almost no barriers to import. Thus, any monetary change would only affect the balance of trade as the monetary approach to the balance of payments points out. The other major role assigned to monetary policy, price stability, is also limited in island economies since extreme openness to trade makes them price-takers in the international markets. Inflation then is seen as imported inflation against which domestic monetary policy has little to do.

In addition to the above doubts about the possibility of monetary policy to contribute to economic growth and price stability in small island economies, some authors argue that monetary policy activism may also cause some adverse results (Caram, 1985). For example, under a flexible exchange rate regime changes in national interest rates would cause higher exchange rate uncertainty and variability which in turn may affect both trade arrangements and financial (in)flows. Others point out that, under a fixed exchange rate regime, there is no possibility to change either interest rates or money supply because these two are determined at the international level by financial flows; that is to say, the money supply is considered to be endogenous so national monetary authorities have no 'monetary sovereignty' at all (Khatkhate and Short, 1980; Carlene, 1986; Worrel, 1991, among others).

The overall conclusion at which most authors arrive is that monetary policy is of little help to overcome the structural problems of small island economies. Caram puts it as follows:

> The real significance of monetary policy lies in its ability to create favourable financial conditions for structural transformation in the real economy. Before all else, monetary policy is concerned with the creation of conditions and can only promote growth to an appreciable extent. An expansionary monetary policy can, by itself, not give rise directly to a sustained growth. A balanced monetary policy does, however, create a climate of confidence and stability which is indispensable for such growth. ... Money and monetary policy are thus of vital importance for the expansion of prosperity in small, open economies. However, they do not achieve miracles. Monetary medicines cannot remedy non-monetary ailments (Caram, 1985, pp.65-66).

Although we share the general point made by Caram (1985), we think this quotation hides an orthodox conception of the monetary policy because of the use which seems to be made of the expressions 'expansionary' and 'balanced' monetary policy. The orthodox approach to monetary policy, explained in Section 2, assumes the existence of a real and a monetary side in the economy, and sees monetary policy as responsible for business cycles in the short run and inflation in the long run. There is not even reference to the banking system nor the role that bank credit may play in the finance of investment. According to this theoretical framework, only real factors determine real variables whereas all that monetary policy can do is to force economy to grow over its long-term natural rate producing instability (business cycles in the short run and inflation in the long run).

Further, this particular view does not consider the possibility for the monetary policy to have different transmission channels depending on the degree of financial development achieved (see Chick, 1986, 1988 for this point). It also assumes that the best way to promote financial stability is by not pursuing an expansionary monetary policy, but a balanced monetary policy which is likely to mean a 'steady and known rate of increase in the quantity of money' (Friedman, 1970, p.48). It is well known however, that at least for financially developed economies, monetary policy works mainly through 'interest rates'. If this is true, then financial stability and credibility can be achieved by different mechanisms depending on whether we are facing a high or low level of financial development.

Sometimes monetary targeting may work, particularly when central banks can unilaterally control the 'exogenous' supply of money. However, once liquidity expansion depends more on banks' and borrowers' behaviour (that is, liquidity preference), central banks can only provide confidence and stability by stimulating the development of sound financial institutions and setting a stable pattern for interest rates along business cycles. Of course, these economic policy prescriptions are more difficult to implement since they do not provide 'fixed' rules for policy makers to follow at any time, but at least they are more appropriate for financially developed economies. Based on this theoretical framework, we analyse the contribution of monetary policy to the economic development of small island economies. The point which is made in the next section is that the effectiveness of the monetary policy depends on institutional factors, such as the stage of banking development, which not only modify the monetary transmission mechanism but also the way the whole economy works.

The Monetary Policy from a Post-Keynesian Perspective: Implications for the Development of Small Island Economies

Contrary to monetarists and Keynesians, to Post-Keynesians, money is integral to the economic process (Dow, 1993), and this means that no clear distinction between real and monetary sides of the economy can be drawn. This is the reason why Post-Keynesian authors need not look for any transmission mechanism since money is not considered as a separate and exogenous variable. It is the distinction between the real and the monetary sides of the economy which forces orthodox monetary economics to look for a transmission mechanism that links both sides. Indeed, it is because of this dichotomy that money is introduced exogenously into the economic analysis only once real forces have determined real variables. Then money comes into play only to lubricate exchange and solve problems associated with barter economies.

On the contrary, to Post-Keynesians, money is not 'exogenous' but 'endogenous'; and for that reason 'money does not enter the system like manna from heaven, nor is it dropped from a helicopter, nor does it come from the application of additional resources to the production of the money commodity' (Davidson, 1978, p.226). To Post-Keynesians, money is credit-driven and demand-determined (Rousseas, 1986; Moore, 1988; Wray, 1990; Arestis, 1992; Davidson, 1994) and enters the system through two different ways: through an 'income generating process or a portfolio change process' (Davidson, 1978, pp.226-7). In the portfolio change process, money comes through 'fiscal and open market operations initiated by monetary authorities' (Arestis, 1992, p.180) and therefore can be considered as exogenous (Wray, 1990, chapter 3). However, in the income generating process, money appears at the very beginning of the production process because 'production takes time and purchase of inputs has to be financed prior to the sale of the output' (Arestis, 1992, p.180).

If the endogeneity of money means that 'money and monetary institutions are an inseparable part of the real sector of the world' (Davidson, 1978, pp.213-4), then there is no need to look for any transmission mechanism for monetary policy since money takes part in the production process and does not come at the end of it to facilitate the exchange of goods produced in the past (Lavoie, 1984, p.773). The endogeneity of money means that it is money and particularly credit money which bridges the time-gap which arises in the production process, so it is not a shortage of saving that could constraint investment but a shortage of liquidity and finance (Davidson, 1992, p.51).

In fact, the endogeneity of the money supply explains why banks play a crucial role in economic growth; they are responsible for the provision of credit prior to production. Therefore, banks are not intermediaries that 'allocate a predetermined amount of savings among alternatives uses, but active agents that, by financing investment, force resources to be used to put investment in place, thereby fostering the development of the economy' (Minsky, 1993, p.82).

However, it must be noticed that the endogeneity of the money supply does not necessarily imply a horizontal or perfectly interest rate elastic money supply, as Moore (1988) has pointed out. The endogeneity of the money supply means that its control does not only depend on the central bank's decisions but also on the financial behaviour (i.e., expectations and liquidity preference) of borrowers and lenders. Table 5.1 summarises the relationship between the endogenous/exogenous character of money and the elasticity/inelasticity of the money supply, as well as the effect that monetary policy, banking development and liquidity preference may have on such variables.

Table 5.1 shows that, at lower stages of banking development, there can only exist an elastic supply of liquidity when central banks are implementing a loose monetary policy and, at the same time, both banks and borrowers are willing to lend and borrow, respectively. But in all other cases, either because central banks are pursuing tight monetary policies which make banks' reserves scarce, or because banks and borrowers are unwilling to lend and borrow respectively, an inelastic supply of liquidity is likely to exist. However, a high stage of bank development does not necessarily mean that an elastic supply of liquidity exists, but it rather reinforces the fact that liquidity expansion relies much more on banks and borrowers' liquidity preference than for lower stages of banking development. The overall conclusion could be that the money supply is sometimes horizontal and, depending on some factors, sometimes vertical (Wray, 1990, pp.91-3).

From this theoretical perspective, it is clear that the analysis of the objectives, instruments and effectiveness of monetary policy cannot be developed without considering context-specific aspects. As Dow suggests, to Post-Keynesians, 'it is impossible to establish any one set of axioms which is broad enough to support an adequate theoretical structure'; hence, 'any problem requires to be analysed from a variety of angles (historical, political, sociological and psychological)' (Dow, 1993, pp.12-14).

Indeed, this is particularly true in the case of monetary policy. Chick (1986, 1988) suggests that the relevance of any monetary theory changes along with the stage of banking development as well as the goals, instruments and effectiveness of monetary policy. If the working of a monetary economy and its banking system evolves with economic development, then no one monetary theory can have a universal applicability. It might be that certain monetary policy actions that work under some circumstances may not work when these circumstances change. This could explain why monetary policy sometimes works and sometimes does not. In this regard, Chick distinguishes up to six different scenarios for the banking system and monetary policy (Table 5.2).

Table 5.1 Endogeneity of money supply and liquidity expansion

Degree of endogeneity	Monetary policy	Stage of bank dev	Liquidity Preference		Liquidity Expansion
			Banks	Borrower	
Exogenous	Tight	Low	Regardless	Regardless	Inelastic
Exogenous	Loose	Low	Low	Low	Elastic
Exogenous	Loose	Low	High	Low	Inelastic [a]
Exogenous	Loose	Low	Low	High	Inelastic [b]
Exogenous	Loose	Low	High	High	Inelastic [c]
Endogenous	Regardless [d]	High	low	Low	Elastic
Endogenous	Regardless [d]	High	high	Low	Inelastic [a]
Endogenous	Regardless [d]	high	low	High	Inelastic [b]
Endogenous	Regardless [d]	high	high	High	Inelastic [c]

Notes to the table:

[a] Banks may decide not to lend despite having funds available because of their high liquidity preference. Instead, they would prefer risk-free investments such as public bonds, large companies rather than small ones, etc. Some credit rationing may exist.

[b] Although banks are willing to lend, borrowers may decide not to borrow because of their unwillingness to invest. Factors such as, high economic instability, low profitability, higher risks, etc. may explain this kind of conservative behaviour.

[c] In this case, both borrowers and lenders are unwilling to run into debt and to lend, respectively. Banks decide not to lend nor borrowers to borrow. This situation is labelled as 'defensive financial behaviour' (see Dow, 1992, for a full account of such a concept and an application to the Scottish case), a situation where the low availability of credit will be explained by both a weak supply and demand for credit.

[d] Once the banking system reaches some level of development, then monetary authorities lose their power to perfectly control liquidity. Nevertheless, monetary authorities may still exert some effect on the liquidity of the system by affecting banks' and borrowers' financial behaviour. Hence, monetary and financial policy may play this role at this stage, and these influences should be considered.

Source: Dow and Rodriguez-Fuentes (1998).

Table 5.2 Chick's stages of banking development: Implications for monetary policy effectiveness

Banking development	Banking system characteristics	Monetary policy implications
Stage 1	Banks intermediate between savers and investors. Investment spending is limited by saving; deposits limit bank lending.	Monetary policy is effective to control liquidity and lending as these depends on banking reserve requirements.
Stage 2	Claims on deposits are widely used as means of payments. Deposit multiplier applies. Bank reserves determine lending	Same as Stage 1.
Stage 3	Inter-bank lending arises but, as a whole, deposit multiplier still applies.	Same as Stage 1.
Stage 4	Central monetary authorities act as 'lender of last resort'. This makes bank lending less dependent on banks' reserves. It is banks' liquidity preference (and not reserves) what determines lending expansion. The former causality between reserves and lending is thus reversed.	From here on it is banks' willingness and not reserves that determines how much lending is given. However, monetary policy may still exert some effect on lending practices providing it affects banks' behaviour (liquidity preference).
Stage 5	Liability management and increased competition among banks characterises this stage. Banks seek for lending opportunities rather than wait for customer to come in.	Same as Stage 4.
Stage 6	Securitisation and other banking practices (off balance-sheet operations) make banks less vulnerable to central banks interventions (monetary control).	Monetary policy is ineffective to control liquidity since lending and, therefore, monetary expansion depends more on borrowers and banks' liquidity preference. However, monetary policy may affect these behavioural parameters ('expectational effect').

Source: Adapted from Chick (1986, 1988).

In Stage 1, banks act as intermediaries between borrowers and lenders, and lending is constrained by deposits. At this stage, the banking multiplier applies. As bank deposits begin to be widely used by the public (see Stage 2), bank lending depends more on bank reserves than on deposits. At this stage, the multiplier still applies, but works faster than at Stage 1. Central bank controls bank lending by affecting banking reserves; hence, the supply of credit can be easily controlled by monetary authorities. Stage 3 is characterised by interbank lending. Although bank lending still depends on bank reserves, this only applies for the whole banking system since interbank lending allows some banks to lend in excess to reserves.

In Stage 4, the 'lender of last resort' facility provided by central banks allows banks to extend credit beyond reserves when demand for credit is considered to be profitable for banks. From here on, both banks and lenders' liquidity preference plays an important role in the process of creation or destruction of credit. However, this does not necessarily mean that central banks cannot control lending expansion, as they can still affect banks and borrowers' liquidity preference through monetary policy and financial regulation. In fact, monetary policy at this stage works in a very different way. It is not the case anymore that central banks control liquidity by establishing tighter reserve requirements or higher interest rates. Despite being a market phenomenon, liquidity expansion or destruction can be still affected by central banks.

Furthermore, it is important to notice that the effect of monetary policy on lending expansion is now more indirect and works through the response that certain monetary measures (financial regulation included) may have on banks and lenders' liquidity preference. In Stages 5 and 6, this tendency is reinforced by factors like financial innovation, liability management and increased competition between banks and other financial institutions (see Chick and Dow, 1988, for the implications of this framework for economic development).

If the former argument is valid, then the analysis of the effectiveness of monetary policy cannot be evaluated from a pure theoretical perspective since the issue will depend itself on certain factors ('the state of the economy') which can only be explicit in a specific context. Chick puts it as follows:

In monetary theory ... the main theme is the effects on the economy of variations in the quantity of money. The literature is extensive but inconclusive. ... Perhaps it is inconclusive because the effect of a change in the quantity of money is contingent upon the state of the economy at the time of the change and upon who issues the money and in exchange for what. ... A change in the quantity of money, however, never occurs in isolation: it always comes into the system in exchange, as half of some transaction, and its effects depend partly on what the other half is. An expansion of government-issued money may result from an increase in the government's purchases of new goods and services, a direct stimulus to demand, or from an exchange for interest-bearing debt outstanding, in which case the effects are more roundabout. Bank money is expanded through increases in bank lending, so the effect of the change depends partly on what the borrower does with the proceeds of his loan (Chick's quote extracted from Arestis and Dow, 1992, pp.159-60).

If we accept the former argument then the crucial issue is not to determine *whether* money is neutral or not for small island development, but *when* and *why* it is neutral. It is not a question of whether the money dropped from the helicopter ('exogenous money') and caused an increase in either the real or the nominal output, or both. And this is not the question because 'it matters who receives the money' (Dow and Earl, 1982, p.285).

On the other hand, once the endogeneity of the money supply and the stages of banking development are considered, the possibilities for monetary policy to affect the economy are expanded (Dow and Rodriguez-Fuentes, 1998). Thus, in addition to the traditional 'direct effect' that monetary policy has on liquidity (displacement of the LM curve within the ISLM model), we have to consider the 'indirect effect' that central banks' interventions may have on agents' financial behaviour (both lenders and borrowers' liquidity preference).

The direct channel of monetary policy would apply at lower stages of banking development and would work through the banking multiplier model, which assumes exogenous and complete control of money by central banks. This concept would match with the most restrictive view of monetary policy and would only work in banking systems at low stages of development. However, as banking systems develop and central banks experience a reduced capacity to control liquidity, the indirect channel becomes the most important way for central banks to affect liquidity. The indirect channel applies to a highly developed banking system and, at this stage, monetary policy would affect the liquidity of the system by means of changes in behavioural parameters that have always been considered as fixed.

Authors such as Chick (1985) and Kaldor (1986) have raised the possibilities for the monetary policy to affect the economy through behavioural changes. For example, Kaldor pointed out that 'the major effect of changes in interest rates is to be found in their repercussions on the behaviour of financial institutions rather than that of private individuals' (Kaldor, 1986, p.13), whereas Chick states that monetary authorities have relied, to some extent, on the *expectational effect* that an exogenous monetary intervention may have on agents' expectations, and that a change in interest rates is not essential to the transmission of monetary policy (Chick, 1985, pp.90-91).

It is thus within this Post-Keynesian theoretical framework where we should consider the contribution monetary policy can make to economic development of small island economies. As we have tried to show above, no monetary policy can assure economic growth because the final effect of any monetary change depends both on what 'the other half' of the transaction is doing (the use that new money is put into) and its impact on economic agents' financial behaviour (i.e., liquidity preference). As regards the first effect, monetary policy could well contribute to economic growth if it successfully manages to drive funds into economic activities (through financial regulation and selective credit policies) which reinforce local economic structure. If the monetary authorities not only fail to do this but also contribute to the diversion of funds towards speculative activities (increasing interest rates and facilitating an 'adverse selection' effect), then monetary policy would be among the factors responsible for the maintenance of the underdeveloped state of the economy. Financial regulation and selective credit policies could help to make sure that financial resources are not driven into speculative activities which normally generate 'financial bubbles' that typically raise the rate of interest and disturb non-speculative activities. Therefore, financial regulation should not only be aimed to achieve financial 'efficiency and stability', as orthodox monetary theory claims, but also the 'functionality' which is needed in order to make sure that banks act as 'active agents that by financing investment, force resources to be used to put investment in place, thereby fostering the development of the economy' (Minsky, 1993, p. 82).

As regards the incidence of monetary policy on agents' liquidity preference, monetary authorities can counteract what Dow (1992) has labelled as 'defensive financial behaviour'; that is a situation of high liquidity preference on behalf of both lenders and borrowers which reduces the availability of funds to local projects and drives local financial resources away to 'safer positions' (i.e., 'capital flight'). One policy rule could be to set a stable pattern for interest rates along business cycles, and not use interest rates exclusively to achieve price stability. From this broader perspective, no concrete monetary policy rules can be given which assure economic growth, but at least it is clear that monetary authorities can and have to do well 'their half' of this 'complicated job'. This means, in other words, that the financial sector needs to be properly regulated and supervised.

Conclusion

The aim of this chapter has been to analyse how monetary policy can contribute to the development of small island economies. We have argued that most literature on this topic usually considers monetary policy to be a 'powerless instrument' to promote economic growth for several reasons. For some authors, monetary policy is ineffective because they consider money to be neutral for economic growth. To others, monetary policy is ineffective because of the structural characteristics of small island economies: openness and economic dualism between traded and non-traded sectors. We have argued in the chapter that none of these two approaches have explicitly considered the implications of certain institutional aspects for the transmission mechanisms of monetary policy.

Although we acknowledge that monetary policy alone can not solve structural problems of small island economies, we have suggested that it could help to overcome such structural problems by means of the provision of proper finance to let investment grow and thereby to improve the productive capacity of the economy. The point we wanted to make in the chapter is that the possibilities, goals and instruments of monetary policy depend on certain institutional factors, such as the stage of banking development (Chick, 1986, 1988), which make some monetary theories (and their economic policy prescriptions) suitable for some economic scenarios but not for others. What this implies is that the effectiveness of monetary policy not only depends on structural characteristics (openness and duality) which reduce the possibilities for monetary activism in small island economies, but also on certain institutional aspects (banking and financial development) which make it impossible to properly address this issue without taking them into consideration.

References

Ally, A. (1975), 'The Potential for Autonomous Monetary Policy in Small Developing Countries', in P. Selwyn (ed.), *Development Policy in Small Countries*, Croom Helm, Beckenham, pp.115-33.

Arestis, P. (1992), *The Post-Keynesian Approach to Economics: An Alternative Analysis of Economic Theory and Policy*, Edward Elgar, Aldershot.

Arestis, P. and Dow, S.C. (eds) (1992), *On Money, Method and Keynes: Selected Essays of Victoria Chick*, Macmillan, London.

Blejer, M.I. (1988), 'Growth, Investment, and the Specific Role of Fiscal Policies in Very Small Developing Economies', in A. Jorge and J. Salazar-Carrillo (eds), *Foreign Investment, Debt and Economic Growth in Latin America*, Macmillan Press, London.

Caram, A.R. (1985), 'Guidelines for Monetary Policy in Small Developing Countries', in G. Kamiramides *et al.* (eds), *The Economic Development of Small Countries: Problems, Strategies and Policies*, International Conference on Small Countries, Malta.

Caram, A.R. (1993), 'The Repercussions of Financial Imbalances in Surinam', *World Development*, Vol. 21, pp.291-99.

Chick, V. (1973), *The Theory of Monetary Policy*, Basil Blackwell, Oxford.

_____ (1985), 'Keynesians, Monetarists and Keynes: The End of the Debate or a Beginning?', in P. Arestis and T. Skouras (eds), *Post-Keynesian Economic Theory. A Challenge to Neo-Classical Economics*, Wheatsheaf Books, M.E. Sharpe.

_____ (1986), 'The Evolution of the Banking System and the Theory of Saving, Investment and Interest', *Economies et Societes 20: Monnaie et Production*, Vol. 3, pp.111-26.

_____ (1988), 'The Evolution of the Banking System and the Theory of Monetary Policy', paper presented at the Monetary Theory and Monetary Policy: New Tracks for the 1990s symposium, Berlin. Reprinted in S.F. Frowen (ed.) (1993), *Monetary Theory and Monetary Policy: New Tracks for the 1990s*, Macmillan, London.

Chick, V. and Dow, S.C. (1988), 'A Post-Keynesian Perspective on the Relation between Banking and Regional Development', in P. Arestis (ed.), *Post-Keynesian Monetary Economics: New Approaches to Financial Modelling*, Edward Elgar, Aldershot.

Crusol, J. (1986), 'La Politique Monetaire dans les Tres Petites Economies Insulaires: L'experience des Iles de la Caraibe Anglophone Barbade, Jamaique, Trinidad et Tobago', *Mondes en Developpement*, Vol. 14, pp.109-22.

Davidson, P. (1971), 'A Keynesian View of Friedman's Theoretical Framework for Monetary Analysis', *Journal of Political Economy*, Vol. 80, pp.854-82.

_____ (1978), *Money and the Real World*, 2nd edition, Macmillan, London.

_____ (1992), *International Money and the Real World*, 2nd edition, Macmillan, London.

_____ (1994), *Post-Keynesian Macroeconomic Theory: A Foundation for Successful Economic Policies for the Twenty First Century*, Edward Elgar, Aldershot.

Dow, S.C. (1985), *Macroeconomic Thought: A Methodological Approach*, Basil Blackwell, Oxford.

_____ (1987), 'Post-Keynesian Monetary Theory for an Open Economy', *Journal of Post-Keynesian Economics*, Vol. 9, pp.237-57.

_____ (1990), *Financial Markets and Regional Economic Development: The Canadian Experience*, Avebury, Aldershot.

Dow, S.C. (1992), 'The Regional Financial Sector: A Scottish Case Study', *Regional Studies,* Vol. 26(7), pp.619-31.

_____ *Money and the Economic Process,* Edward Elgar, Aldershot.

Dow, S.C. and Earl, P.E. (1982), *Money Matters: A Keynesian Approach to Monetary Economics,* Martin Robertson, Oxford.

Dow, S.C. and Rodriguez-Fuentes, C.J. (1998), 'The Political Economy of Monetary Policy', in P. Arestis and M.C. Sawyer (eds), *The Political Economy of Central Banking,* Edward Elgar, Aldershot.

Francis, C. (1986), 'Monetary Policy in a Small, Open, Dependent Economy: The Case of the Bahamas', *Social and Economic Studies,* Vol. 35(4), pp.111-28.

Friedman, M. (1956), 'The Quantity Theory of Money: A Restatement', in M. Friedman (ed.), *Studies in the Quantity Theory of Money,* University of Chicago Press, Chicago.

_____ (1969), *The Optimum Quantity of Money and Other Essays,* Macmillan, London.

_____ (1970), *A Theoretical Framework for Monetary Analysis,* National Bureau of Economic Research, New York.

Kaldor, N. (1986), *The Scourge of Monetarism,* 2nd edition, Oxford University Press, Oxford.

Khatkhate, D.R. and Villanueva, D.P. (1978), 'Operation of Selective Credit Policies in Less Developed Countries: Certain Critical Issues', *World Development,* Vol. 6, pp.979-90.

Khatkhate, D.R. and Short, B.K. (1980), 'Monetary and Central Banking Problems of Mini States', *World Development,* Vol. 8, pp.1017-25.

Lavoie, M. (1984), 'The Endogenous Flow of Credit and the Post-Keynesian Theory of Money', *Journal of Economic Issues,* Vol. 18, pp.771-97.

Minsky, H.P. (1993), 'On the Non-Neutrality of Money', *Federal Reserve Bank of New York: Quarterly Review,* Vol. 18(1), pp.77-82.

Moore, B.J. (1988), *Horizontalists and Verticalists: The Macroeconomics of Credit Money,* Cambridge University Press, Cambridge.

Rousseas, S. (1986), *Post-Keynesian Monetary Economics,* Macmillan, London.

Worrel, D. (1991), 'Fiscal and Monetary Policies in Small Economies', in W. Yin-Kann and Y. Sengupta (eds), *Increasing the International Competitiveness of Exports from Caribbean Countries,* Economic Institute of the World Bank.

Wray, L.R. (1990), *Money and Credit in Capitalist Economies: The Endogenous Money Approach,* Edward Elgar, Aldershot.

Chapter 6

Development Policy Options for CARICOM in an Era of Free Trade

Marie Freckleton and Nikolaos Karagiannis

Introduction

A trend towards increasing trade liberalisation has been a marked feature of the international environment in recent years. This trend was strengthened by the Uruguay Round trade agreement that extended the process of multilateral trade liberalisation beyond trade in industrial products traditionally covered by the General Agreement and Tariffs and Trade (GATT). As a result, agriculture, textiles and clothing, services and intellectual property are now subject to multilateral trade rules. The intensified competition generated by trade liberalisation is giving rise to the creation of regional trade blocs as countries seek to enhance their endogenous competitiveness and integrate into the global economy.

The process of trade liberalisation has been accompanied by changes in the structure of world trade, with trade in services becoming increasingly important. This marked change in the structure of world trade is being driven by innovations in telecommunications and information technology that facilitate cross-border trade in services. More than this, technological-industrial dependence has been consolidated, and export production is determined by demand from the main hegemonic centres. Foreign financing has become necessary in two forms: to cover the existing deficits, and to 'finance' development by means of loans. Caribbean nations encounter unyielding domestic obstacles to their self-determined self-sustained growth, which lead to the accumulation of deficits.

Indeed, the small countries of the Caribbean Community face unprecedented challenges in the new trade environment. The preferential trade arrangements that have supported the region's inefficient industries are being eroded by multilateral trade liberalisation. In addition, the region is involved in negotiations for free trade within the Free Trade Area of the Americas (FTAA) and with the European Union. The survival of the economies of the region therefore depends on their ability to adjust to a more competitive trading environment.

The chapter is organised as follows. Section 2 reviews post-war development strategies in CARICOM. Section 3 outlines important features of the new trade environment. Strategic options for CARICOM are presented in Section 4. Finally, conclusions are presented in Section 5.

Post-War Development Strategies

Caribbean development since the end of World War II can be partitioned into four phases. The first phase, the 1950s and 1960s, was characterised by the advocacy of the promotion of industrialisation and diversification of local production as means of overcoming the traditional Caribbean problem of dependence on agriculture. In some countries, the emergence of modern export industries in the mineral sector was a strong sign of this development thrust.

The theoretical insights underpinning this strategy were provided by W. Arthur Lewis who saw industrialisation as a vital part of a programme for agricultural progress by providing new jobs.[1] From this point of departure, Lewis sought to set out a policy of industrialisation for the Caribbean designed to overcome the dual problems of markets and resources: the region was short of capital, industrial power was expensive and the available raw material base limited, but wage rates were low by the standards of the developed world. Many favourable industries were based not on the use of local raw materials but on the processing of imported inputs. However, regional import substitution, whether on a national or regional basis, would account for only a small part of the industrial output necessary to generate full employment; for this reason, export-oriented industrialisation was the main requirement. To attract foreign manufacturers, Lewis recommended the implementation of a package of investment incentives modelled upon the Puerto Rican experience. Eventually, the inflow of foreign investment would produce sufficient profits, generate sufficient local savings, and transmit sufficient skills to local people to set in motion self-sustaining growth (Payne and Sutton, 2001, p.4).

Lewis' prescription for industrialisation had an immediate impact on newly-emerging Commonwealth Caribbean nations. Indeed, foreign capital responded to the entreaties of the region's governments and flowed into the area in substantial amounts, bringing in its wake several manufacturing industries. By 1967, manufacturing contributed 15 per cent of the GDP in Jamaica and 16 per cent in Trinidad, while the figures for Guyana and Barbados were 13 per cent and 9 per cent, respectively.[2] However, the industries established were 'final-touch' firms based on the assembly of imported inputs. They had relatively little value added, and generally failed to penetrate export markets. Besides, the industries that were set up produced few jobs, had often limited commitment to local development, and sometimes shifted their operations to other locales offering new or better packages of inducements and conditions.

The attempts to industrialise were accompanied by the promotion of tourism. In some islands, tourism was heralded as the road to prosperity even though this sector was vulnerable to vagaries of world markets and the international political economy. As the industry was geared to the affluent North American (and, to a lesser degree, European) societies, it was able to compete only by maintaining high standards of accommodation and hospitality. This required reliance on foreign capital and imports, especially of food, and brought about inflated import bills and profit repatriation. To a considerable extent, therefore, tourism became an enclave within the Caribbean economy having few linkages with, and contributing little to, the development of other sectors.

In general, as the Commonwealth Caribbean Regional Secretariat admitted in 1972:[3]

> [The post-war era of economic growth represented] a continuation of the centuries-old pattern of West Indian economy - growth without development; growth accompanied by imbalances and distortions; growth generated from outside rather than within; growth without the fullest possible use of West Indian manpower, entrepreneurial capital and natural resources; growth resting on a foreign rather than indigenous technological base; and growth accompanied by imported consumption patterns.

In the 1980s, as far as the Caribbean was concerned, the United States managed to reshape the agenda of politics and political economy to the point where it was able to lay down the parameters of what could be done and even what could be articulated. In accordance with the broad tenets of neoliberalism, its main goal in respect of economic development was to create in the region a growing number of market-based economies capable of competing successfully in international export markets. Besides, the neoliberal policy package was enforced by the International Monetary Fund and the World Bank under the 'structural adjustment' prescription. This policy prescription was premised upon squeezing the state, increasing profit margins, weakening trade unions, eliminating inflation through the adoption of monetarist macroeconomic management, and boosting growth by means of supply-side policies.

The international recession of 1980-82 severely reduced demand for a number of the region's main exports - particularly bauxite, petroleum products and sugar - and lowered the number of tourists visiting Caribbean islands. This recession created, in effect, three crises in one in nearly all Caribbean economies: balance of payments constraints, fiscal imbalances, and a national debt crisis. Desperate for financial support, Commonwealth Caribbean nations turned to the IMF and other multilateral financial institutions. As a result, their governments were forced to follow the neoliberal prescription during the 1980s. The favoured measures were always the same: devaluation of the currency, the deflation of domestic demand, privatisation of state-owned enterprises, and liberalisation of foreign exchange and import controls. After following this prescription, the economy in question would be ready to return to the international market-place able to achieve higher levels of exports and economic growth.

However, the social costs of such neoliberal policies, measured in terms of unemployment, inflation and sharply declining living standards, were immense. Furthermore, at the end of the 1980s, Caribbean economies still faced fundamental structural problems associated with the character of their production base as well as with the distribution of their economic assets.

The 1990s were characterised by what might be called 'the consolidation of the neoliberal revolution', tempered only by the realisation that more attention had to be paid to human resource development if the new technological imperatives of a globalising economy were not to pass the region by. Development was seen as a market-driven private sector-led process. Therefore, the role of the state should be to meet the demands for 'good governance' imposed by the international financial institutions, and thereby fashioned to serve efficiently the logic of deregulated competitive markets and integrated global production, led and directed by transnational corporations. This orthodoxy was best expressed by the Prime Minister of Barbados Owen Arthur in 1996:[4]

> Generally, the strategy has to accept the reality of the globalisation of economic forces rather than hanker after a less complicated but impoverished past. The strategy must also recognise that the Caribbean countries, singly and as a group, must make the transition from the old age of preferences to the new age of reciprocity in its international economic relationships. In so doing, it must be designed to minimise the costs and dislocations associated with the transition, and to put in place mechanisms that can allow the region to exploit the market opportunities which are being created by the international liberalisation of trade and the formation of mega trade blocs.

CARICOM states have achieved limited success in transforming their economies, and many of the manufacturing units in the region are little more than 'enclave' operations of larger extra-regional firms. As such they tend to transfer only limited skills to the region and are always vulnerable to recession. Additionally, subsidiary manufacturing units are always easier to close down than those closer to the home base of the company concerned, and history has shown that the Caribbean area is vulnerable to just this sort of action. Yet, there is a widening gap between these firms (mainly transnationals) which typically reside in the Caribbean islands, which are integrating at a faster pace with the global economy, and other firms in the slower integrating Caribbean countries.

The tourism industry has been the only major sector that has grown steadily in importance during the 1980s and 1990s within CARICOM. Indeed, the sector has provided employment for a sizable proportion of the population of the region and is the main source of export earnings for some countries (see Table 6.1). However, tourism has further subjected Caribbean economies to outside dependence, making them highly vulnerable. The result of this dependence makes the Caribbean more susceptible to external shocks as well as more dependent on foreign exchange. This dependence exacerbates the region's instability in employment and national income levels (Higgins, 1994, p.5). Furthermore, the growth of tourism (and other services) has had negligible effects on the development of manufacturing industry. In fact, the benefits from tourism growth have been inadequately exploited because of insufficient linkages with commodity production sectors, and failure to upgrade complementary and related service industries such as communication, information services and banking. As a result, there are few linkages between the sectors of Caribbean economies as well as a serious lack of diversification in production.

Table 6.1 CARICOM selected economic indicators

Country	GDP *per capita* (US$ 2000)	Agriculture (% of GDP)	Manufacturing (% of GDP)	Tourist spending (% Of total EX)	Annual average (%) growth rate of EX, 1990-2000
Antigua & Barbuda	9,216	4.0	2.3	63.7	-0.7
Bahamas	14,822			70.7	6.6
Barbados	9,682	3.7	5.2	51.7	3.9
Belize	2,913	19.0	13.7	30.4	6.2
Dominica	3,753	18.0	8.8	34.1	0.5
Grenada	4,049	7.7	7.7	29.2	0.4
Guyana	912	29.9	2.6	7.0	9.0
Haiti		29.0			3.9
Jamaica	2,851	7.0	15.5	37.3	2.2
Montserrat	6,841	1.3	0.8	53.6	5.6
St. Kitts & Nevis	7,381	2.8	10.4	37.4	0.5
St. Lucia	4,562	7.7	5.1	76.2	-8.5
St. Vincent & Grenadines	3,009	10.7	6.0	42.3	-5.3
Suriname					
Trinidad & Tobago	6,190	2.0	8.1	4.4	6.6

Source: UNCTAD, 'Handbook of Statistics' (2002), and authors' calculations based on national statistics.

The International Trade Environment

The international trade environment has experienced fundamental changes over the last two decades. These have included structural shifts in the composition of trade, increasing trade liberalisation and the emergence of regional trade blocs.

Trade in services accounts for an increasing share of world trade. This structural change in world trade is changing the determinants of competitive advantage. The main catalysts for the rapid growth of trade in services are the innovations in telecommunications and information technology, which have made services more tradeable across international borders. With the growing importance of services in international trade, technology and intellectual property rights are becoming important sources of competitive advantage. Developing countries that are lagging behind in technology are therefore at a disadvantage. At the same time however, the increasing demand for cross-border transfer of services is opening new opportunities for developing countries with the required technological capabilities to diversify their exports by developing new service exports.

Trade liberalisation is critical to the process of globalisation. Consequently, countries seeking to integrate into the global economy have found it necessary to undertake unilateral trade liberalisation initiatives often in the context of externally imposed structural adjustment programmes. The process of trade liberalisation accelerated with the Uruguay Round multilateral trade agreement that took effect on 1 January 1995. Furthermore, the ongoing negotiations under the Doha Development Agenda are expected to lead to further intensification of the process of trade liberalisation. This is likely to intensify international competition. The impact on developing countries will depend on their ability to meet the challenges of a more competitive trading environment.

The Uruguay Round trade agreement extended the process of multilateral trade liberalisation beyond trade in industrial products traditionally covered by the General Agreement on Tariffs and Trade (GATT). Under the agreement, trade in agriculture and textiles and clothing are to be integrated into GATT rules. In addition, trade in services, intellectual property rights and trade related investment measures are now subject to multilateral trade rules. Hence, the Uruguay Round Agreement has several adverse consequences for CARICOM countries. Under the agreement developed countries made commitments to reduce the trade weighted average tariff on industrial production by 40 per cent (GATT, 1994, p.82). Given the dependence of CARICOM countries on preferential access to the markets of industrialised countries, CARICOM states will suffer erosion of those preferences. The region's dependence on imported food means that implementation of the agreed reductions in agricultural subsidies could lead to higher prices for imports such as wheat and dairy products. Most of the benefits of increased competition in international markets for textiles and clothing are expected to accrue to the more efficient producers in China and South-East Asia, whereas the relatively inefficient producers within CARICOM are expected to lose market share.

Moreover, the Agreement on Trade Related Intellectual Property Rights (TRIPS) established minimum standards for the protection of intellectual property rights. Provision was also made for the extension of Most Favoured Nation (MFN) and national treatment to intellectual property rights. The stronger protection of intellectual property rights will make it more difficult for CARICOM countries to gain access to new technology. CARICOM countries will face increased costs for license fees and royalty payments. Opportunities for technological advancement through imitation are likely to be significantly reduced. These issues have serious implications for the pace of economic development in these countries given the growing importance of technology as a determinant of competitive advantage.

More importantly, the Uruguay Round Agreement imposes new constraints on the domestic policy autonomy of developing countries. For example, the General Agreement on Trade in Services (GATS) provides opportunities for developing counties to expand exports of services, but it also limits the flexibility of domestic policies with respect to issues such as movement of labour and capital. Similarly, the agreement on Trade Related Investment Measures (TRIMS) reduces the control of developing countries over foreign investment in their economies. As noted by UNCTAD (1994, p.158), 'The disciplines of the Uruguay Round Agreement may deprive latecomers of the opportunity of emulating the successful strategies of other developing countries which deployed a wide range of policy measures to strengthen competitiveness and "catch-up" with developed countries'.

In response to the pressures of neoliberal globalisation, regional trading blocs have emerged. Unlike the old regionalism that was essentially inward looking and protectionist, the new regionalism is being driven by the need to integrate into the global economy. Regional integration allows for improved competitiveness and facilitates the harmonisation of economic policies demanded by the imperatives of globalisation. Membership of regional blocs like the proposed Free Trade Area of the Americas (FTAA) will require significant adjustment on the part of CARICOM states, and will entail further erosion of policy autonomy. However, choosing to remain outside these blocs is not a viable option given the risk of marginalisation. The dilemma facing CARICOM is that while reciprocal free trade with stronger economies is likely to promote polarisation, the new trade environment does not favour special arrangements for weaker economies.

In summary, CARICOM's production and trade are inconsistent with the requirements of the changing international economy. The region's production remains concentrated in primary commodities and labour-intensive manufactures, while knowledge-intensive industries comprise the most dynamic aspects of global production and trade. Similarly, CARICOM's continued dependence on preferential treatment for a significant share of its exports is at variance with the growing trend towards full reciprocity in world trade. Inadequate technological infrastructure and low levels of human capital mean that CARICOM countries are unable to compete in the dynamic areas of international trade and therefore continue to be integrated into the global economy as suppliers of primary commodities, 'sun, sea and sex', and cheap unskilled labour.

Strategic Options for CARICOM

Strategic Intervention and Planning

There is need to recall that it is not necessarily the case that free trade imposes a beneficial discipline in a world of dominant, transnational corporations. On the contrary, nations can face severe socio-economic problems (e.g., unemployment/ underemployment, de-industrialisation, stagnation) by the actions of hegemonic centres, dominant financial institutions and transnationals. But can Caribbean nations effectively control these powerful transnational organisations? Obviously, there are difficulties - due to the asymmetry of power - but there is also a source of leverage: TNCs need access to markets in order to sell their products. Caribbean nations can deny, or threaten to deny, access to local markets.

More than this, access should be tied to local production within Caribbean countries, which should also imply a willingness to intervene in international trade - a movement away from 'free' trade towards 'managed' trade. Hence, there is a basis for recommending international regulations on TNCs; but it is also a basis for establishing a role for national strategic planning. Without such intervention,

Caribbean territories can be involved in a negative-sum game (Cowling, 1990, pp. 12-13).

Further, a free market system allows the short-term perspective of the financial institutions to impinge decisively on the growth prospect of industrial production (which must, of necessity, take the long view). For example, investment spending in R&D or human resource development can be adversely affected by uncertainty about the future, which may be exacerbated by the short termism of an unfettered market system. R&D may also be inhibited by a significant divergence between private and social returns as well as by long-term and uncertain pay-offs. However, not to emphasise the modern factors of industrial competency 'may leave local industries in a vulnerable position, as falling behind rivals may threaten survival' (Cowling, 1990, p.14). These central tendencies within modern market economies point to the requirement for national strategic planning in order to achieve efficiency in the allocation and utilisation of national economic resources.

Strategic planning has not been seen to be pivotal in Caribbean economies; thus, it has not been developed in a systematic or coherent fashion as a centrepiece of governments' approach to economic policy making. State interventions have usually been seen as 'reactions' to pressing problems, and the policies which flow from these interventions appear to be consonant with the *market failure* analysis. While appropriate macroeconomic policies can contribute much towards enhancing the performance of local economies, such policies only deal with the 'symptoms' of deeper structural problems. For this reason, the construction of a production-oriented approach and more emphasis on strategic industrial policy are seen to be necessary to resolve these deeper problems.

Today development means strategy, and a coherent, national strategic planning system should be an essential element of any efficient economic system. In fact, Caribbean economies need broad industrial strategies, which should involve conscious attempts by Caribbean governments to coordinate public policies more rationally in order to reach more fully and rapidly the desirable ends for future development, competitiveness and efficiency. Such economic strategies should be imposed, but leaving the market system to do what it is good at doing: handling the myriad, incremental changes which are required within these broad strategies, and, of course, running those industrial sectors and activities which do not require strategic intervention (Cowling, 1990, p.17). In fact, strategic industrial policy takes the form of modelling, targeting, restructuring and repositioning: support of 'propulsive' sectors, whose rapid growth would have substantial, long-term effects on the socio-economic development, endogenous competency and competitiveness of Caribbean economies, while considering issues of scale and scope.

Obviously, for purposes of designing endogenous competency strategies to achieve the development of productive forces as well as the transformation and diversification of Caribbean economies, technically proficient strategic planning is absolutely essential. Indeed, strategic planning is a pragmatic attempt to increase Caribbean countries' long-run capacity to transform themselves by building up the infrastructure and the requisite skills. It is these national strategic planning systems that can give Caribbean countries their internal autonomy, determine their capacity for self-determined self-sustained growth and development, and create a dynamic basis for engagement in the world economy through export promotion.

Moreover, an important consideration is the capacity-creating aspect of state spending. Caribbean governments should rely heavily on higher levels of state investment. Indeed, planned investments in knowledge, technological innovation, training and research must provide the industrial requisites to thoroughly support the prioritised sectors and activities, and boost the overall competency and growth of Caribbean economies. The key issue here is that investment responsibilities should be closely tailored to the needs of the private sector (clearly, private investment in plant, facilities, supporting infrastructure, etc. is highly desirable and essential).

Strategic Industries: Issues of Selection

Initially, it is important to differentiate between sectors which are strategically important in the functioning of a national economy but which may be left to their own devices, and those which are strategically important but require significant state intervention if their strategic role is to be fully developed. The dividing line between these two sets of industrial sectors may be determined by the history of the economy, its current level of development, and its future prospects (Cowling, 1990, p.19). On this account, we limit strategic intervention to those parts of Caribbean economies where government intervention is going to have its most significant potential impact on their overall dynamism and intensive economic growth. By recognising differentiation of sectors and industries, policy can address the problems that are rooted in the development of these sectors and industries, and thus become effective.[5,6]

In some sectors, the Caribbean already has a strong basis on which to build (such as tourism, food production/processing, etc.). For these sectors to thrive, the quantity and quality of industrial investment must be raised through planned action. Such through plans should be designed to consolidate and improve existing production lines, as well as create new types of economic activities. In fact proactive industrial policy takes the form of industrial modelling (or targeting). This involves restructuring, rejuvenation and repositioning of both 'old' and 'new' sectors and activities in order to achieve economic diversification, endogenous growth and competitiveness.

In the case of agriculture, the region cannot continue to rely on its traditional exports (such as sugar, bananas and rice) as these may be uncompetitive and are highly dependent on preferential trade arrangements. The erosion of preferential margins and the possibility of the dismantling of the Lomé preferences make clear that restructuring and diversification are essential to the survival of the region's agriculture. Agro-processing is one manufacturing sub-sector that has potential for expansion. In addition to providing food supply for the tourism industry and niche markets abroad, there is also potential for exports of pharmaceutical and food additive products processed from regional agricultural products. Opportunities for diversification are being created by the increasing demand for organic foods. This niche market should be targeted by CARICOM.

While most CARICOM countries lack an adequate supply of arable land to facilitate economies of scale in agricultural production, organic foods offer the advantage of being amenable to small scale production.[7] Successful production of organic foods for export will require investment in the training of farmers as well as implementation of the strict quality standards required in this market segment. The basic infrastructure such as roads, irrigation systems, and market information systems needed to support agricultural production will also have to be improved.

In order to maximise the benefits from tourism, the sector must provide an effective stimulus for local agriculture and agro-industrial production. Traditionally, linkages between tourism and local agricultural production have been relatively weak. This problem has been attributed to several factors including the centralised purchasing arrangements of transnational hotel chains, the unavailability of local agricultural supplies, the poor quality of domestic agricultural products, and the preferences of tourists.[8] However, opportunities for increasing the linkages between tourism and domestic agriculture are now opening up, and the mutually beneficial relationship between tourism and agro-industry can provide the foundation which alternative endogenous development strategies can build on. The development of new tourism market segments - such as heath tourism and heritage tourism - is increasing the number of visitors who wish to consume the region's traditional cuisine and domestic agricultural products (Henshall-Momsen, 1998). But it has to be recognised that strengthening linkages between agro-industry and tourism will also require improvement in product quality and efficient distribution systems, and access to credit for farmers.

Thus, it is imperative to develop and strengthen these links between tourism and agro-processing industry, as there is a potential and market opportunities for the growth of specific local industrial sectors and activities (food processing and beverage, organic farming, biological extracts and derivatives),[9] which will set up incentives and open up possibilities for a wide range of new economic activities, for the following reasons:

- there is an increasing demand for a range of food products (domestic demand plus exports to the large North American markets), particularly processed products not currently produced in the Caribbean region. Consequently, they will significantly enhance local food production capabilities and reduce the imported food. There is also an increasing demand for leisure, recreation and holidays from the travelling public;
- they will allow the local capture of a high percentage of value added, and thus generate profits and contribute to the process of capital accumulation. They will also encourage the reinvestment of profits within the local economies;
- Caribbean economies can have some significant prospective competitive advantage in these industries - higher capability to compete internationally will be responsible for their endogenous growth, thereby establishing an expanding market share and contributing to their balance of payments (and foreign exchange earnings);

- the targeted sectors will better utilise domestic resources and offer solutions to the serious problems in the traditional sectors of Caribbean islands;
- they will boost the structural transformation and diversification of Caribbean countries, and will develop and promote stronger intersectoral linkages, with multiple short and, especially, long-run productive effects resulting from investments on infrastructure and the 'accelerators';
- the propulsive sectors will enhance the local skill/knowledge base, introduce the know-how and innovation, stimulate technological progress/technical change, develop a pool of expertise, create managerial and entrepreneurial talents and increase productivity and, in turn, will impart - through their complementarities and linkages with the other sectors and activities - the momentum for 'Economic Take-Off';[10,11]
- the developmental state approach is a realistic and feasible suggestion for the endogenous competency and overall development of Caribbean economies (which can be successful) and does not require much; rather, it requires employment of existing resources in different ways, a 'wiser' public finance and different state policy choices.

Furthermore, the growth process is expected to lead to a widening of the local markets,[12] which in turn will require and/or bring about a better transportation and communications system. Thus, after resources have been developed and/or put to use, changes in technology and modern production techniques will broaden the Caribbean production base, will provide sufficient stimulus to the mobilisation of resources of all kinds and/or the inducement to invest, will bring about a net addition to the effective use of resources and, therefore, to the overall growth of the region.

Obviously, increasing and improving capital equipment and infrastructure, improving human capital and R&D status or pursuing a restructuring strategy for the Caribbean will take a long time. The effectiveness of such a comprehensive policy is a solution in the long term, combines the cooperation of government, private sector, research institutions and funding institutions, and can create dynamic competitive advantages. Such thorough knowledge-based strategies would have to be spawned by the University of the West Indies (UWI), and place emphasis on infrastructural development, machinery and capital equipment, technical change, technology generation and transfer, technology acquisition and know-how from abroad (where necessary), a higher level of education and research, learning-by-doing and training courses, continuous development of scientific manpower, better management and marketing methods.

The application of modern production techniques and technology offers some possibilities for CARICOM to overcome the limitations of small size and develop competitiveness in existing and new industries. In particular, the information revolution offers some possibilities for the diversification of the region's export base through the development of new service exports. The dominant service export - tourism - is a highly volatile industry; hence, overdependence on this industry is likely to promote economic instability. Opportunities for the diversification of the region's exports of services have not been fully exploited. Non-tourism exports from CARICOM are concentrated on the low skilled segment of the information processing industry. The Bahamas and Barbados are the only significant exporters of financial services, while Jamaica and Trinidad and Tobago export recreational services (music). Exports of knowledge intensive services such as professional and educational services remain undeveloped; yet, these are the services that may offer higher value and for which there is growing demand in the world market. The dilemma facing CARICOM states is that their ability to quickly develop knowledge-intensive services is constrained by an inadequate human resource base. Increased investment in human capital will be necessary to facilitate promotion of more knowledge-intensive services in the medium and long term.

However, the transfer of these planned strategies for Caribbean economies to new environments may be self-defeating in the absence of cautious interventionist policies required for their effective implementation. Active state policies (e.g., aggregate demand management policies, investments on, and thorough plans for, the accelerators of competitiveness) are needed to complement these strategies.

Growth Poles, Clusters and Cooperation

Growth pole strategies in the Caribbean would seek to promote specific propulsive industries and sectors with economic dynamism or high potential, which would then be capable of spilling their expansionary forces into depressed neighbouring areas within the region, in order to counterbalance the power and interests of western multinational or transnational firms.

Growth pole strategies and policies would create greater external economies and economies of scale, thereby dealing with issues of scale and scope. Indeed, the existence of these external economies would create conditions and opportunities conducive to faster growth of existing and incoming industry in the Caribbean and, consequently, would make the growth centres more attractive for new industrial development.

Similarly, Caribbean states may emphasise *clusters* as important engines of growth. The effects of these industrial clusters will be to bring together key players in economic development, upgrade technological infrastructure and the quality of skills, accelerate learning and innovation, induce the exchange of important market and technical information, stimulate the formation of new businesses, improve managerial capacity and entrepreneurship, reduce investment risks, and increase profit margins and economic growth rates.

Proactive Developmental State policies will give priority to those industries and sectors that are viable, warranted, advantageous, and strategically important in a long-term perspective but, more or less, vulnerable in the short or medium term without significant state intervention. Such industries require nurturing and have to be provided with the resources and commitment to allow them to grow and mature. Therefore, Developmental State action has not only to select sectors and industries for state attention and support but also to improve their appropriate developmental environment.

These kinds of policies must be strategically focused, and must be directed towards mobilising market forces, building up world-market-standard industries and systematically developing efficient economic locations. Indeed, modern businesses have to improve continuously, emphasise organisational innovations, and develop the capacity to respond quickly to changes in demand in existing and new markets in the world economy. However, the need to focus attention on the expansion of new products/services and exports for the international market should not diminish attention to be given to other sectors and products. Consolidating existing local production lines and improving the competitiveness of traditional exports (where feasible) should remain an important objective. Expanding existing services (such as tourism) to include new products is also important, as there may be linkages and complementarities between new and old sectors and activities (Bernal, 2000, pp. 110-11).

Also, an important notion, which mainly emerges from the New Competition view, is that - contrary to the perfect competition analysis - economies like Japan, NICs and Italy that are able to generate effective long-term-oriented cooperative arrangements, have created prosperous industries and dynamic sectors. In this sense, the cooperation among local industries in areas that are normally subject to strong competition might be of great importance, and may counter-balance the rules of the foreign dominated markets and shape production-oriented investment strategies. As technical inefficiencies and failures to adequately develop and use new products and processes often occur in Caribbean economies, the solution is likely to require cooperation between different firms as well as between firms and governments.

Institutional Changes

It has been often argued (by Stone, Edie, *et al.*) that Caribbean governments have been using the state's power to promote particular interests for both personal and electoral advantage (i.e., 'pork barrel' intervention) and special-interest-group preferences (appear to) count more than the preferences of the majority of these countries' individual citizens. In addition, Caribbean governments have not credibly precommitted to particular 'national purpose' policies and merely react to demands and actions of private actors, pressure groups and political parties. In fact, political institutions have been largely undermined by growing demands of powerful interests and distributional conflicts, while corruption and collusion seem to be endemic (Ahrens, 1997, p.142). This convergence of economic and, especially, political functions in Caribbean states has had disastrous effects in their economic sphere. In contrast, strategic and developmental goals should be neither responsive nor reducible to various political pressures and private interests, and Caribbean governments should design to influence private economic decisions in line with their view of an appropriate industrial and trade profile for their economies.

For these important reasons, it is unlikely that significant state intervention would be warranted given the inadequate capacity and competence of government institutions in the Caribbean region; the institutional impediments to the countries' endogenous development, industrial competency and competitiveness. Therefore, the pursuit of interventionist strategies as well as successful and effective policy reforms (i.e., a set of wide-ranging changes) would require the politico-institutional structures and means to formulate, implement and enforce developmental policies and production-oriented interventions in key sectors of Caribbean economies.[13]

Weak governments are usually captured by powerful interests, and can hardly implement institutional structures that decisively promote structural changes and economic reforms. In addition, changes in the structure of class relations during the last decades induced erosion of political institutions in the Caribbean. In contrast, Developmental States are distinguished by 'strong' politico-institutional structures. Building strong technostructures and embedding them into networks of cooperative and consultative relations with targeted dynamic firms and other social segments is both feasible and operational in CARICOM countries.[14,15]

To do so, determined developmental elites, which surround themselves with skilled development planners and technocrats, are absolutely necessary in order to devise and implement effective national strategies. In addition, it is essential for Caribbean governments to reduce 'pork barrel' intervention and patronage so as to insulate decision makers and technocrats from the excessive influence of powerful interests and societal pressure.

Moreover, competitive wages for well-educated, well-trained technocrats can attract more talented individuals and increase capacity, effectiveness, integrity and professionalism. Indeed, the executive technostructure must be in a position to recruit from among the best and the brightest people of outstanding talent based on meritocratic criteria. Once the central bureaucracy acquires a reputation for attracting the most competent and talented, the system can develop a momentum of its own. It continues to attract such people (even at lower salaries than the private sector) because selection is based on meritocracy. Its personnel can be motivated by the belief that what they are doing promotes the national development and welfare. This sense of 'national mission' can motivate the executive technostructure to stay focused and use its powers in line with 'national purpose' goals. The more the government intends to intervene and to play a leading role, the more important are the staffing, responsibilities, professionalism, authority and motivation of the central core. On the other hand, external pressure on appointments and patronage should be eliminated (Wade, 1990, p.371).

To be successful, Developmental State planning must be democratic, and the institutional structure must allow for participation at all levels. In fact, democratic planning includes participation as one of its defining features - not simply as a goal but as an aspect of the process itself. Participation by the social partners and the establishment of a state-business-society interface through institutionalised channels can improve the organisation of production, and help restrain the power of various groups which have access to government decision-making in Caribbean nations.

By establishing the appropriate participatory institutional network, policies and strategies can be designed and incentives created to channel resources and decision-makers' commitment into those productive activities that are compatible with sustained economic development and prompt private firms and industries to carry out long-term investment spending in the Caribbean (Ahrens, 1997, p.118). Hence,

Developmental State policies need to be accompanied by institutional reforms, which not only lay the foundation of effective implementation and enforcement of production-oriented policies but also create the suitable environment for the endogenous development of Caribbean territories.

Policy Dilemmas

The Caribbean is not a homogeneous area; spatial disparities within the region are very significant. There are great differences in output/income, in employment/unemployment, or in levels of development between different Caribbean countries, between the regions of each country, and between the various regions and islands of the Caribbean as a whole. In addition, due to political and economic associations between the Caribbean countries and developed Western countries (as well as the Caribbean islands' proximity to North America), inequalities in economic terms generate inequalities in political power between the former and the latter. Hence, free trade and international competition favour the 'rich' and the 'strong' economies (usually at the expense of the less-developed ones).

In a recent report on trade initiatives and foreign direct investment (FDI), the CARICOM Secretariat set out an elaborately reasoned position on the appropriate path for future trade policy initiatives (CARICOM Secretariat, 2000). The substance of this position is that FDI, now universally sought after, can make an important contribution to export development and product differentiation through the provision of capital, management, technology, and marketing know-how by TNCs. However, in their negotiations with other countries and group of countries, Caribbean nations should not assume that there exists any 'ideal development strategy that uses FDI' (CARICOM Secretariat, 2000, p.259).

The Secretariat locates the logic of today's proactive policy towards FDI in a context of globalisation and in the fact that increasingly fierce competition for opportunity may be explained by the high degree of dependence on foreign direct investment. This is accentuated by: (1) persistently low levels of savings; (2) the unattractiveness of Caribbean small island economies to international private bank loans and portfolio investment flows; and, (3) the significant decline in overseas development assistance (ODA). To pursue this strategy successfully, it is suggested that Caribbean nations: (1) develop and sustain an enabling environment; and (2) harmonise FDI-related measures in the context of a regional single market and economy, and evolving extra-regional, hemispherical and multilateral (global) free trade arrangements.

Vital gains from these specific recommendations are that 'they are a source of information for prospective investors and a means of signalling that the Caribbean remains open for business', and that 'such stability in the macroeconomic regime gives comfort to businessmen engaged in long-term investment' (CARICOM Secretariat, 2000, p.282). Besides, the Secretariat argues that a regional investment code could thus be a useful instrument for stimulating intra-CARICOM flows and attracting inward flows from the rest of the world. In this regard, the Secretariat perceives significant potential for foreign investments to flow from the proposed FTAA (CARICOM Secretariat, 2000, p.272).

However, one caution expressed by the CARICOM Secretariat concerns the dangers of portfolio investment, given its volatility. Combined with free transfer of dividends and repatriation of capital and profits, portfolio FDI can destabilise the regional financial markets (CARICOM Secretariat, 2000, p.279). In addition, the Secretariat urges that, given the problem of small size and associated vulnerability, there is therefore need for special assistance to be provided to small countries. The general thrust of the Secretariat's argument is that countries in the region need to win preferential treatment on many fronts (CARICOM Secretariat, 2000, p.280).

Among the specific issues considered by the Secretariat are those related to the relevance of GATS, TRIPS and TRIMS, all arising under the umbrella of the WTO. The positions adopted on these issues by countries in the region are likely to have significant implications for foreign investment strategy in the services sector where it is envisaged that the bulk of the development efforts will have to be concentrated in the future.[16]

In a similar vein, the Regional Negotiating Machinery (RNM) advocates the need to be 'sensitive to the peculiarities of size' (Caribbean RNM, 2000, p.3). In the context of the need to diversify, the RNM seems to promote focus on services. Indeed, the RNM advocates concentration on services and related areas rather than securing preferences for trade in goods (Caribbean RNM, 2000, p.4). This view, together with the significant share of services in employment, makes all new trade policy initiatives under GATS, TRIPS and TRIMS important to the Caribbean. In this light, it is proposed that these agreements should be closely scrutinised by Caribbean nations.[17]

However, the growth in dominance, interests and ambitions of transnationals corporations pose a significant threat for Caribbean countries. To achieve their own objectives, transnationals can switch investment and production, or threaten to do so, whenever conditions in any country appear disadvantageous. Consequently, communities in the Caribbean can suffer from the unrestricted activities of TNCs. Without intervention, local societies are involved in a negative-sum game. For this important, and other reasons, Caribbean states need national strategic planning systems within which to approach and position TNCs and foreign investments, and alter policy in their national interest. Otherwise, TNCs' strategies will inevitably become the national strategies of Caribbean territories, and this may have little correspondence to what is best for local communities (Cowling, 1990, pp.12-13).

The failure to thoroughly identify and aggressively pursue the key trade and development policy requirements of endogenous competency in Caribbean economies is perhaps the most important deficiency of the analyses and proposals guiding the WTO, and those of the CARICOM Secretariat, the RNM, as well as many governments in the region. With a local capacity to create domestic capital (which is broadened here to include investment in the production of knowledge, technological development and institutions for productive purposes)[18] Caribbean industries can create increasing returns, engineer product differentiation, and systematically and continuously deploy such initiatives to penetrate markets using strategic supply-side policies, no matter what the wind of change may be in the centuries-old international debate about free trade.

Four hundred and fifty years of failure to change its structure is an important indication of the Caribbean technological dependence in established production systems, in a world capitalist economy driven by fierce competition through rapid technological change. Consequently, a major lesson of Caribbean history is that competing in the international arena requires integration into the world economy on different terms - economically, institutionally and politically - than those offered by metropolitan centres, transnational corporations and foreign investors of various types. In fact, Caribbean economies may have to integrate up to the point where it is useful for them to do so, for promoting self-reliant technological initiatives, endogenous competency, diversification and product differentiation. This may well require relatively less, not more, integration into the world capitalist system. Should Caribbean governments choose to seek 'close' or 'strategic' integration with the world economy seems to be an interesting question which may result in serious policy dilemmas.

Finally, a key question for Caribbean countries is whether economic integration leads to the reduction of regional income inequalities and other regional disparities. The political drive to unite the Caribbean region has taken insufficient account of the problems posed by regional disparity, and efforts to encourage 'convergence' are in effect attempts to impose the removal of various 'distortions'. To hold the whole Caribbean region together, economic gains must be widely distributed; but, in the long run, problems of political will are also very important. Designing actions and policies that will, at the same time, reduce spatial disparities within the Caribbean and be politically acceptable will indeed be very difficult.[19,20]

Conclusion

The new trade environment presents formidable challenges and dilemmas for the small vulnerable states of the Caribbean Community. The intensified competition generated by multilateral trade liberalisation and the emergence of regional trade blocs is increasing the risk of economic marginalisation of CARICOM states. Fundamental changes in economic management are required in order for these economies to adjust to the more competitive trade environment.

The region's experience with neoliberal economic policies during the last two decades or so, suggests that the 'invisible hand' cannot be relied on to promote the required economic adjustment. A strategic approach encompassing high quality state intervention and industrial targeting are viewed as necessary to ensure the survival of the region in the face of the unprecedented changes in the international trade environment. The strategic approach will have to be underpinned by strong government commitment to economic development, and collaboration among state, business and civil society.

Recent neoliberal calls for globalisation, further liberalisation and deregulation, minimalist state and good governance seem to entirely miss the point: in today's circumstances, Caribbean societies will not be able to build their own capabilities or make speedy transitions from poverty without activist states which approximate the model of a developmental state (ideally, but not necessarily, the 'western democratic type'). Without such states, the human cost of the 'New Liberal Order' may be immense in the Caribbean. In short, contrary to the current orthodoxy, development requires better state action, and this is most likely achieved from Developmental State policies.

Notes

1. Lewis, 'The Industrialisation of the British West Indies', 1950, p.7.
2. Commonwealth Caribbean Regional Secretariat, *CARIFTA and the New Caribbean*, 1971, p.10.
3. _____ *From CARIFTA to Caribbean Community*, 1972, p.17.
4. Arthur, 'The New Realities of Caribbean International Economic Relations', 1996, pp. 47-48.
5. The 'infant industry' argument for intervention is very important and relevant here, as full exposure to competition is likely to precipitate a dramatic reduction in the size of these firms. In addition, research suggests that nations which do best in the global arena are those which manage change and use their institutional arrangements to protect their national economies from international vagaries and disorder (Tyson, 1992; Chang, 1994; Singh, 1995, 1998; Boyer and Drache, 1996 - among others).
6. It is argued here that, even under the current conditions of neoliberal globalisation and the pressures from international organisations such as WTO, World Bank and IMF, governments still have room for Developmental State policies. In a rather similar vein, Chang claims that:

   > Intelligent governments should try [...] to use TNCs in a strategic way in order to acquire necessary capital, technology, marketing networks, and so on. What exactly the 'strategic way' means will depend on various factors, such as the country's relative bargaining position, the technological nature of the industry, the role of the particular industry concerned in the bigger scheme of industrial development, and so on (Chang, 1998, p.111). An intelligent government pursuing a strategic industrial policy will not have a 'uniform' policy towards TNCs across industries, as many neoliberal economists recommend. Each industry serves different functions in the greater scheme of industrial development, and it would be foolish to have either uniformly restrictive or uniformly liberal policies towards TNCs across different industries. This also means that the same industry may, and indeed should, become more or less open to FDI over time, depending on the changes in the various internal and external conditions that affect it (Chang, 1998, pp.111-12).

7. Indeed, organic farming has a rigorous basis in science and can be seriously considered.
8. For further details see, Henshall-Momsen, 1998.
9. Also, special emphasis should be placed on particular productive activities in mining (such as Petroleum/Energy in Trinidad and Bauxite in Jamaica).
10. What is proposed here, however, is rather more profound: Caribbean nations should look to develop specific knowledge-based growth-oriented activities across all major sectors in order to restructure and transform their economies.
11. A number of local commodities could have a high value to weight ratio in order to overcome the problem of the high transport costs associated with island production.

12. Clearly, stopover visitors expand the domestic markets. Indeed, the growth of demand for an authentic Caribbean flavour (i.e., tourist consumption plus food and beverage souvenirs) provides the opportunities for the growth of supply of local specialties by local producers.

13. In fact,

> Institutions can formalise the commitment to such [developmental strategies], and their structure, procedures, and personnel can act to ensure that such commitments cannot easily be reversed, but they are simply ratifying [plans] already established. The history of planning [in the region] shows how fragile was the commitment, despite the creation of many new institutions [in Caribbean territories], and [the lack of teeth of these institutions was quite obvious]. With clear goals, and a determination to pursue them, institutions with teeth should be forthcoming (Cowling, 1990, p.23).

14. 'Embeddedness' does not mean cozy relations between the state and individual private firms, but a strategic government-business interface that is distinguished by transparent consultation, cooperation, and coordination mechanisms (Ahrens, 1997, p.126).

15. There will be no need for vast bureaucratic machines in Caribbean states: the approach is clearly entrepreneurial. This radical approach allows 'considerable autonomy in determining the mode of operation, and adjusting it as experience accumulates'. The main objective is the creation of dynamic local economies rather than sticking to sets of rigid rules imposed by central bureaucracies (Cowling, 1990, p.25).

16. CARICOM Secretariat (2000), *Caribbean Trade and Investment Report 2000: Dynamic Interface of Regionalism and Globalisation*, CARICOM Secretariat and Ian Randle Publishers, Georgetown (Guyana) and Kingston (Jamaica).

17. Caribbean Regional Negotiating Machinery (RNM), 'Report of the Reflections Group on Trade', Montego Bay, Jamaica, 25-26 September 2000.

18. See James, V.N., Henry, R.M. and Barclay, L.A. (2002), 'The New Trade Initiatives and Caribbean Realities'.

19. The past history of intra-regional cooperation is not such as to raise hopes very high.

20. Of course, there is the question of financing the above investment spending. A number of recommendations may be considered: (1) an appropriate redistribution of available (existing) funds from government consumption to government investment; (2) changes of the structure of taxation; (3) higher levels of savings generated by higher levels of income; (4) the use of government bonds; (5) available pension funds; (6) the 'arrest' of tax evasion and black economy; and (7) a higher degree of capacity utilisation.

References

Ahrens, J. (1997), 'Prospects of Institutional and Policy Reform in India: Towards a Model of the Developmental State?', *Asian Development Review*, Vol. 15(1), pp.111-46.

Baker, D., Epstein, G. and Pollin, R. (eds) (1998), *Globalisation and Progressive Economic Policy*, Cambridge University Press, Cambridge.

Beckford, G. (1972), *Persistent Poverty: Underdevelopment in Plantation Economies of the Third World*, Oxford University Press, Oxford.

_____ (1975), *Caribbean Economy: Dependence and Backwardness*, ISER, Kingston.

Benn, D. and Hall, K. (eds) (2000), *Globalisation: A Calculus of Inequality*, Ian Randle Publishers, Kingston.

Bernal, R.L. (2000), 'Globalisation and Small Developing Countries: The Imperative for Repositioning', in D. Benn and K. Hall (eds), *Globalization: A Calculus of Inequality*, Ian Randle Publishers, Kingston, pp.88-127.

Boyer, R. and Drache, D. (eds) (1996), *States against Markets: The Limits of Globalisation*, Routledge, London.

Caribbean Development Bank (CDB) (2001), *Annual Report*, CDB, Bridgetown, Barbados.

Chang, H-J (1998), 'Globalisation, Transnational Corporations, and Economic Development: Can the Developing Countries Pursue Strategic Industrial Policy in a Globalising World Economy?', in D. Baker, G. Epstein and R. Pollin (eds), *Globalisation and Progressive Economic Policy*, Cambridge University Press, Cambridge, pp.97-116.

Clayton, A (2001), 'Developing a Bio-industry Cluster in Jamaica: A Step Towards Building a Skill-Based Economy', *Social and Economic Studies*, Vol. 50(2), pp.1-37.

Commonwealth Caribbean Regional Secretariat (1971), *CARIFTA and the New Caribbean*, Georgetown.

_____ (1972), *From CARIFTA to Caribbean Community*, Georgetown.

Cowling, K. (1990), 'The Strategic Approach to Economic and Industrial Policy', in K. Cowling and R. Sugden (eds), *A New Economic Policy for Britain: Essays on the Development of Industry*, Manchester University Press, Manchester, pp.6-34.

Cowling, K. and Sugden, R. (eds) (1990), *A New Economic Policy for Britain: Essays on the Development of Industry*, Manchester University Press, Manchester.

Evans, P.B. (1992), 'The State as Problem and Solution: Predation, Embedded Autonomy, and Structural Change', in S. Haggard and R.R. Kaufman (eds), *The Politics of Economic Adjustment*, Princeton University Press, Princeton.

_____ (1995), *Embedded Autonomy: States and Industrial Transformation*, Princeton University Press, Princeton.

GATT (1994), 'Outcome of the Uruguay Round for Developing Countries', *Development Issues*, Vol. 34, World Bank, Washington DC.

Heizer, J. and Render, B. (1996), *Production and Operations Management*, 4th edition, Prentice Hall, New Jersey.

Henshall-Momsen, J. (1998), 'Caribbean Tourism and Agriculture: New Linkages in the Global Era?', in T. Klak (ed.), *Globalisation and Neoliberalism: The Caribbean Context*, Rowman & Littlefield, Lanham.

Higgins, K.J. (1994), *The Bahamian Economy: An Analysis*, The Counsellors, Nassau.

Karagiannis, N. (2002a), *A New Economic Strategy for The Bahamas: With Special Consideration of International Competition and the FTAA*, UWI Printers, Kingston.

_____ (2002b), *Developmental Policy and the State: The European Union, East Asia, and the Caribbean*, Lexington Books, Lanham.

Lalta, S. and Freckleton, M. (eds) (1993), *Caribbean Economic Development: The First Generation*, Ian Randle Publishers, Kingston.

Leftwich, A. (1995), 'Bringing Politics Back: Towards a Model of the Developmental State', *Journal of Development Studies*, Vol. 31(3), pp.400-27.

Lewis, A.W. (1950), 'The Industrialisation of the British West Indies', *Caribbean Economic Review*, Vol. II, pp.1-61.

Lopez, J. (1998), 'Growth Resumption and Long-run Growth in Latin American Economies: A Modest Proposal', *International Papers in Political Economy*, Vol. 5(1).

Onis, Z. (1991), 'The Logic of the Developmental State', *Comparative Politics*, Vol. 24(1), pp.109-26.

Owen, A. (1996), 'The New Realities of Caribbean International Economic Relations', Lecture in the *Distinguished Lecture Series*, UWI, St. Augustine.

Payne, A. and Sutton, P. (2001), *Charting Caribbean Development*, Macmillan Caribbean, London.

Polanyi-Levitt, K. (1991), *The Origins and Consequences of Jamaica's Debt Crisis: 1970-1990*, Consortium Graduate School of Social Sciences, Kingston.

Poon, A. (1993), 'Caribbean Tourism and the World Economy', in S. Lalta and M. Freckleton (eds), *Caribbean Economic Development: The First Generation*, Ian Randle Publishers, Kingston, pp.262-79.

Thomas, C.Y. (1974), *Dependence and Transformation: The Economics of the Transition to Socialism*, Monthly Review Press, New York.

_____ (1978), 'The Non-capitalist Path as Theory and Practice of Decolonisation and Socialist Transformation', *Latin American Perspectives*, Vol. 5, pp.10-36.

UNCTAD (1994), *Trade and Development Report*, United Nations, Geneva.

_____ (2001), *Handbook of Statistics*, United Nations, Geneva.

Wade, R. (1990), *Governing the Market: Economic Theory and the Role of Government in East Asian Industrialisation*, Princeton University Press, Princeton.

Chapter 7

Caribbean Tourism and the FTAA

Ian Boxill, Diaram Ramjee Singh and Marjorie D. Segree

Introduction

The vicissitudes of global capitalism and of geopolitics have led countries to find various ways to achieve economic growth. To this end, more countries, particularly in the developing world, are entering into Free Trade Associations (FTAs). As suggested by Hu (2002), free trade has emerged as one of the most important macroeconomic trends in the 21st century, as witnessed by the 107 of the 206 countries in the world that have entered into Free Trade agreements. Based on WTO estimates, Hu (2002) noted that the trade volume of FTA during 1993-97 accounted for 42 per cent of the world trade.

This relatively new development paradigm has resulted in a situation in which CARICOM countries are busily attempting to strategically reposition themselves within the world economy. To this end, CARICOM has been slowly moving towards a Caribbean Single Market and Economy (CSME) while, at the same time, making overtures to be part of other regional FTAs, such as the North American Free Trade Association (NAFTA) and the Free Trade Area of the Americas (FTAA). The FTAA, which is likely to be a reality in a few years, will most probably supersede all other economic integration arrangements in the Americas, thereby making it the most important regional economic bloc for CARICOM. Because CARICOM countries are largely tourism-dependent economies, regional governments see tourism as one of the most viable industries within this new trade bloc. In this chapter, we discuss some of the possible impacts of the FTAA on the Caribbean economies, with particular emphasis on the tourism sector. We also suggest an alternative to the current tourism development model that is being pursued within the region.

Elements of the FTAA

The brainchild of President George Bush Sr., the FTAA, was first announced back in 1990. Bush envisaged a western hemisphere where there would be totally free trade, and the signing of the NAFTA treaty by the USA, Canada and Mexico, is believed by many to be the first step in this direction. In 1994, at the Summit of the

Americas held in Miami, the United States along with the other 33 countries of the Americas committed themselves to the establishment of a Free Trade Area of the Americas by the year 2005.

In 1997, the participants met in Belo Horizonte, Honduras, to agree on an Official Plan of Action regarding trade negotiations. Twelve working groups were formed, with responsibility for organising and leading negotiations and preliminary discussions. The Working Groups are as follows: Market Access; Investment; Customs Procedures and Rules of Origins; Standards and Technical Barriers to Trade; Intellectual Property Rights, Services and Competition Policy; Subsidies, Antidumping and Countervailing Duties; Government Procurement; Sanitary and Phytosanitary Measures; and Dispute Settlement.

In 1998, a meeting was held in San José, where ministers of trade of the various countries outlined the structure and objectives of the FTAA, which later became the Declaration of San José. This was ratified at the second Summit of the Americas in Santiago de Chile later that year. The general objectives of the FTAA are as follows:

- the promotion of prosperity through economic integration and free trade;
- the establishment of a free trade area where barriers to trade and investment will be gradually eliminated;
- to assist small economies to realise their potential through market openness, and to foster growth and development;
- the preservation and strengthening of the democracies of the Americas;
- to eradicate poverty;
- the preservation of the environment for future generations;
- to encourage the free movement of labour for specialised workers;
- the harmonisation of tax and monetary policies; and,
- the establishment of supra-regional institutions to administer the arrangement and facilitate the resolution of disputes.

Non-trade issues like culture, education, human rights, and science and technology are covered under the FTAA. According to Harker *et al.* (1996), the objective of the FTAA is to build and strengthen the substantial advances already made by the countries of the Americas in the areas of trade liberalisation and economic integration. The problem of size in relation to small economies is of particular interest to those charged with the implementation of the FTAA. As a result, a committee was set up to address the concerns of small economies as they relate to negotiations.

Small economies like those in the Caribbean region can benefit from the implementation of the FTAA but they can also be affected negatively given their characteristics. Economies of the Caribbean are open and fragile. These economies produce a few export products, for which they enjoy special access to overseas markets. Added to this the islands and coastal territories of the Caribbean are disaster prone. Indeed, the impact of a natural disaster can wreak havoc on these economies because they produce a few primary commodities for export. The size of the local market restricts the production of some goods. A number of these economies depend on trade taxes to finance their budget. The 'smallness' of these economies is, therefore, a major constraint whether we classify them in terms of size, population or GDP. The possible opportunities and benefits of the FTAA for CARICOM countries are therefore questionable. This of course begs the question: why the interest in creating an FTAA, especially coming on the heels of NAFTA?

The FTAA as Ideological and Economic Hegemony

The Free Trade Area of the Americas represents yet another practical manifestation of the growing intellectual and policy hegemony of neoliberal economic thought (Gosovic, 2001; NACLA *Report on the Americas*, 2003). Since the collapse of communism, trade liberalisation and the formation of regional economic blocs have multiplied across the world. The main objective of this process is to open markets in the periphery and semi-periphery to trade by transnational corporations, which operate from the large industrialised nations of the world (NACLA *Report on the Americas*, 2003).

Liberalisation, privatisation and trading blocs have also been seen by the US government and multilateral lending institutions as the only viable path of growth and development for the world economy (NACLA *Report on the Americas*, 2003). Indeed, there is nothing inherently wrong with the formation of trading blocs. Trading blocs like CARICOM have come into existence to foster the social and economic development of the region. The formation of the CSME is really a reaction by Caribbean governments to perceived global economic challenges emanating mainly from the trading blocs such as NAFTA and the FTAA. The CSME is both an economic and political arrangement, with an implicit objective of some type of political integration.

However, the FTAA is of a different order, in that it is neither reactive nor concerned with the social welfare issues (on the previous page, the list of objectives of the FTAA included poverty eradication!). It is an extension of neoliberal thinking aimed at fully integrating the region into the global capitalist economy, mainly on terms that are advantageous to the large transnationals, most of which are located in the USA. According to Dore,

> Neoliberalism has not always ruled the world. In Latin America [for example], the wholesale privatisation of state companies, from water supplies to electricity grids, from manufacturing to telecommunications, is of recent origin (Dore, 2003, p.20).

The central intellectual tenet of this move towards liberalisation is that we live in a globalised world - an inevitability of western-inspired progress. In its most vulgar form this type of social and economic determinism suggests that we have somehow reached 'the end of history'. In a scathing critique of this Global Intellectual Hegemony (GIH), Gosovic writes:

The 'end of ideology (or history)', 'end of conflict', 'partnership', 'stakeholders', 'opportunities or challenges', 'no more South or North', 'positive or proactive agenda', etc. are among the frequently repeated buzz words and phrases in contemporary international and development-related discourse. The intention is to diffuse and pre-empt any probing questions that may be posed. They are also meant to convey the basic soundness of the system, suggesting that it is the only possible one, the 'best of all possible worlds', non-controversial with respect to the basic structural issues (Gosovic, 2002, p.138).

The dominance of this Global Intellectual Hegemony has resulted in a situation in which Caribbean governments have been moving full speed ahead to sign up with the FTAA, without a critical appreciation of its possible negative impacts on society.

To be sure, there are some advantages to the FTAA, according to economic theory. For instance, free trade necessitates the opening of the markets which, according to the classical theorists of international trade, will lead to countries specialising in producing the goods of their greatest comparative advantage. Open economies allow countries to specialise in the production of goods and services for which there are lower opportunity costs. Specialisation, it is argued, would lead to increase production volume and lower unit cost. It is necessary here to state that when a country specialises in producing the good of the greatest comparative advantage, other countries that do not produce the good efficiently will shift to produce other goods. Through specialisation there will be a reduction in cost per unit because production increases and economies of scale will be reaped. In specialising, the market size will increase leading to an increase in the demand for the produce, and firms will be encouraged to invest. Indeed, the attendant increased in demand resulting from specialisation would provide the kind of economies of scale needed to induce large scale investment, transfer of technology and an increase in productivity needed to achieve sustained growth and development.

Specialisation will also lead to increase in export earnings. Consistent with this idea, some analysts point to possible benefits to be derived from being a member of the FTAA. Some of these include: the development of manufacturing sectors due to economies of scale; investment and capital accumulation because the tradable goods sector is more capital-intensive than the non-tradable goods sector; prospects for technology transfers; increased overall efficiency of the economy on a long-term basis through economic growth; greater economic welfare; and a fall in the price level of intermediate goods required as inputs by the manufacturing industry (see OAS, 'The Road Ahead. The Free Trade Area of The Americas', http://www.sice.oas.org).

Of course, there is a downside to joining the FTAA. And this downside, in our view, is likely to be more devastating to CARICOM countries than the larger non-CARICOM economies. To begin with, most of the above presumed benefits will not apply to most of the small struggling economies of CARICOM, which have little or no manufacturing sectors and which depend on preferential arrangements in agriculture. Furthermore, free trade creates greater competition in the domestic sectors.

The Caribbean sugar producers enjoy special access to the US and UK markets under the sugar protocol. Indeed, this is one of the areas of greatest comparative advantage in the Caribbean. This kind of protectionism has led to inefficient production in this sector. With the advent of the FTAA, sectors like sugar, as presently organised, will not be able to compete in the world market. The fact is that there are countries, outside the Caribbean, that can produce sugar cheaper. Thus, once barriers are lifted, Caribbean sugar will be unable to compete. For the Caribbean countries to survive such competition they will have to find ways to utilise their displaced resources. The reallocation of resources from one market to another will result in huge unemployment. Also it will be difficult for countries to shift resources, as some of these cannot be easily transferred. For example, a sector like sugar that employs a large numbers of persons, shifting labour from sugar production to a new industry that uses computers may require a massive education of the labour force that may not be sustainable in the short run.

But there is a further problem. In a number of Caribbean countries, their governments get the largest part of their revenue from trade taxes. For some countries, as much as 50 per cent (or more) of the budget is financed through trade taxes. With FTAA and free trade, these taxes will be a thing of the past, and governments will experience a decrease in revenue. Hence, they will either have to run deficits or find new and innovative ways to raise revenues.

On the political side, many people fear that becoming a part of groupings like the FTAA will result in loss of sovereignty (Gosovic, 2003). To be sure, many small countries may be forced to implement polices set by supra-national organisations in order to compete in the global market place. This can result in an increase in the role of international organisations in these small economies, thereby reducing the impact of governments in their countries.

At a macro level, there is likely to be an increase in the level of disparity between developed and developing countries because the industrialised nations are technologically advanced and, in many cases, are able to produce goods cheaper than developing nations. The theory of natural comparative advantage is no longer valid as developed nations can now produce close substitutes to goods produced by developing nations at a lower cost. Added to this is the cost of a shift from natural products to synthetic ones. The opening up of markets not only causes competition in the product market but also in the labour market. There will be a movement of labour from the developing countries to the developed countries that are able to pay higher wages hence capturing the more skilled. Consequently, there will be a drain on the resources of the developing countries that will have to invest in human capital and design ways to keep such capital within their boundaries.

In short then, an examination of the pros and cons of joining the FTAA shows that Caribbean businesses are likely to be devastated by competition from North America and possibly Latin America. In the area of manufacturing, we argue that only resource-based industries, such as methanol in the case of Trinidad and bauxite in the case of Jamaica and Guyana, are likely to compete seriously with the large transnationals from abroad. But what about the region's largest and most important industry - tourism?

Recently, the governments of Jamaica, Barbados, and Antigua and Barbuda have argued that tourism will become the driving force for economic development in these countries. To be sure, even without the declarations of these governments, tourism is already the most important industry in their countries (Boxill *et al.*, 2002). And, given its success across the region, tourism is likely to assume centre stage in the development process with the formation of the FTAA.

What is the logic behind this emphasis on tourism? The argument is that globalisation carries the economic benefits of specialisation and the division of labour to the world level. Liberalisation, a process that promotes competitiveness, will permit the reaping of economies of scale and will bring about economic growth and human welfare. Further, if development means expanding opportunities and options, as it has come to be accepted, then unfettered globalisation assures these outcomes. In the case of the Caribbean, it could be argued that specialisation in tourism would increase the inflow of tourists, create additional jobs and improve foreign exchange earnings. Of course, this begs the question: is this likely to happen under the FTAA? We now turn our attention to this issue.

Caribbean Tourism and the FTAA

The travel and tourism industry is one of the world's largest sectors and a major employer (Bernal, 2000; Boxill, 2000). This industry is one of the fastest-growing sectors of the world economy and has a significant impact on all sectors of the economy. It provides employment for a large portion of the global population and makes an important contribution to worldwide Gross Domestic Product. In 1998, the travel and tourism industry contributed approximately 8 per cent to worldwide GDP. It is important to note that the World Tourism Organization (WTO) estimates that by 2010, tourism should generate US$10 trillion.

In the Caribbean, tourism earnings account for approximately 25 per cent of the region's Gross Domestic Product. By 2000, the region recorded over US$ 18 billion tourism receipts with over 20 million tourist arrivals and more than 12 million cruise passenger arrivals (CTO, 2001). There is no doubt that these figures are quite impressive.

Clearly, tourism is CARICOM's most globally competitive industry (Boxill *et al.*, 2003). More and more tourism has been emerging as the engine of growth in many Caribbean countries. In fact, over the last decade, tourism was seen as the main engine of growth in many of the island states within the region because of its perceived potential to earn foreign exchange, create jobs and attract capital investment (see Table 7.1). According to projections by the World Travel and Tourism Council (WTTC, 2002) the regional industry was expected to generate US$ 34.3 billion in economic activity, contribute US$ 7 billion to GDP, produce 2.1 million jobs and account for US$ 7 billion in capital investment, by the end of 2002.

Table 7.1 Forecast of top job creators in the Caribbean, 2002-2012

Cuba	262,800
Dominican Republic	216,500
Jamaica	111,600
Haiti	75,800
The Bahamas	40,400
Puerto Rico	26,500
Curacao	23,800
Barbados	16,900
Trinidad & Tobago	12,800
Guadeloupe	11,400

Source: WTTC (2002), chart 5.

However, due to the terrorist attacks of September 11, 2001 in the USA, while the worldwide loss in travel and tourism demand was 8.5 per cent, the loss in the Caribbean was 13.5 per cent and that translated into around 365,000 total jobs lost. The WTTC analysis found that the greatest job loss in the Caribbean was in the Dominican Republic (192,800), followed by Cuba, Jamaica, Haiti and Puerto Rico, with The Bahamas' 10,200 losses placing it 6th. WTTC also found that the greatest revenue losses following September 11 were sustained by the Dominican Republic (US$ 837.2 million) and Puerto Rico (US$ 589 million), followed by Jamaica (US$ 299 million), The Bahamas (US$ 282.5 million), Cuba (US$ 281 million), Barbados (US$ 169 million), Aruba (US$ 141 million), Bermuda (US$ 133 million), Trinidad and Tobago (US$ 116 million), and Curacao (US$ 113 million) (WTTC, 2002, chart 2).

The gross indicators are not only impressive but point to the importance of the industry to regional economies as well. As noted by Vaugeios (2002), tourism has been one of the few growth sectors in the region. It is undeniable that for many countries in the region tourism has become the main source of foreign exchange earnings. Data published by the Caribbean Tourism Organisation (CTO) showed that visitor expenditure in 2000 ranged from a low of 3.59 per cent of GDP (in Trinidad and Tobago) to a high of 83.06 per cent of GDP (in Anguilla). For the same period, an estimate of total visitor expenditure in the region was put at US$ 19.9 billion (or US$ 979 per tourist). According to Vaugeois (2002), this level of expenditure represented some 50-70 per cent of the region's hard currency earnings. It should be obvious that the capacity of tourism to earn foreign exchange is not in question. The structure of the industry is such that a significant portion of regional earnings is accrued abroad.

According to Jayawardena (2002), this success was neither due to any strategic decisions nor planning by Caribbean governments. The tourism sector drifted into prominence because of the failure of the local traditional economic sectors, such as agriculture and mining, to provide the stimulus needed to generate economic growth. In the early days of the industry, most governments in the Caribbean were generally satisfied to play a non-interventionist role which was limited to legislation, coordination, and the promotion of the various destinations. Most of the tourism legislation in the region, even today, pertained to the establishment of National Tourism Organisations (NTOs) and to specify their roles and functions within the industry (McDavid and Ramjee Singh, 2002).

However, in the late 1960s, governments were forced to assume a direct entrepreneurial role in the industry. In most cases, this new role was dictated by economic pressures. The public ownership of hotels, for example, was largely influenced by the need to save jobs and to prevent the unemployment rates from reaching levels that were considered politically untenable. With the advent of privatisation in the early 1980s, the ownership role of government in the industry declined dramatically. Today, the industry is not only private sector driven but is dominated by foreign ownership, as some 63 per cent of hotel rooms in the region are currently under foreign ownership (Barberia, 2003). However, as Karagiannis (2002, p.156) observes, one of the characteristics of the industry is that it has a large number of small locally owned hotels, many of which find it difficult to compete with the large more established transnationals. It should be noted, however, that it is because of these smaller properties that locals are able to feel that they have a greater stake in the sector.

This, of course, raises the question: what would happen to the region if these small properties were to disappear or be swallowed up by larger entities which are foreign owned? While there can be no definitive answer to this question, it is possible that something similar to what obtains in parts of the tourism corridor of the Riviera Maya, Mexico - where local resentment is high because small entities are marginalised from the decision-making process as the industry is dominated by large international chains, which make their decisions in the metropole - may indeed occur (Boxill and Hernandez, 2002). In the case of the Caribbean, warning shots have already been fired. For instance, Boxill and Frederick (2002) have shown, in the case of Antigua, that when foreign investors develop tourism projects without integrating locals into the planning process, there is likely to be serious social conflict. What is more, the FTAA is likely to lead to a situation in which small local hotels are swallowed up by larger foreign investors. In other words, under the FTAA regime, foreign capital may come to dominate the economies of these countries even more via the tourism sector.

The hegemonic role of foreign capital and ownership in the industry began in the early 1970s, when regional governments took the decision to move towards the construction of all-inclusive enclave resorts. The problem was that the massive capital injection needed to execute these projects was not available in the domestic capital markets. As a consequence, regional governments were forced to rely on foreign owned hotel chains to build and participate in the ownership of these enclave resorts (Barberia, 2003).

The wave of liberalisation, which began in the early 1980s and continues today, will not only serve to entrench and expand the role of foreign capital and ownership, but also create a very competitive regional market environment as new and existing players fight for market share. In such a market it is anticipated that small and medium-sized tourism enterprises, both local and foreign owned, would find it extremely difficult to compete and survive. As a result, the market is expected to be dominated by large sized enclave resorts.

The projected widespread introduction of 'all inclusive resorts' is expected to produce several negative consequences for the region. To begin with, the benefits associated with the network effects of tourism would be severely curtailed, thus resulting in incalculable economic and social costs to local economies. Furthermore, as in the early days of the industry, the role of national governments would, once again, be limited to promotional activities and the provision of investment for infrastructure development in tourism enclaves. The high mass volume tourism associated with 'all inclusive resorts' would perpetuate the region's dependency on specific markets and continue to exclude the masses from sharing in the fruits of the industry. And this for an industry which is so import-dependent.

Leakage of tourism receipts, especially among small island states in the Caribbean, occurs at different stages of tourist spending. According to Karagiannis and Salvaris (2002, p.47), direct imports which are required to sustain the industry and the needs of the visitors account for first round leakages, while the import content of investment and overall economic consumption is responsible for the second round of leakages. Besides, a third round of leakages usually arises when government, national tourism organisations and individual properties engage in overseas promotion in order to sell the destination.

According UNEP (1996), the level of foreign exchange leakage from tourism is due primarily to the high import content of the industry. This is determined to a large extent by the high level of imports, both of construction and consumer goods, reparation of profits, and the amortisation of external debt. Obviously, the level of leakage is expected to vary from country to country depending on the extent to which the domestic economy is able to meet needs of the industry. Currently, data on the leakage rate for the industry are only available for eleven countries in the region. These include (see Table 7.2):

Table 7.2 Leakage rates (%) in the Caribbean, 2002 [*]

Antigua & Barbuda	56
Barbados	66
The Bahamas	85
British Virgin Islands	56
Dominica	45
Grenada	55
Jamaica	50
St. Lucia	62
St. Kitts & Nevis	67
St. Vincent & the Grenadines	33
Trinidad & Tobago	22

[*] Computed by Ramjee Singh, 2002, 2003 (on-going research).
Source: Caribbean Tourism Organisation (CTO), 'Tourism Receipts (Statistical Annex)', 2002.

With the exception of Trinidad and Tobago, the leakage rates for the rest of these economies could be described as excessively high. In most cases, over half of the industry's earnings flow out of the local economy. The exceptionally high import content of the industry does suggest that there are relatively few intersectoral linkages between the domestic economy and the tourism sector. Apart from influencing the industry's net earnings, the leakage rate impacts the tourism income multiplier. The multipliers for several of the regional economies are listed below (see Table 7.3):

Table 7.3 The multipliers for several Caribbean economies [*]

Antigua & Barbuda (1997)	1.06
Barbados (1996)	1.19
The Bahamas (1996)	0.98
British Virgin Islands (1996)	1.16
Dominica (1999)	1.59
Grenada (1996)	1.39
Jamaica (1996)	1.35
St. Lucia (2000)	1.56
St. Kitts & Nevis (1998)	1.00
St. Vincent & the Grenadines (2000)	1.79
Trinidad & Tobago (1999)	2.00

[*] Computed by Ramjee Singh, 2002, 2003 (on-going research).
Source: IMF website, 'Individual Country Report', 1998, 2000 and 2001.

A cursory examination of the data clearly indicates a strong correlation between the leakage rates and the multipliers. In particular, countries such as Trinidad and Tobago, St. Vincent and the Grenadines, and Dominica have larger multipliers because of the lower leakage rate while the opposite is true in the case of The Bahamas, and Antigua and Barbuda. In short, the import content of the industry strongly impacts on the multiplier effect of tourist expenditure in the region. It comes as no surprise that the ripple effects of the multipliers are on the low side.

Cruise ships, which gained prominence over the last two decades, have emerged as an important component of the industry. According to Barberia (2003), the cruise shipping industry has aggressively entered the market and today at least 40 per cent of tourists entering nine of the region's leading destinations participate in cruise ship tourism. At the global level, the Caribbean accounts for over half of all cruise ship tourism. Generally, spending by cruise ship tourists at a destination is significantly lower than stopover tourists. CTO estimates show that stopover tourists, on the average, tend to spend 10 to 17 times more than cruise ship tourists. Cruise ship tourism, which is unregulated and untaxed, has brought few economic benefits to the region. Continued growth in this segment of the industry could spell disaster to Caribbean economies.

Perhaps, the most troubling issue in regard to using tourism as the engine of growth under the FTAA is that it could result in excessive dependency on this sector, leading to more serious problems. Excessive dependence on tourism would increase the vulnerability of local economies while, at the same time, exacerbate their already highly open import-dependent characteristics. However, some may argue that under the FTAA regime the cost of imports for construction and consumer goods will decrease due to reduced tariffs. The counter-argument could be that reduced tariffs (and therefore less government revenue) may also lead to a reduction in the levels of tourism receipts. In addition, the FTAA regime may lead to higher levels of capital outflow from the region.

It should be understood that most states turned to tourism as a means of restructuring and diversifying their economies. To depend on tourism as the engine of growth would be undesirable since it could push these economies back into monosectorial domination. In many CARICOM countries, governments had come to rely on tourism to provide part of their revenue through a variety of taxation measures. Under the FTAA, governments would have to forego these taxes or find innovative ways to raise new revenue within the domestic economy. The additional pressure placed on domestic tax payers can easily lead to social discontent.

It should be made clear that we are not suggesting that tourism should not be seen as a possible option for regional governments which have signed on to the FTAA. In fact, even though Caribbean microstates remain extremely vulnerable to global shifts and fluctuations in tourism industry and financial flows, they have demonstrated a capacity to exploit, at least temporarily, some niches in globalised service markets and to generate a degree of prosperity for their small populations. We are however cautious because single sector growth by its very nature neither maximises the benefits of economic activity to the economy as a whole nor allows this potential leading sector to impart the momentum that is necessary to drive the other economic sectors as the single sector expands. Indeed, insofar as the decision to pursue tourism development as one (but not the only one) targeted sector is adopted, we suggest a thorough approach with a regional orientation, requiring the cooperation of governments which are part of CARICOM. We also suggest that, to achieve the greatest returns from the sector under an FTAA arrangement while at the same time ensuring sustainability, there needs to be an alternative tourism development strategy. The next section turns to an examination of aspects of this alternative.

Towards an Alternative Tourism

A number of writers have suggested that the problem with Caribbean tourism is that it is largely unplanned and used simply as a quick way of earning foreign exchange for the governments' coffers (Hayle, 2002; Karagiannis, 2002; McDavid, 2002). We believe that there is need to think about tourism in a more strategic sense, especially in light of the FTAA. Furthermore, tourism development should be seen as one dimension of a larger set of development policies that may be pursued by a country. We advocate a tourism development policy which respects people's way of life, engages them intellectually, is economically beneficial, and sustains the region's ecological systems. In other words, we advocate a type of tourism development not dissimilar to that advocated for Belize in Boxill (2003), where emphasis is placed on using and developing the intellectual and cultural capabilities of the people of the region, rather simply exploiting the natural resources of the islands (i.e., sea, sand and sun). For this type of tourism to succeed, four factors should be present: a regional approach to tourism planning; careful planning and regulation of the industry; focus on a more diversified product; and greater people/local involvement in the process.

A regional approach to tourism planning would allow CARICOM countries to pool resources and market the tourism product with more diverse features than would be the case if countries were marketed individually (Hayle, 2002). As the Caribbean is highly dependent and vulnerable to changes in the structure of air services, the region is facing the prospect of becoming a 'service taker' in its main market regions. Besides, the growing influence of the major Computer Reservation Systems (CRS) in the USA, Canada and Europe is a further source of concern to the Caribbean. Therefore, the only solution for the region's carriers may be to form cooperative alliances in the key areas of marketing and scheduling with some of the major carriers in order to avoid being entirely left out (as cost effective and efficient marketing and distribution are very important to the success of tourism promotion). In fact, the building of strategic alliances and partnerships within and outside of the tourism industry is expected to enhance the competitiveness of the sector (Poon, 1993, p.273). As Karagiannis points out:

> With cooperative arrangements and regional approaches to tourism, Caribbean islands can share the expenses of creating market intelligence systems, information technology networks, promotion, and public relations campaigns. Indeed, it is these cooperative arrangements and united effort that can considerably increase the strength of the bargaining power of the entire region (Karagiannis, 2002, p.169).

Concomitantly, as a sub-region within the FTAA, CARICOM countries should also increase their competitiveness.

In regard to the issue of proper planning and regulation, a number of writers have argued that careful planning and regulation of the tourism industry should result in a more enhanced and more sustainable product (Boxill, 2000; Hayle, 2002; McDavid, 2002; Karagiannis, 2002). McDavid (2002) argues that the development of the tourism sector should not be left up to the market. Instead, he warns that:

> The free play of the market forces may lead to over-reaching capacity limits and hence a lack of sustainability. Thus, more attention has to be paid to the imperfections of the market and to those specifically necessary interventions that can correct the tendencies towards disequilibria and monopolistic positions in both the public and private sectors (McDavid, 2002, p.68).

Therefore, a precondition for a more competitive and sustainable tourism is greater strategic planning, instead of the practice of *ad hoc* arrangements. Karagiannis suggests that this strategic approach must integrate all elements of the 'new tourism best practice' and would include, among others things, the development of human resources, product development and marketing. He also states:

> The public and private sectors can cooperate in a range of different arrangements, each contributing what it does best and both participating in the financial returns, within the context of a socially defined development agenda (Karagiannis, 2002, p. 165).

But even with proper planning, there is still the need for the region to diversify the tourism product, moving away from the 'sun, sea and sand' model, to one which focuses more on the culture and the heritage of the people. According to Bernal (2000, p.111), if Caribbean tourism is to continue to grow, it must diversify to include new products such as heritage tourism, health tourism and eco-tourism. Also, in a detailed examination of the structure of tourism in the Caribbean, Hayle (2002) points to the need to diversify the tourism product in the region in order to improve the competitive edge of the industry. Karagiannis (2002) asserts that a more diversified tourism product will automatically make Caribbean tourism more competitive. The economic potential for cultural tourism is greater than the current 'sea, sand and sun' model which is currently being pursued by the region (Boxill, 2002a; Nurse, 2002). Nurse is of the view that there is an abundance of artistic talent in the Caribbean which makes the region ideal for cultural tourism as well as for the growth and promotion of the entertainment industry. He observes:

> An important feature of cultural tourism is that of events or festivals. The experience with festivals and other cultural events is that they tend to create a tourism demand that is resilient and less susceptible to economic downturns (Nurse, 2002, p.129).

Indeed, places like Port Royal in Jamaica and Brimstone Hill in St Kitts are world renowned historical sites which attract a large number of visitors, despite the lack of emphasis on heritage tourism in these countries. Imaging what would happen if there was a policy to develop and properly market both the material and non-material culture of these countries.

This new emphasis should lead to greater local involvement in the industry - the fourth feature of this alternative approach - as well as the development of local communities. In addition, a more diverse product, away from the mass 'sea, sun and sand' model, would permit the training of a workforce that would have a greater appreciation for the history and culture of its society. Heritage, cultural, ecological and community tourism are all alternative niches which require community involvement and ownership in order for them to be successfully implemented (Boxill, 2000; Hayle, 2000; Duperly-Pinks, 2003). Indeed, this local involvement would result in a more equitable distribution of tourism earnings throughout the society, and the creation of a positive psychological state for individuals in the various countries (Duperly-Pinks, 2002). More than this, such local involvement should go a long way in creating the much needed organic link between the industry and the people (Boxill, 2002; Hayle, 2002). According to Hayle (2002) and Boxill

(2002), bridging this missing link is important to the industry's long-term survival, particularly in view of the competition from large transnational firms under an FTAA regime.

Therefore, much more attention has to be placed on these important issues, given that the new tourism industry is very complex and volatile. Furthermore, as this highly competitive industry depends on environmental quality, the issue of environmental protection should be accorded a greater priority by policy makers in the Caribbean in order to cope with a product that has already begun to deteriorate (besides, natural disasters have intensified the region's environmental threats). In fact, although the natural environment is the region's main tourism resource, there appears to be a huge gap between this recognition and putting effective controls in place. For this reason, a much closer link is required between tourism policy and environmental control and preservation.

Conclusion

The FTAA is more likely to have significant impacts on the economies of the CARICOM soon after it has been implemented. While the precise nature and extent of these impacts are unknown, we are of the view that many of them will be negative and extensive. According to neoliberal economic analysis, tourism, the industry in which the region enjoys a comparative advantage, would be a major beneficiary of this new hemispheric arrangement. We argue however, that this is rather unlikely unless the region adopts a different approach to tourism. An alternative tourism development agenda would involve greater regional cooperation among CARICOM states, greater emphasis on strategic planning, the creation of a more diversified product linked to the history and culture of the region, and greater local involvement in the tourism development process. While there is no guarantee that these changes would be enough to withstand the fall-out from the likely negative effects of the FTAA, they represent a seemingly viable alternative. In the final analysis, we will really know the true impact of the FTAA after it has been implemented.

References

Barberia, L.G. (2003), 'The Caribbean: Tourism as Development or Development for Tourism?', www.fas.harvard.edu.
Benn, D. and Hall, K. (eds) (2000), *Globalisation: A Calculus of Inequality*, Ian Randle Publishers, Kingston.
Bernal, R.L. (2000), 'Globalisation and Small Developing Countries: The Imperative for Repositioning', in D. Benn and K. Hall (eds), *Globalization: A Calculus of Inequality*, Ian Randle Publishers, Kingston, pp.88-127.
Boxill, I. (2003), 'Towards an Alternative Tourism for Belize', *International Journal of Contemporary Hospitality Management*, Vol. 15(3), pp.147-55.

_____ (2002a), 'The Caribbean World: A Proposal', paper prepared for the University of the West Indies and the Caribbean Maritime Institute.

_____ (2000), 'Overcoming Social Problems in the Jamaican Tourism Industry', in I. Boxill and J. Maerk (eds), *Tourism in the Caribbean*, Plaza y Valdez, Mexico, pp.17-40.

Boxill, I. and Maerk, J. (eds) (2000), *Tourism in the Caribbean*, Plaza y Valdez, Mexico.

Boxill, I. and Frederick, O. (2002), 'Old Road, New Road: Community Protests and Tourism Development in Antigua', in I. Boxill, O. Taylor and J. Maerk (eds), *Tourism and Change in the Caribbean and Latin America*, Arawak Publications, Kingston, pp. 101-110.

Boxill, I., Taylor, O. and Maerk, J. (eds) (2002), *Tourism and Change in the Caribbean and Latin America*, Arawak Publications, Kingston.

Caribbean Tourism Organisation (CTO) (2002), *Statistical Tables 2000-2001*, CTO, Bridgetown, Barbados.

Cepal Review 59, August 1996, pp.98-111.

Duperly-Pinks, D. (2002), 'Community Tourism: "Style and Fashion" or Facilitating Empowerment?', in I. Boxill, O. Taylor and J. Maerk (eds), *Tourism and Change in the Caribbean and Latin America*, Arawak Publications, Kingston, pp.137-61.

'FTAA Summit of The Americas: Fourth Trade Ministerial Meeting', Joint Declaration, San Jose, Costa Rica, March 1998, http://www.ftaa-alca.org.

Girvan, N. (2000), 'Globalisation and Counter-Globalisation', in D. Benn and K. Hall (eds), *Globalisation: A Calculus of Inequality*, Ian Randle Publishers, Kingston, pp.65-87.

Gosovic, B. (2001), 'Global Hegemony and the International Development Agenda', *Cooperation South*, No. 2.

Hayle, C. (2000), 'Community Tourism in Jamaica', in I. Boxill and J. Maerk (eds), *Tourism in the Caribbean*, Plaza y Valdez, Mexico, pp.165-76.

_____ 'Issues Confronting New Entrants to Tourism', in I. Boxill, O. Taylor and J. Maerk (eds), *Tourism and Change in the Caribbean and Latin America*, Arawak Publications, Kingston, pp.229-72.

Hu, A. (2002), 'The Free Trade Agreement (FTA) Policy for North-East Asia Countries and ASEAN: A View from China', paper presented at the 16th International Symposium, Nagoya University.

Jayawardena, C. (2002), 'Cuba: Crown Princess of Caribbean Tourism?', mimeo, presented at the 27th CSA Conference, Nassau, The Bahamas.

Karagiannis, N. (2002), .*Developmental Policy and the State: The European Union, East Asia, and the Caribbean*, Lexington Books, Lanham.

Kempadoo, K. (1999), *Sun, Sex and Gold: Tourism and Sex Work in the Caribbean*, Rowan and Littlefield Publishers, Lanham.

Lalta, S. and Freckleton, M. (eds) (1993), *Caribbean Economic Development: The First Generation*, Ian Randle Publishers, Kingston.

McDavid, H. and Ramjee Singh, D. (2003), 'The State and Tourism: A Caribbean Perspective', *International Journal of Contemporary Hospitality Management*, Vol. 15(3), pp.180-3.

McDavid, H. (2002), 'Why Should Government Intervene in a Market Economy? A Caribbean Perspective on the Hospitality and Tourism Sector', in I. Boxill, O. Taylor and J. Maerk (eds), *Tourism and Change in the Caribbean and Latin America*, Arawak Publications, Kingston, pp.56-81.

NACLA Report on the Americas, Vol.34(3), 2003.

Nurse, K. (2002), 'Bringing Culture into the Tourism: Festival Tourism and Reggae Sunsplash in Jamaica', *Social and Economic Studies*, Vol. 51(1), pp.127-43.

Organisation of American States (OAS) (2002), 'The Road Ahead: The Free Trade Area of the Americas', http://www.sice.oas.org/tunit/Books/Free_Trade/ftch14_e.pdf.

Pereira, A., Boxill I. and Maerk, J. (eds) (2002), *Tourism, Development and Natural Resources in the Caribbean*, Plaza y Valdez, Mexico.

Pattullo, P. (1996), *Last Resorts: The Cost of Tourism in the Caribbean*, Ian Randle Publishers, Kingston.

Poon, A. (1993), 'Caribbean Tourism and the World Economy', in S. Lalta and M. Freckleton (eds), *Caribbean Economic Development: The First Generation*, Ian Randle Publishers, Kingston, pp.262-79.

Schott, Jeffrey (2002), 'The Free Trade Area of The Americas: US Interest and Objectives', http://www.sice.oas.org/geograph/papers/iie/schott0401.asp.

Vaugeios, N. (2003), 'Tourism in Developing Countries: Refining a Useful Tool for Economic Development', mimeo.

PART III
COUNTRY-STUDIES

Chapter 8

The Bahamian Economy in the Era of the FTAA

Nikolaos Karagiannis and Christos D. Salvaris

Introduction

The acute degree of dependency of the Bahamian economy on the world economy in general, and on the economies of its main metropolitan trading partners in particular, is an historical and contemporary fact. This dependency stems not only from the structural features which are shared, to a greater or lesser extent, with all developing economies, but also from the small size of the country, and its current or recent political relationships with colonial powers.

Indeed, the impact on The Bahamas of developments in the world economy is intense and excessive. Underlying this situation are: unstable growth and levels of employment; fiscal difficulties; the poor performance of agriculture coupled with negligible industrial production; large current account deficits; and rising debt and debt service ratios. Not surprisingly, much of the discussion in this chapter focuses on these economic problems.

The posture adopted by the foreign sector in The Bahamas has a fundamental influence not only on the growth rate, but also on the direction of development and ultimately on the form which the country's economic system assumes. Financial institutions, for instance, are in a position to frustrate national objectives and priorities or to encourage the economy to move along paths that have not been the subject of premeditated policy (given the ethos of the institutions in The Bahamas whose presence tend to be motivated more by what they can get out of the existing 'tax haven' situation rather than by any conscious desire to play an active part in changing the fabric of the economy, or stimulating the country's endogenous development). Thus, it is easy for undesirable distortions and relationships to arise, which become effective factors in hampering development efforts.

The first main section of this chapter provides a framework for addressing important development issues of the Bahamian model. The argument deals broadly with the country's development context rather than with specific details. The second part examines possible implications, problems and dilemmas for The Bahamas - should the country join the FTAA. The final sections of the chapter provide notions for an alternative development policy framework as well as policy considerations, based on the Developmental State - New Competition views, while considering structural and functional problems of the Bahamian economy.

The Bahamian Pattern of Growth

The major source of the Bahamian post-war economic upsurge has arisen from the extraordinary expansion of the service sector, principally Tourism and Financial Services. Indeed, Tourism (including associated activities like construction and land development) and to a lesser extent financial activities were the main engines of economic growth during the 1950s and the 1960s. Almost all the capital came from abroad. The closing of the Cuban facilities in the early 1960s boosted a trend that had already begun and opened opportunities which foreign investors and speculators were quick to grasp (Ramsaran, 1983, p.41).

There is no doubt that the growth of tourism in the post-war period has brought a measure of prosperity to several countries, both in the developed and developing world. This is not better illustrated than in The Bahamas where the traditionally high foreign ownership pattern enmeshed with a web of international structures relating to all aspects of the sector. The contribution from this source to Gross National Product amounts to around 70 per cent while the employment contribution, directly and indirectly, is between 50 and 60 per cent of the labour force.[1] However, although numbers have certainly grown in the Bahamian case, this growth has not been accompanied by local industrial development and diversification. In fact, the almost total dependence on external sources for food, materials and equipment made Tourism, and still makes it, largely an 'offshore' activity in which the country plays little more than a peripheral role (Ramsaran, 1983, p.44).

In addition to the rapid growth of Tourism in The Bahamas, the Financial Sector has also experienced a fairly rapid growth over the last four decades, while the Nassau segment has been experiencing the fastest growth rate. Yet, in recent years, The Bahamas has become best known as a centre for offshore banks and trusts and as a functional location for the conduct of the international currency business. This has been helped by the close proximity to the United States and the general openness of the economy, as well as the 'tax haven' status of The Bahamas. In fact Financial Services can generate income and employment and also enhance the 'tax haven' image of the country.

Undoubtedly, the growth in the service sector has led to a significant increase in the level of National Income in The Bahamas, and the country has attained a relatively high level of *per capita* income in recent years (with estimates rising from B$ 1,943 in 1973 to over B$ 11,500 in the early 1990s).[2] However, the certain commonly used economic indices tend to mask a serious state of underdevelopment of the country's endogenous productive activity. Indeed, there are important limitations that are found in the contemporary Bahamian economy (Higgins, 1994, p.8).

First, the major source of the Bahamian post-war economic upsurge has not arisen from any structural transformation in the productive base of the economy or any changes in the structure and functioning of the Bahamian economy, but from the extraordinary expansion of Tourism and international financial activities. In fact the Bahamian pattern of growth has been from the primary production directly to services, with very negligible development of the secondary sector and thus with few, even embryonic, linkages between any of the sectors. In addition, the leakage from the domestic economy of tourist spending has been quite high.

Secondly, also as a result of the expansion in the service sector, The Bahamas exhibits patterns of high consumption, which are an extreme case of 'rising expectations'. Two main direct consequences stand out in this regard: (1) actual levels of domestic savings remain low (and are inadequate to finance higher levels of investment); and, (2) an endemically exaggerated propensity to import and balance-of-payments constraints. More importantly, it is the lack of local initiative in production and supply which is at the heart of the structural imbalance and development disorder in The Bahamas. Exporting is concentrated on a narrow range of primary products, and is highly dependent on the metropolitan markets (mainly the USA). However, the levels of exports of a number of products have seriously declined throughout the 1990s (and continue so until today); other local exports have experienced ups and downs during the same period (Department of Agriculture; Department of Statistics, Nassau, 2000).

Thirdly, while foreign investment can be quite important, it is clear that a country dependent largely on foreign funds may find itself severely constrained in exploiting its potential. Foreign investment may imply foreign control of, and decision making in, important productive sectors and activities. Yet, the foreign sector has been very indifferent to the various needs and problems of the Bahamian economy and society, as it has no natural commitment to the country.

Also, dependence of the Bahamian economy on the foreign sector manifests itself in two very important areas. First, the large role that has been assigned to private foreign capital in the growth process. New foreign investment may assist in alleviating some short-term problems and, in this regard, many see foreign capital as the *panacea* for all the ills facing the Bahamian economy. Depending on the perception of the importance of foreign capital to the Bahamian economy, this could further dictate the whole tone of government's policy and action (i.e., the critical role that foreign decision-making plays in domestic employment, output and income generation). Given the high ratio of foreign to domestic finance in capital formation, the level and rate of accumulation become highly dependent on the volume of foreign capital inflows. Besides, one of the most important effects of foreign investment, particularly in small societies like The Bahamas, is its potential for stunting the growth of local enterprise and initiative, and this too, can perpetuate and deepen the state of dependence (Ramsaran, 1983, p.45).

Second, although the various aspects of the Tourist industry do not involve any high technology and skills for their operation, the country still has to rely, to a significant extent, on foreign skilled manpower and expertise requirements necessary for the functioning of the economic system which has emerged over the last four decades. For this reason, as so much of the Bahamian national output (and income) is dependent on the foreign activity, the rate of domestic accumulation and the transfer of technology from the metropolitan capitalist centres to the local economy will be highly dependent on the pattern and rate of foreign capital inflow.

Fourthly, The Bahamas imposes no personal or corporate income taxation. The result has been that the government of the country has always had to rely heavily on indirect taxes (import duties in particular) for a substantial proportion of its revenue to carry out its administrative functions and other commitments. In fact, the proportion of import duties to state tax revenues has been the largest single contributor (amounting to around 60 per cent on average throughout the 1990s).[3] Heavy reliance therefore has been placed on the foreign trade sector which, because of its size, the high degree of monetisation, and administrative convenience has always been an 'easy target' for taxation in The Bahamas (Ramsaran, 1983, p. 365). Given the pressure on the public expenditure side coupled with a limited tax base, the result has been to further exacerbate the problem of fiscal 'stress'.

Another important point that should be noted about The Bahamas tax system is that it is not the result of a carefully thought-out scheme formulated from a long-term perspective or within an articulated development strategy. The tax structure has evolved largely as an *ad hoc* response designed to meet revenue needs and paying little attention to other considerations. However, in a developing country like The Bahamas where the state has to assume a crucial role in stimulating and guiding the development process, deliberate fiscal action would encourage certain types of activities and sectors (Ramsaran, 1983, p.364).

Fiscal and Trade Challenges Facing The Bahamas

During the first Summit of Americas held in Miami, Florida in 1994, the leaders of 34 countries, including The Bahamas, agreed to begin the process for the gradual removal of barriers and impediments to free trade and investments, leading to the establishment of a Free Trade Area (FTAA) by the year 2005. Further, the leaders agreed that countries would be expected to make substantial progress towards the establishment of a free trade area by 2000. Nevertheless, the proposed Free Trade Area of the Americas is a serious challenge for the Bahamian economy, which may also face serious problems.

International trade has always been an important part of the Bahamian economy. During the last two decades, there have been dramatic changes in the composition of imports and a downward trend in the balance of the Bahamian external trade (there is an increase of over 50 per cent in the country's external trade deficit during the period 1996-2000) (The Central Bank of The Bahamas, 'Quarterly Statistical Digest', Table 9.2, 2003).

The Bahamian economy can be considered to be structurally dependent, since there is a great divergence between the type of goods supplied and the pattern of domestic demand. Due to the extreme openness of The Bahamas, the country has a high preponderance of imports *vis-à-vis* exports. The inevitable result is that the levels of imports (and, consequently, the propensity to import) are high. Without international trade, nevertheless, the economy can only consume what it produces;

with international trade, the economy can consume different quantities of goods from those that it produces. In fact, when a country opens itself up to international trade, it expands its consumption possibilities. The values of non-oil exports to, and non-oil imports from principal trading partners are given in Tables 8.1 and 8.2 which follow.

Table 8.1 Value of non-oil exports to principal trading partners, The Bahamas, 1990-2000 (000, B$)

Region	1990	1995	2000
United Kingdom	14,266	3,966	7,790
EEC/EU Countries	56,001	12,182	43,475
Caribbean Commonwealth Countries	4,409	2,812	3,894
United States of America	80,645	142,614	430,095
Canada	13,003	3,388	7,996
Other Countries	44,132	10,928	30,468
TOTAL	212,456	175,890	523,718

Source: The Central Bank of The Bahamas, 'Quarterly Statistical Digest', Table 9.6, Nassau (2003).

Table 8.2 Value of non-oil imports from principal trading partners, The Bahamas, 1990-2000 (000, B$)

Region	1990	1995	2000
United Kingdom	21,777	8,691	15,322
EEC/EU Countries	37,050	21,730	30,001
Caribbean Commonwealth Countries	5,480	1,638	10,769
United States of America	819,093	1,008,691	1,876,171
Canada	16,823	11,338	19,639
Other Countries	58,271	34,562	92,777
TOTAL	958,494	1,086,650	2,044,679

Source: The Central Bank of The Bahamas, 'Quarterly Statistical Digest', Table 9.5, Nassau (2003).

Another issue, which has to be mentioned, is the importance of the increasing openness of national economies to international competition. Besides, the external environment in which national economies operate is changing rapidly. In fact, the performance of Caribbean economies in the 21st century is now being challenged by the radical changes in the international competitive environment. There is no doubt that an open world trade has steadily increased the degree of openness of national economies to imports and exports which have grown rapidly over time. Hence, the levels of imports and exports, as well as the countries' competitiveness, clearly show that countries differ as to the type and quantity of goods and services they trade (see Table 8.3).

Table 8.3 Value of imports, exports and trade balance, American countries, 1997 (000, B$)

COUNTRIES	Imports	Exports	Balance of Trade
Bahamas	1,622,026	181,393	-1,440,633
United States	1,469,602,201	133,228,887	-1,336,373,314
Canada	10,893,122	3,902,248	-6,990,874
Bermuda	205,739	407,387	201,648
Jamaica	719,175	377,175	-342,000
Trinidad & Tobago	1,113,657	192,304	-921,353
Turks & Caicos	-	65,730	65,730
St. Lucia	2,038	27,144	25,106
Dominica	346	-	-346
Barbados	948,470	194,023	-754,447
British Virgin Islands	-	308,898	308,898
Cayman Islands	58,735	77,276	18,541
Belize	34,378	46,177	11,799
Guyana	-	4,958	4,958
CARICOM Countries (*)	2,854,782	933,510	-1,921,272
Cuba	147,718	-	-147,718
Dominican Republic	179,950	125,188	-54,762
Haiti	84,406	118,177	33,771
Puerto Rico	3,459,604	6,655,123	3,195,519
Honduras	36,928	108,224	71,296
Aruba	573,567	180,221	-393,346
Argentina	115,699	19,786	-95,913
Brazil	403,538	231,617	-171,921
Chile	204,464	121,676	-82,788
Colombia	464,271	39,401	-424,870
Guatemala	214,775	26,747	-188,028
Mexico	10,438,261	3,516,083	-6,922,178
Panama	3,284,559	525,001	-2,759,558
Paraguay	-	3,894	3,894
Peru	20,429	12,039	-8,390
Venezuela	5,410,237	31,113	-5,379,124
Ecuador	3,609,260	3,878	-3,605,382
Costa Rica	111,688	-	-111,688
Nicaragua	2,960	14,532	11,572
Uruguay	-	128,319	128,319
El Salvador	-	13,829	13,829
Bolivia	-	84,739	84,739

(*) There are no available figures for Montserrat.
Source: Department of Statistics, Nassau (2000).

The Bahamas relies heavily on taxes on international trade, and import tariffs are imposed on the importation of products into the country. The largest percentage of state revenue (over 60 per cent) is received from international trade transactions (that is, import and export duties, and stamp taxes on imports and exports). They are levied on an *ad valorem* basis or on a specific basis. Their purpose is solely for raising government revenues given the rigid government spending pattern largely on wages and salaries (i.e., 'Personal Emoluments') coupled with debt repayments, and the fact that The Bahamas imposes no personal or corporate income taxation.

Import duties and tariffs may reduce the volume of imports, affect the balance of trade quickly (or relatively quickly), are generally applied for the purpose of carrying out a particular economic policy, and can be used to serve many functions:

- to reduce the overall level of imports by making them more expensive;
- to protect a new promising industry or 'key' industries until they are sufficiently well-established to compete with more developed industries of other countries (i.e., 'infant industry' argument); and,
- to counter the practice of dumping of other countries.

In 1992, 57.5 per cent of Government Tax Revenue was received from 'Taxes on International Trade', and the categories 'Other Stamp Tax' and 'Departure Tax' followed at 14.6 per cent and 10.5 per cent respectively. In 1995, 'Taxes on International Trade' accounted for 67.2 per cent of the Government Tax Revenue and 'Other Stamp Tax' and 'Departure Tax' for 8.3 per cent and 8.6 per cent respectively. In 2002, 65.3 per cent of Government Tax Revenue was received from 'Taxes on International Trade' and the categories 'Other Stamp Tax' and 'Departure Tax' followed at 7.6 per cent and 7.2 per cent respectively. Table 8.4 shows the composition of the Bahamian Government Revenues in 1992, 1995 and 2002, and Table 8.5 the different types of import duties.

Table 8.4 Government revenue sources: 1992, 1995 and 2002 (B$)

Kind of Tax	1992		1995		2002	
	Millions	%	Millions	%	Millions	%
Property Tax	16.8	3.4	19.1	3.1	40.2	4.6
Select. Service Tax	25.5	5.2	22.7	3.8	48.5	5.5
Business Licences	24.8	5.1	33.3	5.7	59.9	6.8
Motor Vehicle Tax	13.7	2.6	13.0	2.2	18.1	2.1
Departure Tax	50.7	10.5	50.9	8.6	63.7	7.2
Taxes on Int'l Trade	276.6	* 57.5	393.7	* 67.2	574.1	* 65.3
Other Stamp Tax	70.5	14.6	48.7	8.3	67.4	7.6
Other Tax	5.9	1.1	5.9	1.1	7.7	0.9
Tax Revenue	479.8	100	585.5	100	879.7	100
Non-Tax Revenue	53.5		61.5		77.8	
Total	533.3		647.0		957.5	

* Or 51.7%, 59.6% and 59.9% of Total Tax and Non-Tax Revenue in 1992, 1995 and 2002 respectively (around 58% on average throughout the 1990s).
Source: The Central Bank of The Bahamas, 'Quarterly Statistical Digest', various years.

Table 8.5 The different types of import duties

ISIC Code	Wholesale	Tariff Rates
5122	Food, Beverages & Tobacco [1]	10%-35%
5139	Other Household Goods	30%
5141	Solid, Liquid & Gaseous Fuels & Related Products	30%-35%
5143	Construction Materials, Hardware, Plumbing & Heating Equipment & Supplies	35%
5190	Other	20%-45%
5206	Motor Vehicles	45%-65%
5207	Maintenance & Repair of Motor Vehicles	35%
5208	Motor Vehicle Parts & Accessories	35%-65%
5209	Sale, Maintenance & Repair of Motorcycles & Related Parts & Accessories	35%
5210	Automotive Fuel	35%
5219	Other	35%
5220	Food, Beverages & Tobacco in Specialized Stores	35%-55%
5221	Liquor in Specialized Stores	35%-55%
5231	Pharmaceutical Medical Goods, Cosmetic & Toilet Articles	35%-65%
5232	Textiles, Clothing, Footwear & Leather Goods	25%-35%
5233	Household Appliances, Articles & Equipment [2]	35%
5234	Hardware, Paint & Glass	35%
5239	Other Retail Sale in Specialized Stores	35%
5260	Repair of Personal & Household Goods	35%

[1] Turkey, ducks and geese 10%, fish and seafood 30%, citrus and other fruits 20%-30%, vegetables 25%, frozen/preserved vegetables 30%, prepared/preserved meat and seafood 35%, manufactured food products 35%, jam/jelly 20%-35%, juices 30%-50%, and animal feeds 0% (exemption).
[2] Electronics 50%.
Source: Department of Statistics, Nassau (1997, 2000).

As can be seen in Table 8.5, there are different import tariff rates (which vary from 10% to 65%) for different types of goods. The magnitude of the impact of these tariffs varies, and depends on the elasticity of demand for the imported goods, thereby having a strong impact on economic activities and trade in The Bahamas. This is an important issue in the Bahamian context, given that retailing is the final link in the chain of distribution from foreign (mostly US) manufacturers to the Bahamian consumers. Therefore, should the Bahamian Government seek 'close' integration and free trade with the Western Hemisphere and the world economy, the FTAA is expected to have a serious impact on a number of economic activities - most likely at the expense of local productive initiatives, and the development of the country's technological capabilities and endogenous competency.

Towards an Alternative Production and Trade Profile

The direction in which the Bahamian economy is pointed at present seems to be somewhat random, depending on the current state and vagaries of the international market rather than based on long-term development planning. Attention will have to be drawn to the part played by tourism in the Bahamian economy, as the lack of an overall integrated policy has limited its contribution to the country's endogenous development.

In order to maximise the benefits from tourism, the sector must provide an effective stimulus for local agriculture and agro-industrial production. However, the economic benefits from tourism growth have been inadequately exploited due to insufficient linkages with local food, beverage, and other commodity production sectors; and failure to upgrade complementary and related service industries such as communication and information services. The fact that decisions relating to a particular sector (e.g., tourism industry) tend to have broader implications for the national economy as a whole requires a clear examination of the interacting influences between the promising activities from the point of view of endogenous competency, and those that may provide short-term benefits but offer little hope as a secure basis for future national well-being (Karagiannis, 2002, p.15).

In formulating policies for economic restructuring and diversification, it is essential, therefore, to recognise the critical elements of the system in terms of deriving a long-term strategy. Simultaneously, it is necessary to juxtapose certain facts relating to the structure of the Bahamian economy in order to provide what might be called 'an integrated development perspective of the system', and to show the relative position of endogenous strategic components. Failure to do so can easily lead not only to short-run, highly partial considerations, and short-term measures dictated by pressing problems (e.g., balance of payments constraints) but also to the adoption of *ad hoc* approach to development which may be in basic conflict with the goal of a stronger economic fabric.

Prospects for future growth in The Bahamas have been lowered significantly and frustrated due to foreign exploitation and underutilisation of existing resources, and the economic difficulties the country has repeatedly faced with its balance of payments. The underutilisation of part of its productive capacity is proof of this considerable growth potential. As the Bahamian economy operates at well below its level of physical and human capacity, policies to increase aggregate demand can yield substantial economic gains (Karagiannis, 2002, p.61).

Thus, a first requirement of a thorough development strategy is that aggregate demand is sufficient enough to stimulate production up to the adequate rate of capacity utilisation. However, growth of local production must go hand in hand with special consideration of the country's external trade. In connection with this, the competitiveness of the Bahamian economy must come to the fore.

In order to expand industrial production and employment, firms must have the financial means to invest in the necessary machinery, capital equipment, critical kinds of science and technology initiatives, and skills training and upgrading, and short-run bottlenecks preventing a fuller utilisation of capacities have to be taken care of. These bottlenecks may include a lack of the necessary resources and skills, difficulties in obtaining finance, and a lack of business confidence.

Hence, a second requirement of the proposed developmental state strategy is that selective economic policies should provide the resources and stimuli to carry out the investments in both working and fixed capital, infrastructure, and the modern factors of development and competitiveness, necessary to raise output and to improve the production and commercial conditions of industries and hotels at national and local levels. Active fiscal policy ought to carry out the investments necessary to improve the supply conditions of industries and to support the other expenditures associated with the selective policy. Monetary policy ought to ensure that sufficient financial resources are channelled to businesses and to intermediary agencies at reasonable interest rates. In addition, it should be considered that the increase in output would translate into higher profits and savings.

What has been asserted should not be taken to imply a rejection of the problems that could arise with the proposed developmental strategy. But to face them, a sound economic approach ought to complement short-run measures with thorough and technically proficient plans for the future, which include long-term industrial or structural change strategies aimed at diversifying local production, strengthening technological capabilities, and promoting innovation. Greater levels of production, employment and profits that would be achieved in the short term owing to the fuller use of available resources, would actually spur a transition to a more structurally efficient economy. Part of this increased production and income in The Bahamas would go to higher spending on the modern factors of endogenous competency and competitiveness and lead to faster development of skills of the labour force. Not only higher profits would allow additional investments but also a greater proportion of income growth will be channelled towards investment. So, in the future, it would be relatively easier to incorporate more modern technology and increase productivity, while at the same time raising accumulation rates.

Bottlenecks at the firm or macro level often hamper a more efficient capacity utilisation. These bottlenecks have to be seriously considered, would require addressing a number of issues simultaneously, and, accordingly, a medium and long-term development strategy should have as a basic requirement a close link with a deliberate industrial strategy. Indeed, industrial targeting should single out areas of emphasis in selected fields, and should be directed towards strengthening the national industrial core and upgrading international competitiveness. It should be concentrated on a few focal areas having favourable prospects for development, and be selectively designed so as to support a small group of key dynamic firms managed by modern entrepreneurs (Karagiannis, 2002, pp.61-2). Even a small group of key propulsive industries can be instrumental in emphasising the modern factors of endogenous competency and development, exert pressure to adapt on other supply firms, and introduce modern concepts of policy making and labour relations. The various spheres of policy should be directed towards consolidating these focal areas, correcting the imbalances which continually emerge in the wake of restructuring and repositioning, reconciling contradictory elements therein, and smoothing the path for industrial growth.

Obviously, for purposes of designing endogenous competency strategies to achieve the development of productive forces, and the transformation and diversification of the structure of Bahamian production, technically proficient strategic planning is absolutely necessary - indeed, it is inevitable - and should be directed towards the creation of new conditions and processes to be effectively and directly determined by the planning authorities. Strategic planning is a pragmatic attempt to increase the country's long-run capacity to transform itself by building up the infrastructure and the requisite skills. It is this national strategic planning that can give The Bahamas its internal autonomy, and determine its capacity for 'self-determined' 'self-sustained' growth and development. In the development of these strategies, a proactive Developmental State generates not only the capacity to spread the use of modern knowledge and industrial techniques into all elements of the economic transformation so as to spur local industrial activities, but it also creates a dynamic basis for engagement in the world economy through higher levels of exports.

Moreover, tourism is a very volatile industry making excessive dependence on it very risky. Single sector growth by its very nature neither maximises the benefits of economic activity to the national economy as a whole nor allows this leading sector to impart the momentum that is necessary to drive the other economic sectors as the leading sector expands. More importantly, Bahamian exports have never developed on an initial platform of production for internal requirements and domestic needs. Instead, domestic production should be oriented towards satisfying domestic demand in the first instance with export specialisation occurring as an extension of this. The aim should be to bring about a general improvement in the competency and efficiency of the national economy, in the level of technological infrastructure it relies on, and in the quality of workmanship and service, so that more and more activities may become increasingly competitive.

Modern production techniques, precisely because of their flexibility, make it possible to manufacture in small series on a viable basis. Targeting and flexibility are possible, especially if they can draw on modern industrial planning. Assuming predominance of clear focal areas and initiatives carried out by both a competent administrative machine and dynamic local businesses, demand for imported capital and goods could decline and exports of local products expand. Given the growth of production of local industries and the improvement of national competitiveness, a large part of the additional goods produced will be devoted to exports. Therefore, the country would make a greater and better use of its productive resources and capacity, while at the same time easing the constraints on its balance of payments (Karagiannis, 2002, p.62).

In addition, as indigenous technology is the basis for an organic integration of domestic production and demand structures (which means human capital formation coupled with consistent technical progress), investment priorities and the choice of technique are determined by the strategies of transformation and diversification, and by the product choices to which these strategies give rise. The overall purpose is to increase the capacity of the Bahamian economy to respond at the level of the government, businesses, and the population as a whole.

In order to devise and execute effectively national strategies, a small, determined developmental elite, which surrounds itself with skilled development planners and technocrats, is absolutely essential. The government provides the 'national purpose' framework, while the technocrats supply planning and overview. This 'national purpose' can bring together social and political forces in the interests of a socially defined agenda. In addition, the growth-oriented transformation must lead in a corporatist direction and strategic partnership between a Developmental State, forward-looking businesses and various social segments. A broad-based consensus is also required and could afford scope for national strategic planning. Besides, if such thorough alternative strategies are to solve such problems, they presuppose participation. Indeed, participation is an important element ensuring that sufficient motivation, creativity, and human effort are forthcoming to guarantee that such technically proficient strategies can be successfully carried out in The Bahamas.

A Developmental State policy framework may be a more feasible and realistic suggestion in light of the fact that these strata and decision makers which serve the powerful interests of the dominant transnational corporations and the hegemonic centres are those which tend to reject the concept of national development in The Bahamas, and seek to maintain the economic and political order of a dependent productive structure by siding with backward-looking segments, officials and policy makers; by engaging in modern experiments with neoliberalism; and also as a result of balance of payments constraints, and the astonishing technological developments taking place in the leading industrial economies. However, only under such a national strategic planning system and well-conceived and vigorously executed development plans trade will serve a different function because the economy itself will be reoriented to serve different purposes (Karagiannis, 2002, p. 62).

Lastly, any economy is underpinned and imbued by social values, codes of behaviour and ethics, which are in turn reflected in the structure and functioning of government sector institutions and private sector firms. As political will may not be clearly agglomerated and administrative capacity is inadequate in The Bahamas, governments have not been successful in indicating a clear course for the public sector to adopt. However, the adjustment of its social and political conditions to the country's urgent social, economic and developmental needs cannot be avoided. If The Bahamas is to develop growth-oriented learning-based productive activities, therefore, it would be necessary to adopt a number of measures to remodel its key social, economic and institutional factors that will be required to provide the necessary underpinning. More importantly, these thorough development strategies assume a much better state action, and would require an efficient and competent administrative machine. But so does any strategy capable of overcoming barriers and laying down the basis of endogenous competency in any developing economy.

Devising the necessary action to stimulate sustainable tourism development and industrial production, while raising the quantity and quality of productive investment necessary to allow the fullest and most efficient utilisation of existing local resources, seems to be a more sensible way to confront the future. Such an approach seems, certainly, a better option for the endogenous development and overall competency of the Bahamian economy than a frantic search for accelerated 'western-style' modernisation and free market antidote - a 'vision' that decision and policy makers in The Bahamas aspire to. An alternative and, perhaps, more realistic development paradigm would require the pursuit of thorough Developmental State strategies and policies. This is what the Bahamian economy needs (Karagiannis, 2002, p.62).

Developmental State Policy Considerations

Industrial strategy has not been seen to be pivotal in the Bahamian economy; thus, it has never been developed in a systematic or coherent fashion as a centrepiece of the government's approach to economic policy making. State interventions have usually been seen as *ad hoc* responses to pressing problems based on short-run, highly partial considerations, and the policies which flow from these interventions appear to be consonant with the *market failure* analysis. Consequently, the general concept of a developmental role for the state is rather alien to the general economic and political culture in The Bahamas.

Furthermore, interest group politics and patronage in The Bahamas explain why policy is often flawed in both formulation and execution. This convergence of economic and political functions in the Bahamian state, and the primacy of various political pressures and certain private interests, have had disastrous effects in the economic sphere.

During the last 15 years, neoliberal policies have been the central routes to modern economic solutions of the Bahamian economy. However, there are serious doubts about whether these economic policies have been translated into significant economic and social development, endogenous competency, industrial growth and competitiveness. While appropriate macroeconomic policies can contribute much towards enhancing the performance of the Bahamian economy, nevertheless such policies only deal with the 'symptoms' of deeper structural problems. For this reason, the construction of a production-based approach to economic development and a much sharper focus on strategic industrial policy are seen to be necessary to resolve these deeper problems, and would offer a concrete and realistic alternative for the Bahamian economy. Some alternative policy suggestions for the Bahamian development discourse are outlined below.

Macroeconomic Steering

The creation of a free trade area is based on the assumption that through the removal of trade 'distortions', tariffs and other impediments to trade, the market forces will be able to allocate resources efficiently. Hence, governments should progressively eliminate tariffs and non-tariffs barriers as well as other measures that would restrict free trade between FTAA member states.

Should we expect a country like The Bahamas, where around 60 per cent of tax revenue is received from international trade transactions, to immediately reduce or eliminate import and export duties and tariffs? In this case, any reduction in import duties translates rapidly into a decrease in government revenues as customs duty collections decline. However, these public revenues are not only critical for the payment of 'Personal Emoluments and Allowances' and for the repayment of debts, but are also needed to provide essential social services and infrastructure in The Bahamas.

Faced by the difficult realities of budgetary pressure, a proactive fiscal policy would: (1) emphasise a prudent government expenditure management and planning (i.e., long-term planned investments in human capital formation, skills, technical change, technological capacity, R&D, innovation and information); (2) consider alternative sources of government revenue; and, (3) attempt to reduce non-essential over-consumption.

By curtailing high consumption, the amounts of local savings available for investment purposes could be markedly increased. In addition, various national savings plans and savings vehicles can increase the levels and shares of Bahamian savings. The savings thus enforced could be channelled by the government into productive prioritised investments. Furthermore, higher levels of output and income ensuing from a higher degree of capacity utilisation and a better utilisation of equipment can be the source of higher levels of savings required to match higher levels of investment (which will bring about further increase in output and income levels and so on).

Monetary policy on the other hand ought to: (1) provide a stable financial framework for the successful implementation of government policy; (2) ensure that the overall development effort is not to be thwarted by endemic short-termism, 'capital flight' and speculative ventures (that can actually starve the real economy of investment capital); and, (3) ensure that sufficient financial resources are channelled to dynamic industries and intermediary agencies at reasonable interest rates. This will require significant state intervention in the capital market by means of direct control measures and interest rate policies. In particular, the Bahamian government will have to issue direct instructions to the banks, close off the options available for rent seeking and capital flight, and guide prioritised investments by selective credit policies.

As financial institutions have a critically important role in this growth process, it is particularly important that they are well managed, have a clear set of strategic goals, and promote longer time horizons. In this regard, the government must take steps to ensure that the financial services sector is properly supervised (Clayton, 2001, p.16). Hence, appropriate monetary and exchange rate policies to facilitate productive initiatives (as well as higher levels of national savings to finance higher levels of investment) are also essential.

Moreover, for too long, it has seemed as if it is the level of foreign direct investment that is dictating the Bahamian development policy. As foreign direct investment is necessary for the functioning of the economy of The Bahamas, the approach towards foreign investment initiatives should be designed in the context of the long-term strategy for overall development. Besides, to find the appropriate role for foreign investment in the development process is a necessary complement to the strategy for expanding local production.[4]

Investments on the Accelerators

Recent developments in the financial markets have significantly encouraged various speculative ventures and endemic short-termism. These disturbing developments, in conjunction with weak or absent government supervision, can foster a dysfunctional business culture and a 'casino economy' mindset, in which insider trading, conflicts of interest and more direct forms of corruption can increasingly become common (Clayton, 2001, p.16).

In The Bahamas, too, loans and various financial schemes are seen to be partial, inadequate and unsuccessful measures for a successful local development, industrial competency and regeneration. 'Market failure' has usually been the reason for loans, subsidies and other forms of financial support to businesses and industries in The Bahamas. These *traditional* incentive policies offer only marginal solutions and often recommend some temporary assistance, without getting at the root of the problems. Instead, particular emphasis should be placed on government finance and guidance of higher levels of investment spending: investment in people, machinery, technical change and its implementation.

Further, some support the view that high operating costs (high wages) in The Bahamas are a serious barrier which may discourage productive investments. The only logical alternative, then, is to consider the capacity-creating aspect of state spending, and the Bahamian government should rely heavily on higher levels of government investment. Indeed, planned investments on knowledge, technological innovation, training, education/technical education, and work-place experience programmes and research should provide the industrial requisites to thoroughly support the prioritised sectors and activities, and boost the overall competency of the Bahamian economy, towards higher rates of growth and 'high wages - high productivity'. The key issue here is that investment responsibilities should be closely tailored to the needs of the private sector.[5]

While state intervention may have multiple beneficial effects, investment planning at national and local levels is clearly required in order to support and develop indigenous resources, industries and firms; to add to the sum total of investment capital, skills and expertise, technical development, technological infrastructure, and services available; to create and/or enhance the opportunities for local economic development, diversification and/or restructuring; and to improve social welfare in The Bahamas.

Bahamian Food Production

In The Bahamas, the pattern of growth has been from the primary production directly to Tourism and Financial Services, with negligible development of the secondary sector and embryonic linkages between its economic sectors. Besides, the three macroeconomic imbalances (i.e., fiscal 'stress', trade deficit, and the imbalance between savings and domestic investment spending) are tightly linked to the 'development disorder' of the Bahamian economy.

An 'aggressive' export strategy for The Bahamas must seek to strengthen the national capability first, if the economy is to improve its ability to compete at international level. Indeed, The Bahamas must actively trade if the economy is to be prosperous and successful, and factors such as human capital formation and technological infrastructure must be brought to the fore. This mixture of inward and outward-oriented development should constitute the foremost priority of state action.

The proposed development of food industry in The Bahamas shapes the agro-industrial landscape; provides a clear thrust and direction for the development of the country's technological base, scientific and technical expertise, and managerial competence; allows the local capture of manufacturing value-added; promotes diversification; seeks to establish and strengthen the linkages between all sectors and activities of the local economy; is a realistic and pragmatic response to the country's 'development problem'; and, seeks to lessen the dependence of the Bahamian economy.

Strategic Intervention

The mainstream Anglo-American economic analysis focuses on the essential opposition of market and government, and draws a sharp division between state and industry. The 'New Right' argues that there is no constructive role for the state, and that government activity is indeed detrimental to economic development and prosperity (and that the free flow of the market is crucial for economic prosperity).

However, the experience of many of the Newly Industrialised Countries (NICs) suggests the importance of the strategic partnership between the government and private sectors - which can cooperate in a range of different arrangements - each contributing what it does best and both participating in the financial returns, within the context of a thorough development agenda. This institutionalised public-private cooperation will allow the Bahamian state to develop independent national goals, and to translate these broad national goals into effective policy action, in line with its view of an appropriate industrial and trade profile for the Bahamian economy.

Further, demand for industrial products leads to output growth and important efficiency benefits (capital accumulation, mechanisation, structural transformation, reallocation of resources, learning and technical change), which induce further growth of demand. Indeed, the development of industry represents a net addition to the effective use of resources and can contribute to a higher degree of capacity utilisation in The Bahamas. For this reason, industrial strategy should be an important part of government policy making, which means that 'the state adopts a strategic view of future industrial development in the [Bahamian] economy and provides a range of support mechanisms to those sectors deemed to have a key-role to play in the future' (Sawyer, 1992, p.8). Therefore, the Bahamian government needs to undertake selective intervention; focus its attention on increasing growth, competency, productivity and profitability; and restrict its deliberate action to the strategic requirements of long-term economic transformation and diversification.

Politico-institutional Reforms

In this chapter, it is argued that Developmental State policies in The Bahamas must be concerned with the long-term aim of altering (both) the direction and pace of domestic development. However, it is unlikely that significant state intervention would be warranted given the inadequate capacity and competence of government institutions; the institutional impediments to the country's economic development. For this reason, the pursuit of an interventionist strategy as well as a successful and effective policy reform require the politico-institutional structure and means to formulate, implement and enforce developmental policies and production-oriented selective interventions in certain key sectors of the Bahamian economy (e.g., food industry).

First of all, a small, determined developmental elite, which surrounds itself with skilled development planners and technocrats, is absolutely necessary in order to devise and execute effective national strategies. Besides, if the Bahamian state is to become developmental, it is essential for the government to reduce 'pork barrel' intervention and patronage so as to insulate decision makers and technocrats from the excessive influence of powerful interests. This executive 'new look' elite must possess accurate intelligence, inventiveness, commitment and effectiveness, as well as active, strategic and sophisticated responsiveness to a changing economic reality (Evans, 1992, p.148).

Potentially weak central cores or state governments may be captured by powerful interests, and can hardly implement institutional structures that decisively promote structural changes and economic reforms. Also, changes in the structure of class relations during the last decades induced erosion of political institutions in The Bahamas. In contrast, Developmental States are distinguished by 'strong' politico-institutional structures.[6] Building a strong technostructure and embedding it into a network of cooperative and consultative relations with targeted dynamic firms and other social segments is both feasible and operational in The Bahamas.

Secondly, the involvement of business elites and social segments in public policy making through institutionalised channels represents an adequate means to establish a government-business-society interface by which the mutual exchange of information can be encouraged, risk sharing facilitated, bureaucratic autonomy and flexibility enhanced, and a consensual process of policy formulation realised. This combination of social connectedness and bureaucratic autonomy, which Evans (1992, 1995) calls 'embedded autonomy', may represent the institutional basis for effective and accountable government involvement in the Bahamian economy, while being independent of societal pressures (Ahrens, 1997, p.125).

Thirdly, in order to make government activities more effective, both effective procedures and increased participation are of vital importance. Indeed, this new institutional structure must allow for participation at all levels. Furthermore, loose and transparent links between the strategic planning agency and Ministries and

Government Departments involved in the investment planning and industrial strategy (such as Treasury, Education and Training), and sectoral agencies and local authorities/boards would decentralise much of the work of the central core.

To be successful our planning must be democratic. Indeed, our institutional structure must allow for participation at all levels. Participation by the 'social partners' can improve the organisation of production and help restrain the power of interest groups which have access to government decision making (Cowling, 1990, p.28).

Fourthly, preconditions for the practicability and success of these alternative strategies and policies in The Bahamas should include: the government's credible commitment to a production-oriented strategy (which includes agriculture, industry, and the entire services sector); an improved quality of state action; the replacement of the short-term perspective of the Treasury and the financial institutions with one much more favourable to productive investment and industry; recognition of the importance of state capabilities, capacities, efficiency and effectiveness; autonomy, accountability, professionalism and manageability of the executive developmental elite; mechanisms of consensual conflict resolution through transparent and efficient procedures; the organisational design of, and the incentives within, the public sector and the institutional environment: incentives to pursue collective ends while restraining arbitrary action, favouritism and corruption (Ahrens, 1997, p.116).

Lastly, particularly in the course of a fundamental redirection of the existing pattern of development, as in the case of the Bahamian economy, simply matching such a radical policy framework to existing political institutions will be counter-productive. Effective governance is a dynamic process that requires continuing fine-tuning and adjusting institutions and policy solutions to changing political, social, technological and economic environments (Ahrens, 1997, p.119).

To the extent that a chosen path falls short in this respect, this will need changes and adjustments in certain policy areas. However, it is difficult to retain a disposition against change in a world environment where basic conditions are subject to constant mutation. Without these preconditions, therefore, no matter the new structure of institutions, such an alternative policy framework for The Bahamas will founder on short-term expedients, the deficiencies and conservatism of the Civil Service, the power of transnational corporations and foreign interests, or the mindset of the people.

Conclusion

This chapter has argued that in a world of imperfect competition, and inadequate access to modern knowledge and know-how to use it, there are sound analytical grounds for following Developmental State policies and adopting a production, capital accumulation, and innovation-oriented approach. But in such a world, the optimal degree of openness or the optimal degree of domestic competition for an economy may not be maximum openness or perfect competition. In fact, the neoclassical/neoliberal assertions do not correspond to the real world (e.g., 'level-playing field'); consequently, suggestions and solutions which emanate from these paradigms may not be helpful to the Bahamian economic development.

Contrary to the 'current orthodoxy', 'developmentalism' is related to, and concerned with, strategic actions for achieving long-term intensive growth, and knowledge-based investment-led endogenous development and competitiveness in the dynamic international market. Devising the necessary measures to nurture and promote vibrant Bahamian agro-industrial activities that will ensure a greater and better use of existing resources - along with the further development of Tourism and Financial Services - seems to be a more sensible way to confront the future. Such an approach seems, certainly, a better option for the endogenous development and competency of the Bahamian economy, than a frantic search for accelerated 'western-style' modernisation - a 'vision' that decision and policy makers in The Bahamas aspire to. The alternative and more realistic development paradigm would require the pursuit of Developmental State strategies and policies. This is what the Bahamian economy needs.

Notes

1. Department of Statistics; The Central Bank of The Bahamas, Nassau.
2. According to available statistical information.
3. The Central Bank of The Bahamas, 'Quarterly Statistical Digest', various years.
4. Once again, it is maintained that, even under the current conditions of globalisation and the pressures from international organisations such as WTO, IMF and World Bank, governments still have room for Developmental State action.
5. Private investment spending on the accelerators of endogenous competency and growth is also essential and most welcome.
6. 'Strong' in the sense that the government is able to credibly commit itself to 'national purpose' policy making; serious and capable of signalling its commitment to sustainable economic development.

References

Ahrens, J. (1997), 'Prospects of Institutional and Policy Reform in India: Towards a Model of the Developmental State?', *Asian Development Review*, Vol. 15(1), pp.111-46.

Chang, H-J (1998), 'Globalisation, Transnational Corporations, and Economic Development: Can the Developing Countries Pursue Strategic Industrial Policy in a Globalising World Economy?', in D. Baker, G. Epstein and R. Pollin (eds), *Globalisation and Progressive Economic Policy*, Cambridge University Press, Cambridge, pp.97-116.

Clayton, A (2001), 'Developing a Bio-industry Cluster in Jamaica: A Step Towards Building a Skill-Based Economy', *Social and Economic Studies*, Vol. 50(2), pp.1-37.

Cowling, K. (1990), 'The Strategic Approach to Economic and Industrial Policy', in K. Cowling and R. Sugden (eds), *A New Economic Policy for Britain: Essays on the Development of Industry*, Manchester University Press, Manchester, pp.6-34.

Cowling, K. and Sugden, R. (eds) (1990), *A New Economic Policy for Britain: Essays on the Development of Industry*, Manchester University Press, Manchester.

Evans, P.B. (1992), 'The State as Problem and Solution: Predation, Embedded Autonomy, and Structural Change', in S. Haggard and R.R. Kaufman (eds), *The Politics of Economic Adjustment*, Princeton University Press, Princeton.

_____ (1995), *Embedded Autonomy: States and Industrial Transformation*, Princeton University Press, Princeton.

Higgins, K.J. (1994), *The Bahamian Economy: An Analysis*, The Counsellors, Nassau.

Karagiannis, N. (2002), *A New Economic Strategy for The Bahamas: With Special Consideration of International Competition and the FTAA*, UWI Printers, Kingston.

Ramsaran, R.F. (1983), *The Monetary and Financial System of The Bahamas: Growth, Structure and Operation*, ISER, Kingston.

Sawyer, M.C. (1992), 'Unemployment and the Dismal Science', *Discussion Paper Series G92/15*, Leeds University Business School, Leeds.

Wade, R. (1990), *Governing the Market: Economic Theory and the Role of Government in East Asian Industrialisation*, Princeton University Press, Princeton.

Chapter 9

Prospects for Jamaica's Economic Development in the Era of the FTAA

Michael Witter

The International Conjuncture

All analysis of the Jamaican economy and society must begin with the international context. At the dawn of the 21st century:

- There is now a 'uni-polar' world, dominated by a superpower that has been continuously at war with some part of the Third World since 1945. As we write, it has declared a new world war, this time against organisations that it deems to be 'terrorist'. The dangers of this path are obvious: a new crusade against Islam 1000 years after the Great Crusades; a Jihad by Moslems against an international alliance of Christians and Jews; and a great conflict between the white Europeans on one side and the non-white peoples of the world on the other. It will be all the more disturbing to peace and social development if these are interconnected but separate arenas of conflict around the globe. We assume that a global war will delay the economic process of Globalisation by disrupting trade, capital flows, and the growth of international markets.
- The Globalisation of economic activity has impacted Jamaica and the rest of the Caribbean, in the sense of production processes spanning countries, and barriers to entry into national markets breaking down. This global economic activity is facilitated by the information technology and telecommunications revolution, and the growth of air travel.
- The FTAA (Free Trade Area of the Americas), is scheduled to come into being in 2005, assuming that international conditions are sufficiently peaceful to tackle this undertaking.
- The Europeans are withdrawing the preferential access to their markets from their former colonies.
- The new round of the WTO promises to introduce new rules for the world economy which will in effect reduce the sovereignty of Caribbean states even further as it opens all spheres of their economies to international competition.
- Renewed efforts are underway to implement the Single Market in CARICOM.
- Large Caribbean communities exist in the developed North Atlantic countries.

- The unevenness of technological development persists and is accelerating, particularly in the sphere of information technology, between the advanced countries on the one hand and the backward and underdeveloped countries on the other.

As we assume away oblivion, so we must assume that a way will be found to avoid or at least curtail quickly the impending global war, and that conditions will permit the establishment of the FTAA.

The Political Economy of Jamaica

The roots of the radical nationalist critique of the structure and dynamics of the Jamaican economy reach back to Marcus Garvey and before. Its central focus has always been on the exploitation of people who work, and the export of the appropriated wealth to the home countries of the wealthy. In this way, the local economy was deprived of the investment of the surplus or profits that the economy needed to grow. In concrete historical terms, white English people subjected black and other non-white people to colonial political rule and exploited them, primarily on plantations producing cane sugar for export. Further, it was not hard to see that the Jamaican experience was a particular expression of a more general division of international labour in which Europeans colonised non-European peoples for reasons of political and military power and the extraction of wealth.[1] Garvey's travels as a timekeeper for the United Fruit Company to its Central American plantations made him realise that the pattern of exploitation that he experienced in Jamaica was repeated in many countries of the Americas wherever Africans had been enslaved. A generation later, Kwame Nkrumah of Ghana would summarise the role of Africa and the colonial world in the international division of labour as 'hewers of wood and drawers of water'.

The strategy of Jamaican nationalism was to seek political Independence with a view to using state power to break the monopoly over economic resources that the landed colonial elite traditionally enjoyed.[2] The political method of the nationalists was popular mobilisation of Jamaicans against British rule. This was the historically particular expression, the Jamaican version, of the general struggle of the native versus the coloniser that played itself out throughout the colonial world. For the nationalist, race was ultimately the primary analytical category in a struggle conceived of as exploitation of black and brown people of African and Asian origin by white Europeans. The enemy of the nationalists was visible, both in the flesh, and in the symbols of colonial rule.

The Marxist influence on radical nationalist thought was to shift the focus from race to the economic basis of social inequalities. The dominant interpretation of the uprising in 1938 was that labour was demanding better working conditions and justice from the employer classes. In the context of the Jamaican social hierarchy, race and class coincided and penetrated each other so completely that even the separation in analysis of race from class was *not immediately* credible.[3] In colonial Jamaica, the working people were black, and almost all black people had to work for a living. Some worked for wages paid by the predominantly white employer classes. Others worked as small and landless farmers whose input markets and export markets were controlled by the white merchants. Similarly, the wealthy property owners were white and, except for the small number of poor white German immigrants who became small farmers, almost all white people were wealthy.

In between the two, the brown (of all shades) middle class of professionals, administrators, and small property owners buffered and brokered the contradiction between the black dispossessed and the white dispossessors. In the middle of the social pyramid, the brown middle classes were simultaneously beneficiaries and victims of the system of exploitation and oppression. They benefited either directly or indirectly from the exploitation of the black working people - some had been slave owners. Yet, they were themselves victims of exploitation by the ruling propertied classes. This ambiguity in their social role would contribute to both the strength and the weakness of the national movement.[4]

European capitalism by nature was exploitative of its own people, and super-exploitative of subject peoples in the colonial empires. In the case of Jamaica, the Marxist analysis identified the central social relations as the relations between labour and capital, particularly foreign capital. In this analysis also, Jamaica was but a particular expression of a more general phenomenon across the world ruled by a system of imperialism. Because race and class coincided in colonial Jamaica, the Marxist analysis seemed to strengthen the developing radical economic critique, while it deflected some attention from the racial and cultural contradictions. It was, however, suspicious of the nationalist agenda as a 'Trojan horse' for the national capitalists to usurp the power and the privilege of the colonial capitalists without changing the fundamental inequities in the society. But as it turned out, the nationalisation of some foreign enterprises led to the denationalisation of many of the natives. The dynamics of the corporate linkages and culture dominated, and soon the native became the corporate man. In the extreme, the native returned to shut down the very plant that employed him as a native, as his loyalties shifted to the corporate headquarters abroad at the expense of the nation. In the process, he recasts his identity, often into his other.

The radical perspective was honed by way of critiques of the failures of the two governments of the first decade of Independence to improve the social conditions for which the masses had been pressing steadily since the labour uprising in 1938.[5] The highpoint of the influence of the radical critique on public policy was the 1970s when the first government of Michael Manley and the Peoples National Party (PNP) began to implement some of the social and the economic policies that the radical tradition had supported. However, it would be inaccurate and misleading to suggest that the radical thinkers had prepared a programme, which the Manley government implemented. Rather, the focus of the first Manley government on social programmes for the most disadvantaged and vulnerable, the orientation to economic independence, the attempts at land reform, and the democratisation of society coincided with the main lines of criticism that had come from the radical thinkers in the previous two decades. Yet, the radical character of the reforms of the Jamaican government of the 1970s was one of several radical alternatives, many of them of socialist orientation being implemented throughout the former colonial world in search of economic independence. Manley had his own radical influences, beginning at his parents' home, and then later cultivated as a student in England.[6]

Note that democratisation in a society that had historically oppressed black people necessarily stimulated the flourishing of African and African-based cultural expressions, as well as a greater voice for the politics of Black Nationalism and anti-colonialism. Democratisation also facilitated voices in support of the wave of national liberation and anti-imperialist movements that swept much of the ex-colonial world of the 1970s.

The implosion of the Grenadian revolution in 1983 and the subsequent crushing of the government and movement by the USA and its Jamaican-led Caribbean allies stilled the voices of Caribbean radicals. The internecine struggle within the Grenadian ruling regime (actually within the New Jewel Movement) was shocking, revolting and inexplicable. It gave new credence to the arguments of the anti-revolutionary forces that the undemocratic nature of the regime made it prone to violent struggles, and conjured up the Cold War images of internal struggles within communist and socialist regimes.

The implosion of the Grenadian revolution seemed to discredit, delegitimise and invalidate radical Caribbean thought. There was already the widely held view that the Jamaican economic crisis of the 1970s resulted directly from socialist policies of the Manley government. In the midst of the building momentum of the Reagan-Thatcher push for international capitalism, the collapse of the Grenadian revolution seemed to erase any possibilities for CARICOM Caribbean countries to pursue any alternate paths for development. When the USSR collapsed in the early 1990s, the evidence of the failure of socialism was overwhelming even for many radicals.

Caribbean economists, who had led the radical critique for three decades, now led the embrace of neoliberal thought by many Caribbean social scientists.[7] Some of the erstwhile radicals fervently embraced neoclassical orthodoxy, its neoliberal ideology, and eventually its programme of action as articulated in the 'Washington Consensus'. It is still not clear how such a sharp intellectual volte-face occurred. There was no debate around the relative validity of the radical versus the neoliberal ideas. Neoliberal ideas simply blossomed under the ideological umbrella of the World Bank's structural adjustment programme, and the IMF's stabilisation programme in the case of Jamaica. Simultaneously, radical ideas withered, and seemed irrelevant as the governments embraced neoliberal policies and the popular mass movements lost their momentum for social change.

There was also a new generation of graduates of the USA academy who internalised neoliberal thought, with apparently little regard or concern for the ideas of their intellectual forbears in the Caribbean. In the USA itself, neoliberal thought overcame the pockets of radical thought, or simply ignored them, and became a central element in the political reaction to the radical social insurgences of the 1960s. Most important was that in the 1980s and 1990s the USA emerged supreme in a uni-polar world with arguably the most successful economy. The promise of the American way of life was perhaps too hard to resist for many USA-trained economists.

The psychic shock to Caribbean intellectuals from the Grenadian implosion cannot be underestimated. For many years, leading intellectuals seemed to be paralysed on the subject of Grenada, unwilling to engage the issues, almost in a state of denial. And yet, the agenda of issues around which the radical critique had been built persisted and became even more transparent: unemployment and poverty caused by social and economic inequities in an increasingly dependent under-developed capitalist economy. To be sure, the old answers are unlikely to suffice, but are there no insights from political economy into the Caribbean's prospects for socio-economic development in the new millennium?

Post-Independence Economic Development in Jamaica

The Post-World War II class structure of the Jamaican society was clearly defined by Independence in 1962. At the base of the society were the black majority of wage earners, small farmers, casual labourers and the unemployed. Workers were organised into powerful unions, with the major ones closely affiliated to the two major political parties.[8] Through their Unions, they pressed their employers for greater benefits and improved working conditions, and agitated for the state to provide social services and legal support in their struggles with their employers.

The small farmers were never as organised as the wage earners. The Jamaica Agricultural Society, dominated by medium and large farmers, spoke on their behalf, and some rural Members of Parliament took their cases to the government and the public. While there was arguably a rural identity, their consciousness of themselves as a specific social class with corresponding interests was never fully developed nor institutionalised, despite flashes of militant class action such as in the rebellion of 1938. By Independence, both of these social classes had been divided along politically partisan lines as the nationalist movement that had agitated against colonialism turned in on itself.

At Independence, a brown middle class had consolidated itself and was in its ascendancy, occupying the administrative and technical roles vacated by the departing British colonialists, constituting the technocracy in an expanding economy, and winning the trappings of state power on behalf of the masses of black working people. A little more than a decade later, many of them became economically insecure and so politically intimidated or anxious that they began to migrate to North America. Into their social space moved children of the black working classes who had acquired professions, positions of leadership in the public sector, or non-traditional income sources in the late 1970s and 1980s, such as music, ganja exports, and the trade in scarce imported consumer goods.[9]

At Independence too, the propertied classes were primarily big landowners in sugar and banana export production, traditional merchant families, and an emergent manufacturing group with deep family, social and financial ties with the merchants and landowners. They exercised direct and indirect decisive influence on the state of Jamaica through their organisations, and especially through the political forces they supported in both major political parties. Their economic power and political influence gave them considerable power over and within social institutions. Their dominance in these three spheres of society defined them as the ruling classes.

Yet, the ruling classes themselves were junior partners in the ownership and management of the economy. The leading sectors - mining, manufacturing and tourism - that had emerged in the post-World War II period, like the traditional sugar and banana export industries before them, were dominated by North American and European multinational corporations.

Most of the people in the propertied ruling classes were primarily white or of light-skinned non-African origins. The coincidence of race and class caused the society to present itself as a colour-coded hierarchy of social classes. What is more, the structure of the society was quite 'fractal',[10] with each of the social classes exhibiting a similar colour-coded hierarchy of wealth, power and privilege in its structure. This was particularly evident in the range of 'middle classes', where the top merged with the bottom of the non-Black upper classes, and the bottom merged with the top of the Black working classes.

This social structure directed and guided the economic process, and this in turn, generated the wealth and distributed it disproportionately among the social classes to support the hierarchical social structure. The post-World War II economic process in Jamaica began with two decades of rapid growth of bauxite mining for export, manufacturing for a protected domestic market, tourism, and the public sector. Mining displaced some of the small farmers and, together with tradesmen, many migrated to England to exercise the option of British citizenship over citizenship in an independent Jamaica. There was also the beginning of a steady stream of persons to the USA. Today, there are large Jamaican communities all over North America, particularly in the USA, as well as in the UK.

Manufacturing and housing construction attracted rural people into Kingston. By Independence, Kingston had fully developed slum communities - e.g., Back o' Wall - built by those rural-urban migrants who were unable to secure a stake in the expanding urban industrial structure. The residents of these communities were forced to develop own-account livelihood strategies around unstable employment in low paying manufacturing and service jobs, petty trading, and various forms of not-illegal and illegal hustling. Just as their ex-slave ancestors had built villages in the hills after slavery, so too they built their communities on the marginal lands of Kingston. It is these communities that gave birth to popular Jamaican music and in which many African cultural forms, like Rastafari and Revivalism, flourished and acquired urban expressions.

Moreover, there was rapid growth of tourism around resort towns, primarily Montego Bay and Ocho Rios, which transformed semi-rural extended villages into urban centres. In the process, people from surrounding rural communities migrated into the resort areas.

Not only did economic growth lead to the differentiation of the economic activity, but it also stimulated the expansion of non-wage non-rural own-account income earning activities, the growth of the middle class, and the substitution of a small American expatriate community of owners and managers for the British who had departed at Independence.

Norman Girvan identified the inflows of foreign investment to expand the bauxite mining sector, and to a lesser extent tourism, as the financing mechanism for the rapid growth of the Jamaican economy in the 1950s and 1960s. Both were stimulated by the rapid growth of demand in the USA in the immediate aftermath of World War II. The military and space industries as well as the manufacturers of consumer goods needed aluminium. Flush with cashed war bonds, and with the cost of air travel falling, consumers began to demand vacations and leisure in the Caribbean.

It is these capital inflows that created the domestic purchasing power to buy manufactured goods, and supplied the foreign exchange to finance a wide range of imports of capital goods, raw materials and consumer goods. But these investment inflows ended with the decade of the 1960s when the multinational mining companies had completed their infrastructural works. With that, the flow of foreign exchange to sustain the import addiction of the manufacturing sector and of household consumption also ended, and the secular pressures on the Jamaican balance of payments began. Henceforth, the fundamental weaknesses of the Jamaican economy would be exposed:

- import dependence, especially on basic food and energy;
- export concentration in a small number of primary agricultural and mineral products with an equally narrow range of markets;
- technological backwardness;
- a fragile labour regime of fractious forces in which organised labour's suspicion and distrust of owners and managers confronted the capitalists' anxieties over the potential disruption of business and the loss of profits;
- a tendency for the Jamaican business persons to restrict themselves to short-term horizons, to rely on government protection from competition, not to be innovative, and to demand high returns on investment;
- an attitude to work that was more alienated than committed, and that favoured the least effort, responsibility, initiative and creativity when in the employ of someone else, particularly the state;
- a healthy national appetite for imported luxury and basic consumption goods;
- a public sector that had been designed for, and served as the administration of, a colony, and had not yet been transformed into an agency of development and change.

A decade of economic decline and two decades of marginal growth have followed Independence, during which the Jamaican state became indebted to international financial institutions and to a small group of local institutions and individuals. The nationalist agenda of the post-colonial state, and especially its policies of income distribution, were abandoned in the 1980s, and in many cases were reversed, as conditions for international debt financing. Once viewed as the instrument of social and economic development for the working people that brought it into sharp conflict with foreign and local business interests, the state became preoccupied with repayment of the national debt and guaranteeing the security and profitability of investment, particularly foreign investment.

The decade of economic decline was the 1970s. Indeed, investors responded to the government's attempts to assume the leadership of the economic development process by disinvesting and financing hostile political and economic acts to destabilise the government. The decline in foreign investment led inevitably to the slow down of the economy, and in particular to the shrinking of public revenues and the foreign exchange resources of the economy. In the end, the government's attempts at far-reaching social reform floundered for want of financial resources. Consequently, despite the unquestioned achievements in social policy, popular political support for the government and its development strategy and policies was eventually undermined by the economic hardships of austerity programmes, the political tensions of the ideological conflict between the opposition forces and the government, and especially the violence that it engendered.

The decades of marginal economic growth were the 1980s and 1990s. In the 1980s, public borrowing of foreign loans accelerated rapidly in the context of IMF stabilisation and World Bank structural adjustment programmes. The accumulation of debt began in the 1970s as an attempt to sustain production and consumption at levels that the government thought was socially necessary and politically prudent. However, by the 1980s, new debt was financing the repayment of old debt, with lower levels of domestic consumption. Import substitution manufacturing collapsed in the face of competition from imports, while Free Zone export-processing activity flourished. The cultivation of the mass market for tourism brought large numbers of visitors. Like Free Zone manufacturing, the net returns to Jamaica from tourism, as opposed to the companies engaged in these activities, were small. In a parallel fashion, guns to enforce stakes in the international trade in illegal drugs and narco-dollars to be laundered flowed back to Jamaica in return for ganja and later cocaine supplies.

In the 1990s, the wave of financial speculative economic activity that began in the 1980s in the USA swept into Jamaica from the North, and the cocaine trade flowed through from the South. From the North came government loans, laundered narco-dollars, guns, and two kinds of young men. The first kind of returnees was the young graduates in finance and business that began to return home from US universities. They had come of age in the period of speculation on junk bonds and later, on technology stocks in the USA. Their business was making financial deals, and they saw Jamaica as presenting many opportunities since the liberalisation of the economy proceeded rapidly without government regulation. Effectively, these were speculators on changes in the value of financial securities, and not captains of industry searching for profits through the application of new technologies and the penetration of markets.

The second kind of returnees was the deportees, those who ran afoul of the US legal system, particularly for crimes related to the trade in illegal drugs. Like the young financiers, there were many ambitious young men who sought to carve out places for themselves in the business world, and to establish and maintain a lifestyle of opulence.

From the South came the transhipment trade in cocaine. The ganja trade began in the 1970s, boomed in the early 1980s, and by the 1990s it was suppressed, or at least curtailed with the help of the US law enforcement agencies. The cocaine trade has been growing rapidly since the late 1980s. From it came cash for the economy, the opportunities for the rapid accumulation of wealth, and the attendant violence of the competitive struggle among gangs for control of the trade. In addition, a familiar hierarchy of power in the Inner City communities was established on the basis of the inflow of narco-dollars. At the pinnacle was the 'Don' who provided employment for young men as his 'soldiers', funded the consumption of his retinue as well as the less fortunate in the community, and financed the investment of community micro-entrepreneurs.

The organised working class movement had its greatest influence on the state in the 1970s. In the mid-1980s, it confronted the state with a general strike, lost, and has been marginalised since. By the 1990s, it had declined in numbers and political influence. Its leadership abandoned the confrontational industrial relations tactics of the past, and sought accommodations with the employers from defensive negotiating postures. Some went so far as to embrace Globalisation as inevitable and irreversible, and resigned themselves to the invincibility of capital. The focus of their critique turned from the injustice of the employer to the incompetence and inefficiency of the state, and to incentive schemes to enhance the productivity of labour.

The small farmers too had their highpoint of attention from policy makers in Jamaica in the 1970s, in the context of the government's promotion of self-reliance. A far-reaching land reform programme was conceived, announced, partially and inefficiently implemented, but was abandoned when the Manley government lost state power in 1980. For the next two decades, the traditional rural sector received little attention from policy makers. Some relatively powerful groups, such as big poultry and dairy producers, have resisted the import liberalisation policies with mixed success, and cane farmers and sugar producers have relied on a lifeline of cash injections from the government. But the vast majority of small and medium farmers are essentially voiceless, facing competition from imports with a rapidly declining level of subsidies.

It is arguable that the rural communities have benefited from the low prices of consumer goods in the liberalised economy of the 1990s. In fact, the widespread consumption of consumer durables evidences the improvement of material consumption for many people in the rural economy. With the decline of their productive agricultural base, the only explanations for rural survival are the low cost of the imported consumption goods that they purchase, non-traditional sources of income, and remittances from migrant relatives.

Stimulated by the liberalisation of the economy, particularly in the 1990s, and financed by heavy inflows of debt, the financial sector grew rapidly as Jamaican nationals invested borrowed money in the establishment of commercial banks, merchant banks, and building societies. 'Old' capital reconstituted itself in new forms of economic activity, such as financial services and tourism, as the wealth of the plantocracy became increasingly concentrated among fewer of its families.

'New' capital accumulated from non-traditional economic activities, by fair means and by foul, financed investments in service activities, and funded high consumption life styles of the newly affluent.

While professionals and administrators still generally fall within the middle classes, there is now a greater proportion of small entrepreneurs in formal and informal business activities in the middle classes. Therefore, there has been some fluidity in the social structure that has allowed some upward mobility in the lower sections of the social pyramid, but the basic class structure remains with deep cleavages along the lines of wealth, income and social privilege, and persistent divisions along racial and cultural lines.

The Jamaican economy at the turn of the millennium has become a service economy, and the relative contributions of agriculture and manufacturing have declined. The bulk of manufacturing is really the supply of cheap labour services in Free Zone assembly plants. Mining, agriculture and manufacturing together now contribute less than tourism to gross foreign exchange earnings. Approximately two-thirds of the labour force now work in service industries. Yet, many still earn incomes below the poverty line.

Moreover, informal activities have proliferated rapidly in the service sector. These include large-scale activities such as international trading in illegal drugs and laundering money, and small-scale activities such as own-account professional and personal services, and sidewalk-vending. While informal activities can be distinguished analytically, with some difficulty, from formal activities, in practice, informal and informal activities are intertwined, most of the time running parallel to each other but making contact at critical points along the way. For example, informal vendors compete with formal retailers on the sidewalk in front of their stores for customers, even where the same distributors and wholesalers supply both of them. Or, professionals employed in formal establishments often offer their services informally on the side to earn additional income.

At the points of contact between the circuits of informal activities and the circuits of formal activities, capital passes from one economic activity to another as it reproduces itself. Laundering narco-dollars through formal merchandising or financial institutions is an example of capital accumulated in informal activities passing through formal financial activities. Conversely, the payment by formal businesses for protection services to gangsters and bribes for privileges and favours to the authorities are examples of capital accumulation in formal activities that is facilitated by informal activities. Similarly, the 'banker' in the informal partner schemes usually deposits funds saved in a legally registered commercial bank.

Though the centre of gravity of the economy has shifted to service activities and the economy is demonstrably more diversified than it was at Independence, the historic inequalities of ownership and income distribution that has sustained the privileged classes since colonialism remain, sometimes in different forms. Land ownership is still highly concentrated, and as a result, squatting remains the primary social process of reconnecting property-less ex-slaves to the land. The shadow of plantation social relations still hangs over export agriculture and the hotel industry. Foreign capital still dominates the export sector and the financial sector. Even the informal economy is hierarchically structured under the leadership and concentrated power and authority of the Don.

The challenges of education in a world of knowledge-intensive industries and growing knowledge are formidable for a society in which more than 20 per cent of adults are illiterate and the academic achievement of secondary school graduates in language, maths and science is in decline. The under-achievement is particularly evident among young males.

AIDS alone is overwhelming the health services, at a time when the diseases of developed countries, like hypertension and cardiac diseases, are prevalent, and traditional diseases thought to have been eradicated threaten every so often to return.

Housing needs continue to outrun supply, and public infrastructure suffers for want of maintenance and from the pressure of a growing population. Informal housing in squatter settlements, often on environmentally unsuitable areas, has spread around and in the interstices of the urban centres, and particularly Kingston. Most importantly, the relations of dependency that facilitate the appropriation and export of wealth have been multiplied and strengthened.

Dependence in the 21st Century

Jamaica and the rest of the Caribbean are even more dependent today than they were at the start of the 1960s when Cuba seized its sovereignty, and the UK granted constitutional Independence to much of the Anglo-Caribbean. The old dependent political and economic relations persist. The Dutch and the British still have official colonies, and the French and the USA have *de facto* colonies in their so-called overseas Departments (Martinique, Guadeloupe and St. Martin), and in the associated territory of Puerto Rico respectively. With the exception of Barbados and the Dominican Republic, the rest of the Caribbean remains dependent on their traditional exports - sugar, banana, bauxite/alumina and oil.

In almost all cases, a tourist sector has emerged, and in some cases, as in Barbados and Jamaica, the dependency on traditional agricultural exports has been transferred to tourism, the industry that earns the most foreign exchange. The tourist sectors have repeated the historical pattern of dependence on a narrow range of markets, namely, vacationers from North America and to a lesser extent Europe and Japan, and on imports from the same narrow range of markets. Cuba, despite its efforts to diversify its economy, had been blockaded into dependence on sugar for two decades. It has also turned rapidly to tourism in the wake of the collapse of its markets in the Soviet Union and the former socialist countries.

Multinational corporations are even more dominant today than 40 years ago, as is the case throughout a world undergoing Globalisation. But for the brief episodes of nationalisation in Cuba and quasi-nationalization in a few countries in the CARICOM Caribbean in the 1970s, the MNCs have been largely unchallenged in the region. Indeed, some MNCs gave up direct control and the risks attached to that, for the certain returns of management contracts and the control of access to export markets. In Jamaica, Tate and Lyle was contracted to manage the same sugar estates and factories that the government had acquired from them, and in Guyana, Alcan became the sole marketing agent for the bauxite from the mines that were nationalized. A similar story can be told for the nationalised, but soon to be divested, oil wells of Trinidad.

Foreign direct investment shunned Jamaica for more than a decade after the imposition of the Bauxite Levy in 1974. It gradually returned to significant levels by the mid-1980s to establish manufacturing enterprises in the Free Zones, and in the 1990s for the acquisition of divested public enterprises. Investment in the Free Zones proved to be transient, as by the mid-1990s many of them had moved their operations from Jamaica to lower cost Central and Latin American countries. In the case of the divested public assets, foreign interests acquired ownership of the assets without necessarily increasing the productive capacity of the enterprises.

The external debt of Jamaica has risen dramatically from less than US$ 50 million at Independence in 1962, mainly in commercial loans, to over US$ 4 billion, mainly in international institutional loans. Forty years ago, the external debt was the equivalent of 19 per cent of goods and services, and in 2002, the debt exceeds annual foreign exchange earned from exports and tourism by more than 40 per cent.

Technological change has been advancing so rapidly that Jamaica has fallen further behind the advanced countries, and has become far more technologically dependent on them. In the case of information and communication technologies, the dependence is total and more far-reaching than other technologies, as many production and consumption processes now require these technologies. There has been an uneven and halting start to investment in IT service industries, mainly in the low end of the industry and located within the ambit of the Free Zone. This too is foreign owned, highly dependent on imports and oriented to the export market.

Popular consumption of telecommunications services grew dramatically with the introduction of cellular telephones and the curtailing of the monopoly of the British multinational, Cable and Wireless, to facilitate competition. Inevitably, the competitors were international firms, providing an import-intensive service.

There is a new and deepening social cleavage in the Caribbean as elsewhere in the world, between those who have access to the Internet and those who do not. Perhaps, like the radio and TV, access to the Internet too will become universally accessible. In the interim, access enhances the advantages of the elite and binds them even more firmly to the international markets.

By and large, the external debt has financed mass consumption, and the information and communications technology is facilitating the tastes for imported goods and services. In addition, information and communications technology has enabled Caribbean households to consume electronically delivered services, like film, video, television, music, and advertising messages for consumption goods. Crudely put, even the palates of the Caribbean people are now being colonised by fast foods and the culture of rapidly changing lifestyle fashions that modern fast food epitomises. Also, energy dependence for both production and consumption persists with the consumption demands for transportation and cooling rising rapidly.

The process of Globalisation is the increasing interdependence of the economies of the advanced countries through investment and trade flows dominated by the Multinational Corporations of the USA, Europe and Japan. This expresses itself at the level of production in the form of production processes that span several different countries. At the level of markets, liberalisation and the formation of economic unions have integrated domestic markets more closely to the international economy. At the level of investment, modern information and communication technology has facilitated and, in some senses, has helped to forge closer links between the national markets. With the merging of national markets into the large markets of economic unions, consumption patterns are converging across cultures into a transnational culture that is heavily influenced by North American culture.

These changes in the international economy over the past two decades have deepened the dependence of Jamaica and the Caribbean economies on the USA and Europe, and have expanded the scope of external influence on national policy formation. In many instances, the national economy has been undermined by policies of liberalisation that, on the pretext of levelling the playing field, exposed weak national industries to strong international competitors.

Whereas these economies had been protected, first by the colonial authorities against international competition, and after their Independence by nationalist governments to facilitate the growth of national industries, they are now completely open but for selected agricultural sub-sectors. Public policy now promotes export-propelled growth and seeks to woo foreign investors, while removing the protective measures traditionally enjoyed by Jamaican businesses. There has been limited success in attracting investment into export activities other than tourism, Free Zone manufacturing and information technology services.

Capital now has a freer hand in the employment of labour, with the breaking of the power of the labour unions, the flexibility and mobility of capital investments, and the facilitation of government policy. Income to capital accrues in new forms - interest payments, management fees, licences and other technology payments - in addition to the traditional forms of profit and rent. Globalisation has created new opportunities for capital accumulation in entertainment services, primarily music and sport, in financial speculation, primarily on foreign exchange, and the trade in illegal drugs. At the same time, government anti-inflationary policy has provided virtually risk-free high interest yielding securities as attractive investment options.

Also, there are signs of evolving capital-labour relations that are increasingly favouring the use of contracted services from formally independent producers offering services. *Pari passu*, mini and micro-enterprises have been growing rapidly. The technological basis for networking small independent producers through contracts to a central technically equipped marketing organisation already exists. But the viability of these new forms hinges on whether they will increase the productivity of labour, and facilitate the extraction of surplus. In this information technological age, political economy will have to re-visit the theory of 'unequal exchange' to explain the appropriation of surplus value from contracted labour services.

Moreover, the traditional rural sector lags behind technologically, but more so, not surprisingly, in production than in consumption. Rural households are increasingly generating non-agricultural service (e.g., transportation) income. In the broadest interpretation of informal economic activities, small scale domestic agriculture and the related processing and marketing activities of the small farmer's household have traditionally been the base of the informal economy. Hence, there has been a proliferation of informal activities within and around the urban industrial economy, sub-serving capital accumulation in much the same way small-scale domestic agriculture served the plantation sector. Namely, informal economic activities provide supplementary income for many wage earners to enable them to purchase consumption goods. In a minority of instances where income is earned from high-risk illegal activities, such as the cocaine trade, occasional lump-sum earnings facilitate investment, generally in housing and vehicles.

Jamaica and the FTAA

The economic conditions for Jamaica's entry into the FTAA have long been spelled out as complete liberalisation, to the extent of giving up the preferential access to the sugar and banana markets that have been historically important mainstays of the Caribbean economies. Under such conditions, it is unlikely that the present industrial structure of the Jamaican economy can survive for very long. Traditional agricultural export industries will collapse, illegal agriculture (ganja) is already under suppression, domestic agriculture is already losing ground to cheaper imported food, manufacturing will be out-competed by the Central and Latin American economies, and the international tourism market can only become more competitive as other countries turn to this industry to offset the contractions in their national economies. But even this last option is being narrowed as fears of flying and other forms of travel are intensified by the international tensions that have accompanied this phase of Globalisation.

In neoliberal theory, Jamaican labour, land, natural resources, and cultural resources will become cheaper to foreign investors. With the confidence that their investments and the financial returns they yield will be secure, foreign investors will establish new export-oriented enterprises. Jamaican people will be re-employed from dying industries by technologically dynamic industries that produce for the international market.

Again, all of this presupposes both international and domestic peace. Jamaica, for example, beyond the international influences, has its own internal drivers for social disorder. Jamaicans have a history of militant social protest and aggressive individualistic behaviour. Already the economic hardships of the last two decades have stimulated anti-social behaviour that has put much strain on the society's fundamental institutions, such as the family, the school, the labour union, and the political party.

This process of social instability has already begun in other Caribbean countries as well, and there are ominous signs of its appearance in the traditionally tranquil societies of the Eastern Caribbean. Intensified economic hardships resulting from sharp economic declines in a post-NAFTA scenario may well test the cohesion of some Caribbean societies.

The disjuncture between what Jamaica produces and what it consumes has widened since Independence. The danger now is that the chronic import dependence cannot be sustained once the traditional export industries are marginalised without new viable industries replacing them. Jamaica and the Caribbean, around which a world economy developed in the 17th and 18th centuries, are in danger of being marginalised in the Global economy of the 21st century. In fact Jamaica faces a near-to-medium term future of unsatisfied demand for imported consumption and production goods and services because of its declining ability to earn foreign exchange by competing successfully in international markets.

There is however another serious contradiction to be faced. The new forms of dependency, together with the traditional dependent relations, enable the transfer of profits, interest, technology payments and other forms of surplus accruing to foreign owners from the total surplus generated in production. Unless new forms of production replace the traditional industries, there will be little surplus to transfer, in addition to the unsatisfied demand for imported goods.

The most likely scenario is that some Caribbean territories will develop new industries, primarily around tourism, financed by foreign investment. Initial gains in the establishment of off-shore financial activities have been set-back by OECD blacklisting of some countries in the region. While this industry earns foreign exchange, it does not employ much labour and is prone to penetration by money-laundering activities. Some countries will participate in the illegal exchange of drugs for guns between North and South America, despite pressure from the USA-led international campaign against the smuggling of illegal drugs. And some will hang onto dying industries for want of viable alternatives.

Prospects for new manufacturing are poor, for want of cheap labour and energy resources, and the requisite investment. The Caribbean has some experience, and a few countries (e.g., Dominican Republic, Jamaica for about 10 years) have had significant economic growth in Free Zone export processing. Such activities are large employers of low wage, primarily female, labour, with no integration back into agriculture or linkages with other industries.

The economic rationale for the Single Market and Economy in CARICOM is to create a regional market as an export base for Caribbean firms to compete in the wider international market. Many market opportunities for agro-industrial products have been identified but are yet to be tapped, since the problems of agro-industry are those that all manufacturing activities share in addition to the vagaries of the supply of agricultural products.

While several Caribbean countries, especially the continental countries and Jamaica, have excellent agricultural potential in high-value markets for exotic foods, there are a host of historical challenges that the agricultural sectors in the region have still to overcome. It has long been argued persuasively that the transformation of agriculture requires land reform, affordable finance, accessible, affordable and appropriate technology, international marketing capabilities, low labour costs, affordable and reliable air cargo transport, and insurance and other ways to cope with the risks of financial losses due to natural forces, like hurricanes.

Trinidad and Tobago with its huge petroleum and natural gas reserves, and its emergent regional manufacturing prowess, is somewhat of an exception in the CARICOM Caribbean. But while progress has been made in diversifying the economy away from its dependence on petroleum exports, the dependence remains a major challenge to sustainable economic development. If, for any reason, the current cartelisation of the international petroleum industry is broken, small producers like Trinidad will find it more difficult to extract economic gains from this resource.

Opportunities

In theory, there are many opportunities open to Jamaica and the Caribbean in the FTAA and the evolving international economy. Specifically, Jamaica can compete successfully in tourism services, cultural products and services, - such as, exotic food and drink, music and other forms of entertainment, - and bauxite and alumina. In addition, there are opportunities in the new IT-intensive service industries that Jamaica can tap. The challenge is to find the mechanism to mobilise the country's resources in a focused national campaign to tap these opportunities efficiently so as to establish and maintain a competitive edge in the international economy.

The current dominant policy approach is to allow the markets to determine the allocation of investment and resources, with the state playing the role of facilitator to private investors. So far, capital has preferred the higher and less risky gains of government debt instruments to the certain challenges with uncertain outcomes of investing in production. Ultimately, it will require an appropriate social partnership among the state, the foreign and local investors, and civil society to mobilise resources for international competitiveness.

The Jamaican business community has historically feared and resisted the state being the dominant partner. In the last two decades, the antagonistic relationship between the state and the business community of the 1970s has been transformed into a tentative live-and-let-live relationship. While the state has committed itself to being the junior partner, the Jamaican business community is yet to commit its ideas and resources to a long-run vision of Jamaica in which it assumes leadership of the process of economic development. The foreign business community appears to be more secure *vis a vis* the state, because of the more welcoming posture of the governments of the past two decades as well as the guarantees of the international financial institutions and the WTO. But the crime rate and the costs to business of social inefficiencies - poor infrastructure, bureaucracy, security, for example - are still deterrents to investors.

Civil society has been coalescing around issues of social justice and the environment, but little attention has been paid to developing social ownership of productive activities or fostering more productive labour regimes to make the expected profitability of investment in Jamaica attractive to entrepreneurs. The coop movement, except for the Credit Unions, remains dormant. Organised labour has moved from its traditional confrontational approach to accepting junior partnerships with employers, paying more attention to the productivity of labour in the traditional labour regime than to the search for alternative forms that empower labour.

Micro and mini-enterprises proliferate in a range of livelihoods, primarily trading and personal services, in a network of formal and informal activities. Many persons who lost their jobs in the two-decade long structural adjustment process have turned to self-employment in small and micro business activities. This form of organising economic activity may well suit the Jamaican producer who exerts far more effort and commitment in his own employ than in the employ of someone else. In the era of the miniaturisation of technology, in addition to the availability and accessibility of telecommunications and information technology, networking mini and micro enterprises around central marketing organisations with the requisite technical expertise may offer some potential as a form of industrial organisation for Jamaican economic development.

Until Jamaica fashions an appropriate social compact to guide, facilitate and direct focused productive activity by the society as a whole, economic conditions will continue to deteriorate until the value of Jamaica's human and natural resources is cheapened sufficiently to attract a new wave of foreign investment into export production of goods and services. Consequently, the historic pattern of dependent capitalism based on cheap natural and human resources will persist and deepen, and with it poverty and underdevelopment will continue to be reproduced.

However, the pace at which the FTAA, EU-ACP, and WTO processes have been proceeding leaves little time for Jamaica to reposition itself to take advantage of the opportunities of competitive hemispheric and global markets. Recently, sections of the regional private sector began to call for more urgency in the establishment of the CSME, as a base for engaging the FTAA. The hard-line postures of the USA and EU governments and the international financial and trade institutions are conceding little leeway by way of 'special and differential treatment for small economies' for Caribbean economies to adjust to global competition.

Cuba has been an outstanding example in using mobilisation around national causes to withstand the economic shock of the loss of 70 per cent of its export earnings in one year, and the decade of adjustment that followed. It has managed the impacts of natural disasters by focused social action. It is ironic that Cuba may be better able to compete successfully in the global economy despite four decades of economic blockade than the rest of the Caribbean that has deepened its connections with the international economy over the same period.

Notes

1. Beckford (1972), *Persistent Poverty*; Girvan (1971), *Foreign Capital and Dependent Underdevelopment*; Best (1968), 'A Model of Pure Plantation Economy'.
2. In its extreme form, repatriation to Africa was the preferred option to the country's political Independence.

3. See Ken Post, 'Arise Ye Starvelings, and Strike the Iron'.
4. See Beckford and Witter (1980), *Small Garden ... Bitter Weed*.
5. The New World Group, based at the University of the West Indies at Mona in Jamaica, exemplified this.
6. See Michael Manley, 'Search for Solutions'.
7. In a lecture given to the symposium in honour of Lloyd Best in Trinidad in September 2002, Kari Polanyi-Levitt, one of the major contributors to radical economic thought in the Caribbean, also made this observation.
8. The Bustamante Industrial Trade Union (BITU) was, and still is, affiliated to the Jamaica Labour Party (JLP). The National Workers Union (NWU) and the Trade Union Congress (TUC) were, and still are, affiliated to the Peoples National Party (PNP).
9. This is non-traditional activity for Black Jamaicans, having been the province of Europeans from the beginning of colonialism, as well as the Chinese and Lebanese merchants who immigrated to Jamaica in the 20th century.
10. The connotation of 'fractal' here is a structure consisting of components that are miniature forms of the whole.

References

Beckford, G. (1972), *Persistent Poverty: Underdevelopment in Plantation Economies of the Third World*, Oxford University Press, Oxford.
_____ (1975), *Caribbean Economy: Dependence and Backwardness*, ISER, Kingston.
Beckford, G. and Witter, M. (1980), *Small Garden ... Bitter Weed: Struggle and Change in Jamaica*, ISER, Kingston.
Best, L. (1968), 'A Model of Pure Plantation Economy', *Social and Economic Studies*, Vol. 12(3).
Girvan, N. (1971), *Foreign Capital and Dependent Underdevelopment*, ISER, Kingston.
Girvan, N. and Jefferson, O. (eds) (1971), *Readings in the Political Economy of the Caribbean*, New World Group, Kingston.

Chapter 10

The Demand for Imports in Jamaica: 1972-2000[1]

Dillon Alleyne

Introduction

Trade liberalisation is now a feature of globalisation and will directly impact the Caribbean with the implementation of the Free Trade Area of the Americas (FTAA) in 2005. The FTAA aims to unite the economies of the countries of the North, Central and South America, and the Caribbean. Goods and services imported from all participatory countries once they meet the prerequisite criteria would qualify for duty free status. Given the vulnerability of many countries of the region, new development strategies will have to emerge.

The importance of trade and in particular imports, to growth and development is not disputed. In the case of Jamaica, this is particularly so as imports may embody inputs with new technologies for production and accumulation. At the same time, there may be components of imports, which may be less efficient than their domestic substitutes thus limiting the growth of domestic resources. In fact, one of the elements of Jamaica's new trade regime is to 'displace imports, i.e., steadily reduce the share of imports in [the] economy relative to the growth of output'.[2] The assumption is that local productive capacity will replace the current level of imports if the incentives to import are changed.[3]

This discussion, however, has taken place outside the context of an empirical examination of the degree of substitutability or complementarity between imports and domestic factors of production. This is important since some components of imports may help to enhance productivity growth, and this has implications for employment generation and the balance of payments.

Craigwell and Boamah (1993, p.212) have correctly pointed out that the literature in the Caribbean has followed the traditional approach of expressing the demand for imports as a function of real income and relative prices. For example, works along such lines are Cox and Worrell (1978) and Joefield-Napier (1984) for Barbados, Gafar (1988) for Trinidad and Tobago, Gafar (1979) for Guyana, and Freckleton (1988) for Jamaica and Guyana. The methodology of these studies assumes that imports are either final goods for consumption or intermediate goods which can be separable from other primary factors of production. The point raised here is that this must be a testable hypothesis since imports are a vital factor in many aspects of production.

Wang (1998, p.121) in examining this issue argued that for most resource poor countries importation of raw materials and intermediate parts as well as exportation of manufactured outputs are vital for their economic growth. He points out that the conventional approach, however, is to view import demand as a function of income and relative prices, and the quantity of imports is viewed as a solution to the consumer's optimization problem.[4] Burgess (1974a, p.226), who modelled imports as a primary factor of production for the United States, has argued that the approach that views imports as final goods with no close domestic substitutes, rules out any income distribution effects resulting from changes in import prices. His treatment of imports as an input in the production process explicitly assumes that most internationally traded goods are actually intermediate goods, and even consumption goods go through commercial channels before reaching the final consumer. While much of the research in this area has been done for developed countries,[5] a number of studies have also been done for developing countries. Among the developing country studies are Mohabbat, Dalal and Williams (1984) for India, Henry (1989) for Pakistan, Liu (1986), Lin (1992) and Wang (1998) for Taiwan, Kang and Kwon (1988) for South Korea, and Craigwell and Boamah (1993) for Barbados.

These studies, which utilise a translog specification, reject separability between primary factors and imports, and cast doubt on specifications in which the demand for imports is a function of import prices and aggregate output with capital and labour the only inputs. They also suggest that, for developing countries, imports and capital services are substitutes.

This chapter aims to investigate the hypothesis that imports are separable from primary factors of production in Jamaica, and to do so, a three input - two output translog cost function is estimated. This function allows for testing a wide variety of hypotheses without imposing these *a priori* as in the case of the Cobb-Douglas or the CES (Computable Elasticities of Substitution) production functions. Following Craigwell and Boamah (1993), real output is divided into tradable and non-tradable goods produced by three factors of production.[6] These factors are imported materials, capital and labour services. The share equations are derived, and price elasticities of demand for inputs are estimated based on the model estimated for the period 1972 to 1998.

The rest of the chapter is made up of four sections. Section 2 examines the translog model as well as the data requirements. Section 3 reports the estimation technique, testing and the results. Section 4 compares the results with those of a number of similar studies. The chapter ends with a summary and some concluding remarks.

Methodology and Data

The translog function, which was introduced by Christensen, Jorgensen and Lau (1973) is a second-order Taylor series approximation to any arbitrary production or cost function. The function avoids some of the limitations of the homothetic Cobb-Douglas and CES production functions, thus allowing for variable elasticities of substitution.[7] In addition, homothetic functions are characterised by linear expansion paths in which factor shares of output or relative input demands are independent of the level of output. Under the translog specification, homotheticity is a hypothesis that can be tested, in which case one can determine under what conditions it reduces to any of the other specifications. Another advantage of the translog function is that separability between inputs and outputs, or between domestic factors and imports, is not imposed *a priori* but may be tested as an hypothesis. A final advantage is that the translog approach allows us to derive estimates of the Allen Elasticities of Substitution (AES) between imports and other primary inputs, as well as between labour and capital, again without any prior restrictions.[8]

It is well understood that the optimisation problem which the firm faces in profit maximisation is equivalent to minimising the cost of production at a given output level by choosing inputs at given prices. This duality property means that the parameters in the production function can be recovered from the cost function. Under the cost function approach, input quantities are endogenous and output and input prices are exogenous. Although production and cost functions are primal-dual in nature under assumptions of optimality, there are advantages to using the cost function.

Biswanger (1974a) suggests various reasons why the cost approach should be employed, and among these are the following. First, while it is difficult to impose homogeneity of degree one on the production process, the cost functions will be homogenous in prices. In addition, the parameter estimates in the cost function are easier to estimate relative to the production function, and they bypass multi-collinearity problems inherent in the production function. Finally, it allows the employment of the Samuelson-Shephard[9] Lemma from which one can write the input demand functions and marginal cost in terms of relative cost and revenue shares respectively.

The translog function has been criticised on several grounds. For example, the criticisms centre on its unstable nature (Wales, 1977; Caves and Christensen, 1980; Lau, 1986), as well as claims that it generates elasticity estimates which are not plausible (Anderson and Thursby, 1986). However, if the parameter estimates meet certain conditions such as regularity[10] and concavity in input prices, the translog cost function can be used to approximate known cost and production functions with reasonable results.

In this study, the cost approach is employed and we consider a production function such that,

$$Q = F(K, L, M) \tag{1}$$

where Q is gross output and K, L and M are inputs of capital, labour[11] and imports. The output Q is disaggregated into tradables Q_T and non-tradables Q_N. Among the other assumptions of this model are that input and output markets are competitive and production agents behave optimally.[12] Corresponding to the production function is a cost function of the form

$$C = C(W_k, W_L, W_M, Q) \tag{2}$$

where $W_j, j = K, L, M$ are the price of capital, labour and imports respectively. The translog cost function can be written as a logarithmic Taylor expansion to a second order of a cost function as follows:[13]

$$\ln C = \alpha_0 + \Sigma_i \, \alpha_i \ln Q_i + \Sigma_j \, \beta_j \ln W_j + 1/2 \Sigma_i \, \Sigma_r \, \delta_{ir} \ln Q_i \ln Q_r$$
$$+ 1/2 \Sigma_j \, \Sigma_s \, \gamma_{js} \ln W_j \ln W_s + \Sigma_i \, \Sigma_j \, \rho_{ij} \ln Q_i \ln W_j \tag{3}$$

where i,r = T(tradables), N(non-tradables); s = L, M, K. We also impose the symmetry restrictions such that $\delta_{ir} = \delta_{ri}$ and $\gamma_{js} = \gamma_{sj}$.

It is assumed that the conditions for the cost function (3) hold, and that the cost function is positive and homogenous of degree one in input prices and concave. Monotoniticy in input prices requires that $\partial \ln C / \partial \ln W_j > 0$, and concavity in input prices requires that the Hessian matrix of second derivatives in terms of factor prices must be positive semi-definite. Sufficient conditions for these to hold are the restrictions.

$$\Sigma_j \, \beta_j = 1, \Sigma_i \, \rho_{ij} = 0, \Sigma_j \, \gamma_{js} = \Sigma_j \, \Sigma_s \, \gamma_{js} = 0 \tag{4}$$

If we assume the condition of constant returns to scale, the translog approximation further requires the following restrictions:

$$\Sigma_i \, \alpha_i = 0, \Sigma_i \, \rho_{ij} = 0, \Sigma_i \, \delta_{ij} = 0 \tag{5}$$

One could estimate the cost function directly, but gains in efficiency can be realised by estimating it simultaneously with the optimal, cost minimising input demand equations. Differentiating (3) with respect to input prices, one can use Shephard's Lemma to derive the cost share equations. That is,

$$\partial \ln C / \partial \ln W_j = (W_j / C)(\partial C / \partial W_j) = W_j X_j / C = S_j \tag{6}$$

where X_j are the cost minimising quantities demanded, C is cost, W_j are input prices, and S_j are the cost shares with j = K, L, M and $\Sigma_j \, S_j = 1$. The revenue shares can be derived in a similar fashion (Diewert, 1971, pp.483-4). The input and revenue share equations can be written as:

$$S_L = \frac{\partial \ln C}{\partial \ln W_L} = \beta_L + \gamma_{LL} \ln \frac{W_L}{W_K} + \gamma_{LM} \ln \frac{W_M}{W_K} + \rho_{TL} \ln \frac{Q_T}{Q_N}$$

$$S_M = \frac{\partial \ln C}{\partial \ln W_M} = \beta_M + \gamma_{MM} \ln \frac{W_M}{W_K} + \gamma_{LM} \frac{W_L}{W_K} + \rho_{TM} \ln \frac{Q_T}{Q_N}$$

$$S_K \equiv \frac{\partial \ln C}{\partial \ln W_K} = 1 - S_L - S_K \tag{7}$$

$$R_T = \frac{\partial \ln C}{\partial \ln Q_T} = \alpha_T + \delta_{TT} \ln \frac{Q_T}{Q_N} + \rho_{TL} \ln \frac{W_L}{W_K} + \rho_{TM} \ln \frac{W_M}{W_K}$$

$$R_N \equiv \frac{\partial \ln C}{\partial \ln Q_N} = 1 - R_T$$

In this formulation R_T is the revenue share of tradable goods, and S_L and S_M are the cost share of labour and imports respectively. In order to estimate the parameters of the model we must specify a stochastic framework. We can add a random error term u_i to each of the three cost share equations. Since the revenue and cost shares all sum to unity, the error term at each observation must be unity. This implies that n-1 equations are linearly independent for both the cost and revenue shares formulations. This means that at every observation the residuals will sum to zero across equations. The implication being that the residual cross-products matrix will be singular making it impossible to implement a system method of estimation mentioned below. The solution is to delete the cost share equation for capital services and the revenue share equation for non-tradables. Due to the imposition of the symmetry restrictions with respect to the $\delta's, \rho's, \gamma's$, there are only nine independent parameters in the system to be estimated. Estimation of these together with the summation conditions will yield all the parameters in the cost function except the intercept.

Economic theory does not tell us *a priori* what sign or magnitude the estimated parameters should take; however, the γ_{ij} can be used to calculate the Allen elasticities of substitution (AES) between inputs i and j. Uzawa (1962) has shown that the AES can be written as $\sigma_{ij} = CC_{ij} / C_i C_j$ where

$$C_i = \frac{\partial C}{\partial W_i} \quad \text{and} \quad C_{ij} = \frac{\partial^2 C}{(\partial C_i \partial C_j)}$$

Note also that $\eta_i = \sigma_{ii} S_i$ is the own price elasticity of demand for the ith factor. In terms of the parameters of the model and the cost shares, Christensen and Greene (1976) have shown that the results for the AES and the own price elasticities of demand, using the fitted values of the cost shares and the coefficients, are as follows:

$$\sigma_{ML} = (\gamma_{LM} / S_M S_L) + 1$$

$$\sigma_{MK} = -(\gamma_{MM} + \gamma_{LM}) / S_M (1 - S_M - S_L) + 1$$

$$\sigma_{LK} = (\gamma_{MM} + \gamma_{LM}) / S_L (1 - S_M - S_L) + 1 \qquad (8)$$

$$\eta_i = (\gamma_{ii} + S_i^2 - S_i) / S_i; \quad i = L, M$$

$$\eta_K = -(S_M \sigma_{MK} + S_L \sigma_{LK})$$

As pointed out by Craigwell and Boamah (1993, p.214), the elasticities of substitution vary with the cost shares. At the same time, they are non-linear functions of the estimated parameters and cannot be computed exactly, but approximate estimates can be found.[14] The data required for estimation are total cost of production, the revenue share of tradable goods, the cost shares of labour and imports, the ratio of tradable to non-tradable goods, and the ratios of the price of labour and imports to capital services. These variables are computed over the period 1972 to 1998 and the quantity and price ratios are scaled to one in base year 1974. Further details of the data construction and sources are reported in the Appendix.

Estimation, Testing and Results

We assume that the errors are multivariate normal with mean vector zero and a constant covariance matrix Ω. This specification can be justified in economic terms by the assumption that firms are making random errors in choosing their inputs. These errors may however be correlated across inputs; therefore, estimation by single equation methods would be inefficient. A systems approach may be more appropriate to account for the correlation across equations. A non-linear Zellner estimation procedure is employed in order to estimate the parameters of the model (Zellner, 1962). Kmenta and Gilbert (1968) have shown that the estimation results are not invariant to the share equation dropped; however, invariance can be got by iterating the estimation procedure until there is convergence. These estimates are equivalent to the maximum likelihood estimates. As these are maximum likelihood estimates, we use the likelihood ratio (LR) test to test a number of restrictions on the model. This test is computed as:

$$-2\log[L(\Pi_0) - L(\Pi)] \sim \chi_{(r)}^2$$

where Π_0 and Π are the log-likelihood of the restricted and unrestricted cost functions, and r is the number of restrictions to be tested under the null hypothesis.

The parameters in equation (3) were tested against the hypothesis of constant returns to scale, homogeneity in prices and symmetry, and these were found to hold. As a result, this model was used as the unrestricted parameter model against which a variety of hypotheses regarding separability were tested. The second column of Table 10.1 reports the parameter estimates for this model which we call the unrestricted estimates.

Table 10.1 Estimates of the parameters of the revenue and cost shares of the translog cost function

Parameters	Unrestricted Estimates	Input-Output Separability	Linear [(K, L), M] Separability	Non-Linear [(K, L), M] Separability
α_T	.405968 (20.811)	.296989 (13.387)	.376234 (20.230)	.356419 (9.904)
δ_{TT}	-.176650 (-3.139)	.136489 (3.576)	-.158001 (-2.474)	-.06903 (-.94135)
ρ_{TL}	-.243731 (-5.276)	0	-.242520 (-4.390)	-.165704 (-7.2550)
ρ_{TM}	-.118618 (-5.430)	0	-.059393 (-8.468)	-.047773 (-2.1687)
β_L	.281665 (17.831)	.194707 (10.719)	.253569 (14.413)	.244175 (9.3850)
β_M	.277352 (22.203)	.235638 (19.682)	.274955 (32.020)	$1+\gamma_{LM}*\beta_L/\gamma_{LL}$
γ_{LL}	-.045131 (-1.004)	.152458 (10.324)	-.084507 (-1.534)	.006086 (.854137)
γ_{LM}	-.07834 (-4.273)	.015683 (1.738)	0	-.018633 (-.86150)
γ_{MM}	.037033 (1.918)	.075096 (5.513)	0	$\gamma_{LM}^2/\gamma_{LL}$
Log-likelihood	173.549	158.429	164.605	168.075

Note: t-ratios are in parentheses.

We then test for input-output separability which essentially means the imposition of two independent restrictions $\rho_{TL} = \rho_{TM} = 0$ (see Berndt and Wood, 1975). This means setting the coefficients of the terms which show the interaction between inputs and output prices to zero. The estimates of the parameters are shown in column 3 of Table 10.1. The χ^2 statistic with 2 degrees of freedom obtained from the likelihood function is 30.2, which is greater than the critical 5 per cent value of 5.99, and so the hypothesis of input-output separablility is comprehensively rejected. This result is similar to that found for Barbados (see Craigwell and Boamah, 1993), but the opposite was accepted in the case of India (Mohabbat, Dalal and Williams, 1984). The implication is that the technology is not separable between inputs and outputs, and that the cost minimising bundles of inputs for given factor prices is not independent of the level of output in the Jamaican case.

The next test is for linear separability between primary factors, capital, labour and imports. Berndt and Christensen (1973) showed that a necessary and sufficient condition for linear separability is that the Allen partial elasticity of substitution (AES) between capital and imports, and between imports and labour equal unity, that is, $\sigma_{KM} = \sigma_{ML} = 1$. In terms of the parameters of the model, this translates to the two restrictions $\gamma_{LM} = \gamma_{MM} = 0$. The calculated χ^2 value with 2 degrees of freedom for the likelihood function is 17.88 and, given the critical value of 5.99 at 5 per cent, this leads to a rejection of the hypothesis of separability between imports and primary factors. The rejection of linear separability also implies the rejection of global separability, that is, $\sigma_{KM} = \sigma_{ML} = \sigma_{KL} = 1$. This means that a Cobb-Douglas function which implies global separability must be rejected and cannot adequately represent the production technology of Jamaica.

The final test is for non-linear separability between primary factors and imports. This test, in terms of the parameters of the model, implies that two independent restrictions must be imposed on the model, and these are:

$$\beta_M = 1 + \gamma_{LM} * \beta_L / \gamma_{LL} \text{ and } \gamma_{MM} = \gamma_{LM}^2 / \gamma_{LL}$$

In column 5 of Table 10.1 the parameter estimates of the model including the restrictions is reported. The χ^2 value of the likelihood function is 10.94, which is greater than the critical value; thus the hypothesis of non-linear separability is again rejected.[13] In the light of the rejection of both separability hypotheses between primary factors and imports, it would not be correct to specify a relationship in which import demand is a function only of import prices, aggregate prices and a price index of domestic value added in which primary factors were the only inputs. The AES and own price elasticities of demand were derived using the fitted cost shares and the parameter estimates.[15] Table 10.2 reports the AES results for selected years and, following the criticism made by Anderson and Thursby (1986), the elasticities at the mean are also reported for the whole period 1972-1998.

Table 10.2 Allen's partial elasticity of substitution for selected years

Year	σ_{LK}	σ_{MK}	σ_{ML}
1972	1.1173	1.4726	.2400
	(.0179)	(.0226)	(.0145)
1975	1.1795	1.3986	.0193
	(.0274)	(.0289)	(.0174)
1978	1.2583	1.3577	-.2658
	(.0395)	(.0345)	(.0209)
1981	1.2295	1.3733	-.1737
	(.0351)	(.0334)	(.0192)
1984	1.3047	1.3135	-.3088
	(.0466)	(.0299)	(.0285)
1987	1.2438	1.3355	-.1206
	(.0372)	(.0279)	(.0244)
1990	1.2165	1.3552	-.0533
	(.0331)	(.0279)	(.0217)
1993	1.2827	1.3500	-.3556
	(.0432)	(.0359)	(.0220)
1996	1.2900	1.3662	-.4553
	(.0443)	(.0403)	(.0201)
1998	1.1998	1.4124	-.1291
	(.0305)	(.0352)	(.0158)
Mean	1.2292	1.3600	-.1331
	(.0305)	(.0226)	(.0162)

Note: Asymptotic standard errors are in parentheses.

The elasticities of substitution between labour services and capital, σ_{LK} [16] and imports and capital services, σ_{MK} are positive while in the case of imports and labour, σ_{ML} is positive for seven out of 27 years and negative for the remaining years. This means that elasticities between labour and capital services and between imports and capital services are substitutes while imports and labour services are complements.[17]

On average, the degree of substitutability between capital services and imports is greater than that between capital services and labour, and both show elasticities in excess of 1. With respect to partial elasticity between labour and imports, the results suggest that between 1972-1976, (the exception being 1974), they were generally substitutes and after 1976 they were complements. This means that after 1976, the demand for labour reacted positively to any reduction in import prices. Mohabbat, Dalal and Williams (1984, p.597) attribute this finding in the case of India to the changing composition of imports. The elasticities varied between .019

and .240 when the factors were substitutes, and between -.053 and -.455 when they were complements.[18] Since σ_{MK} is greater than σ_{ML} throughout the period, it can be noted, following a demonstration by Burgess (1974b), that if $\sigma_{MK} > \sigma_{ML}$ an increase in import prices possibly due to increased tariff rates will redistribute income from capital to labour raising the share of capital income in total income. It also means that, when import prices increase, firms can substitute more capital for imports relative to labour for imports.

Finally, the own price elasticities of demand for capital (η_K), labour (η_L) and imports (η_M) were also computed for selected years, and these are reported in Table 10.3. The own price elasticities of capital are negative and inelastic and the same obtains for imports. In the case of capital, the elasticities varied between -.6179 and -.8240 becoming slightly more inelastic since the 1970s. The own price elasticity of labour (η_L) was fairly rigid, varying between -1.0155 and -.7541. The own price elasticity of imports η_M are also fairly rigid varying between -.5942 and -.6307. The values have become more elastic since the 1980s.

Table 10.3   Own price elasticities of capital, labour and imports for selected years

Year	η_K	η_L	η_M
1972	-.8240	-.7541	-.6070
	(.0518)	(.1145)	(.0560)
1975	-.7275	-.8531	-.6132
	(.0422)	(.1425)	(.0580)
1978	-.6540	-.9458	-.6187
	(.0365)	(.1777)	(.0601)
1981	-.6734	-.9121	-.6195
	(.0379)	(.1638)	(.0604)
1984	-.6568	-1.0155	-.5943
	(.0367)	(.2107)	(.0524)
1987	-.6926	-.9524	-.5942
	(.0393)	(.1805)	(.0524)
1990	-.7071	-.9151	-.5998
	(.0405)	(.1649)	(.0539)
1993	-.6371	-.9700	-.6201
	(.0354)	(.1885)	(.0607)
1996	-.6179	-.9664	-.6307
	(.0342)	(.1868)	(.0657)
1998	-.6859	-.8637	-.6297
	(.0388)	(.1460)	(.0652)

Note: Asymptotic standard errors are in parentheses.

Given the fact that the elasticity of labour has become fairly elastic over time, this may possibly reflect a decline in the impact of trade unions in wage negotiations.

Comparative Results

There are no comparable results for Jamaica but there are a few studies for other developing countries. The results can be compared with the Craigwell and Boamah (1993) study for Barbados, Mohabbat, Dahal and Williams (1984) for India, and Henry (1989) for Pakistan. In the latter two studies, output was decomposed into consumption and investment goods rather than in our case into tradable and non-tradables. The studies all reject linear separability between imports and primary factors. Note however that Henry (1989) could not reject non-linear separability in his study of Pakistan, while Mohabbat, Dalal and Williams (1984) accepted input-output separability for India. In the case of Jamaica, the results clearly show strong complementarity for the elasticity of substitution between imports and labour as was the case for India. At the same time, the own price elasticity of labour was elastic while the opposite was found in Craigwell and Boamah (1993) for Barbados. Another point to note is that the demand elasticities for capital are closer to that of India than Barbados for which they were relatively inelastic.

Finally, while the study for Barbados found that labour and imports are substitutes, in the Jamaican case they were complements. The implication of this balance of payments policy is quite interesting. The reduction in imports clearly will have an impact on the level of output; adjustments in the trade balance require a careful disaggregation of imports to determine what areas of imports may not be necessary for output expansion.

Summary and Conclusion

This chapter utilised a translog cost function to estimate the demand for imports over the period 1972 to 1998 in Jamaica. In this model imports are regarded as a factor of production with other primary factors as capital and labour. On average, the degree of substitutability between capital services and imports is greater than that between capital services and labour and both show elasticities in excess of 1.

The model rejects linear separability between outputs and inputs implying that factor demand is sensitive to changes in the composition of output. This finding is in line with Craigwell and Boamah (1993) for Barbados but at variance with that of Mohabbat, Dhal and Williams (1984) for India. This may reflect the restructuring that has been taking place since the 1980s with the rise of the service sector and restructuring in manufacturing and financial services.

The model also rejects, as in the case of Barbados, both linear and non-linear separability between capital, labour and imports implying that neither the Cobb-Douglas nor the CES production function may be appropriate for estimating import demand in Jamaica. It is also the case that demand functions that have traditionally been employed, in which imports are explained by import prices and a real output which is dependent on capital and labour only, may be misspecified.

The paper also found that capital services and labour, and capital and imports are substitutes in production. But labour services and imports are complements from about 1976, which suggests that a reduction in imports due possibly to an increase in import prices will also affect the amount of labour employed in some sectors negatively. Since access to imports for most developing countries is limited by the availability of foreign exchange, the study of the substitution possibilities between imports and domestic factors is an important first step in shaping policies which can help to conserve foreign exchange without constraining growth.

Notes

1. I wish to thank Professor Alfred Francis, of the Department of Economics at Mona, for useful comments on this paper and also Damien King for access to the capital stock data. The errors and omissions remain mine. I must also thank Ms. Nadine Pryce for valuable research assistance, and the Research and Publications Committee for a grant which facilitated this research. I would like to thank Ms Annette McKenzie from the Statistical Institute of Jamaica (STATIN) for assisting in the construction of the gross value added for tradable and non-tradable goods and their respective prices after 1992.

2. 'Adjusting Trade Policy to Meet the Challenges of the New World Order', *A Policy Discussion Paper*, Ministry of Foreign Affairs and Foreign Trade, 14 June 2001, p.8.

3. James and Celestin have made an alternative case for Caribbean economies arguing that what is important is the development of local technological base for productivity growth as a means of reducing imports rather than changes in relative price of imports. They argued as follows:

    > A free trade regime of any sort being discussed currently will give a distinct advantage to countries that make technology rapidly, and undertake related capital accumulation, with the advantage enhanced by the multiplier effects of increasing returns.
    > If Caribbean nations do not become strong creators of technology and capital, their development paths will diverge from those of the current world leaders. Then, opening up of trade along the lines being promoted by the WTO will reinforce the current tendency to specialise in traditional import intensive activity or labour and natural resource intensive activity and the growth of employment will suffer accordingly. In this context, it is hardly likely that a change in the terms of trade would correct the income paths and provide a corrective financial flow that will restore convergence in income growth rates (especially industrial sector growth rates) in the long term with those of technology creating countries. The slackening of the balance of payments constraint drives the system, not through prices and the exchange rate, but rather through production, innovation, increasing returns, and the trade multiplier and accelerator, and it is through the latter that the system will be driven towards any balance of payments equilibrium, assuming such a condition exists and is attainable in the short run (James and Celestin, 1998).

4. Burgess (1974a, p.221) argues that it must be rejected that imports are separable from primary factors in the input function, and concludes that:

    > When imports are intermediate goods, it is inappropriate to specify a functional relationship for gross value added in which the primary factors enter as the sole inputs.

Conventional specifications of imports demand functions which employ a single measure of domestic value added involve serious errors of aggregation (Burgess, 1974a, p.221).

5. See Burgess (1974a); Denny and Pinto (1978); Kohli (1978).
6. Mohabbat, Dalal and Williams (1984), decompose output into consumption and investment goods, while Wang (1998) makes use of the decomposition of consumption, investment and export goods. In this study, tradable goods comprise of export agriculture, manufacturing and tourism while the rest of the sectors constitute non-tradables. Some of the sectors may have some imported elements; however, a finer distinction could not be made based on the available data from the Statistical Institute of Jamaica (STATIN).
7. A major limitation of the Cobb-Douglas production function is that the elasticity of substitution σ_{ij} between any two pairs of inputs i and j must always equal one. While the CES is more general in that it may take on other values, it is still required to be the same for all observations and for all possible pairs of inputs i and j. In addition, the translog does not constrain the partial elasticities to be positive only, as in the case of the Cobb-Douglas and the CES.
8. See Berndt and Christensen (1973); Berndt and Wood (August 1975).
9. See Samuelson (1965); Shephard (1970).
10. The regularity conditions are as follows:

(1) $C(y; p)$ is a positive real valued function, defined and finite in y for all finite $y \geq 0, p \gg 0$.

(2) $C(y; p)$ is non-decreasing, left continuous function in y and as $y \to \infty, C(y; p) \to \infty$ for $p \gg 0$.

(3) $C(y; p)$ is non-decreasing in p.

(4) $C(y; p)$ is positively linearly homogenous in p for all $y > 0$.

(5) $C(y; p)$ is a concave function in p, for all y>0 (see Allen and Hall, 1997, p.21).

11. Total employment includes all the workers on the payroll, and we follow the approach of not accounting for age and education among workers. This may be inappropriate since labour quality may have improved over the sample period (see Alleyne, 2001).
12. This function is consistent with Hicks-neutral technical change. As Mohabbat, Dalal and Williams (1984, p.604, footnote 10) and Craigwell and Boamah (1993, p.221, footnote 3) have pointed out, the introduction of a Hicks neutral technical change term would not alter the share equation in formula (3). Following Binswanger (1974b, p.964, footnote 2), Hicks technical change is defined as 'neutral', 'labour-saving' or 'labour-using' depending on whether, at a constant capital-labour ratio, the marginal rate of substitution stays constant, increases or decreases. Neutrality is a homothetic inward shift of the unit isoquant.
13. Among the early works along this line are Berndt and Christensen (1973); Berndt and Wood (1975). For an explicit derivation of the translog function as an approximation about a point see Denny and Fuss (1977).

14. Note that the last expression in (8) is derived from the fact that $\sum_j S_j \sigma_{ij} = 0$. The elasticities of substitution are nonlinear functions of the parameters and their standard errors cannot be exactly estimated. Under the assumptions that the shares are constant and equal to the means of their estimated values approximate estimates can be found (Humphrey and Moroney, 1975). The standard errors for the AES were computed as:

$$SE(\sigma_{ij}) = SE(\gamma_{ij})/S_i S_j ....i \neq j; \quad SE(\sigma_{ii}) = SE(\gamma_{ii})/S_i^2 ...i = j.$$

For the own price elasticities of input demand, the asymptotic standard errors are:

$$SE(\eta_{ij}) = SE(\gamma_{ij})/S_i ....i \neq j; \quad SE(\eta_{ii}) = SE(\gamma_{ii})/S_i ....i \neq j.$$

The estimates were computed using the program LIMDEP.

15. Craigwell and Boamah (1993, pp. 214-5) and others point out that rejection of linear separability implies that a partial Cobb-Douglas structure would not hold. Rejection of complete global separability means that a complete Cobb-Douglas structure will not hold. Rejection of both linear and non-linear separability would imply that no consistent indices of (K, L), (K, M) or (L, M) exists for the data, and this means that Cobb-Douglas and CES functions are rejected.

16. In order that the cost function corresponds to a well-behaved technology, the fitted shares must be positive and the Hessian of second derivatives must be negative semi-definite. These were found to be satisfied.

17. The elasticity of substitution between labour and capital is given by the formula:

$$\sigma_{LK} = \partial \ln(K/L)/\partial \ln(F_L/F_K)$$

where F_L and F_K are the marginal products of labour and capital respectively. Assuming cost minimisation, this can be written as:

$$\sigma_{LK} = \partial \ln(K/L)/\partial \ln(P_L/P_K)$$

18. When the elasticities are positive the factors are substitutes, and when they are negative they are complements.

References

Allen, C. and Hall, S. (1997), *Macroeconomic Modeling in a Changing World: Towards a Common Approach*, John Wiley and Sons Inc., New York.

Alleyne, D. (2001), 'The Dynamics of Growth, Employment and Economic Reforms in Jamaica', *Social and Economic Studies*, Vol. 50(1), pp.55-125.

Anderson R.G. and Thursby, J. (1986), 'Confidence Intervals for Elasticity Estimators in Translog Models', *The Review of Economics and Statistics*, Vol. 68(4), pp.647-56.

Berndt, E.R. and Christensen, L. (1973), 'The Internal Structure of Functional Relationships: Reparability, Substitution and Aggregation', *Review of Economic Studies*, Vol. 40, pp. 403-10.

_____ (1975), 'Technology, Prices, and the Derived Demand for Energy', *The Review of Economics and Statistics*, Vol. 57(3), pp.259-68.

Berndt, E.R. and Wood, D. (1975), 'Technology Prices and the Derived Demand for Energy', *The Review of Economics and Statistics*, Vol. 57(4), pp.556-65.

Binswinger, H.P. (1974a), 'A Cost Function Approach to the Measurement of Elasticities of Factor Demand and Elasticities of Substitution, *American Journal of Agricultural Economics*, Vol. 56, pp.377-86.

_____ (1974b), 'The Measurement of Technical Change Biases with Many Factors of Production', *American Economic Review*, Vol. 64(6), pp.965-76.

Burgess, D.F. (1974a), 'A Cost Minimisation Approach to Import Demand Equations', *The Review of Economics and Statistics*, Vol. 56(3), pp.225-34.

_____ (1974b), 'Production Theory and Derived Demand for Imports', *Journal of International Economics*, Vol. 56, pp.679-733.

Caves, D.W. and Christensen, L.R. (1980), 'Global Properties of Flexible Functional Forms', *American Economic Review*, Vol. 70(3), pp.422-32.

Christensen, L., Jorgensen, D.W. and Lau, L.J. (1973), 'Transcendental Logarithmic Production Frontiers', *The Review of Economics and Statistics*, Vol. 55(1), pp.28-45.

Cox, W. and Worrell, D.(1978), 'Import Structure and Economic Growth in Barbados: 1957-1977', mimeo, Central Bank of Barbados, November.

Craigwell, R. and Boamah, D. (1993), 'Substitution Possibilities between Imports and Traditional Factors of Production for a Small Open Economy', *North American Journal of Economics and Finance*, Vol. 4(2), 211-23.

Denny, M. and Pinto, C. (1978), 'An Aggregate Model with Multi-product Technology', in M. Fuss and D. McFadden (eds), *Production Economics: A Dual Approach to Theory and Application*, Vol. II, North-Holland, Amsterdam, pp.249-76.

Diewert, W.E. (1971), 'An Application of Shepherd Duality Theorem: A Generalised Leontief Production Function', *Journal of Political Economy*, Vol. 79, pp.481-507.

Gafar, J. (1988), 'The Behaviour of Import Demand in a Developing Country: Guyana, 1954-1974', *Research Papers No.10*, Central Statistical Office, Trinidad and Tobago, pp.51-67.

_____ (1979), 'The Determinants of Import Demand in Trinidad and Tobago: 1967-1984', *Applied Economics Letters*, Vol. 20, pp.310-313.

Henry, M.C. (1989), 'An Econometric Analysis of Substitution Possibilities between Domestic and Imported Factors of Production in Pakistan, 1970-1987: A Translog Approach, *Working Paper No.4771*, University of the West Indies, St. Augustine.

Humphrey, D.B. and Moroney, J.R. (1975), 'Substitution among Capital, Labour and Natural Resource Products in American Manufacturing', *Journal of Political Economy*, Vol. 83, pp.57-82.

International Monetary Fund (IMF) (2000), *International Financial Statistics*, IMF.

James, V. and Celestin, L. (1998), 'Production and Prices in a Caribbean Economy', Policy Research and Development Institute, Scarborough, Tobago.

Joefield-Napier, W. (1984), *The Demand for Imports: The Case of Barbados, 1954-1970*, ISER, Kingston.

Kmenta, J. and Gilbert, R.F. (1968), 'Small Sample Properties of Alternative Estimators of Seemingly Unrelated Regressions', *Journal of American Statistical Association*, Vol. 63, pp.1180-1200.

Kohli, U. (1978), 'A Gross National Product Function and the Derived Demand for Imports and Supply of Exports, *Canadian Journal of Economics*, Vol. 11(2).

Lau, L.J. (1986), 'Functional Forms in Econometric Model Building', in Z. Griliches and M.D. Intrilligator (eds), *Handbook of Econometrics*, Vol. III, Elsevier, Amsterdam.

Mendes, M. and McLean, R. (1999), *Essential of Jamaican Taxation*, CFM Publications, Department of Management Studies, University of the West Indies, Kingston.

Ministry of Foreign Affairs and Foreign Trade (2001), 'Adjusting Trade Policy to Meet the Challenges of the New World Order', *A Policy Discussion Paper*, 14 June, Kingston.

Statistical Institute of Jamaica (STATIN) (2002), *National Income and Product Accounts*, STATIN, Kingston.

Samuelson. P.A. (1965), 'Using Full Duality to Show that Simultaneous Additive Direct and Indirect Utilities Implies Unitary Price Elasticity of Demand', *Econometrica*, Vol. 33, pp.731-96.

Shepherd, R.W. (1970), *Theory of Cost and Production Function*, Princeton University Press, Princeton.

Wales, T.J. (1977), 'On the Flexibility of Functional Forms', *Journal of Econometrics*, Vol. 43, pp.183-93.

Wang, E. (1998), 'Sensitivities of Import Demand and Export Supply in an Open Developing Economy: The Evidence from Taiwan', *International Economic Journal*, Vol. 12(1), pp.121-39.

Zellner, A. (1962), 'An Efficient Method of Estimating Seemingly Unrelated Regressions and Tests for Aggregation Bias', *Journal of American Statistical Association*, Vol. 57, pp.348-68.

Appendix: Data and Sources

The total costs were apportioned among the wages bill, returns to capital and the cost of imported input. In the case of revenue, the shares were computed as the ratio of gross value added in each output category in the tradable Q_T and non-tradable Q_N sectors to total value added. These were computed as R_T and R_N respectively. The data for the gross value added and their prices, plus the wage index were computed from various years of the *National Income and Product Accounts*, Statistical Institute of Jamaica (STATIN). The import price index W_M was computed from the indices of *External Trade* for the years 1969-1979, 1980-1989 and 1988-1998, STATIN.

The capital stock series was taken from a series computed by Damien King, and was computed as $K_t = K_{t-1} + I_t - D_t$, where K_{t-1} is the stock at the end of last year and I_t and D_t are the gross investment and depreciation calculation. His initial capital stock series began in 1949 and was computed as the average of gross investment over the years 1950-1959. The rental cost of capital was computed to reflect elements of price, capital gains and the level of depreciation, and was computed as:

$$W_{kt} = r_t q_{t-1} + \delta q_t - (q_t - q_{t-1})$$

where W_{kt} is the user cost of capital services, r is the opportunity cost of holding capital and measured by the government bond yield, δ is the depreciation rate, q is the capital asset price and $(q_t - q_{t-1})$ is the capital gain. The government bond yield was taken from the annual *International Financial Statistics* (IMF, 2000), and q the implicit price deflator for Gross Capital Formation was calculated from the stock of capital at current and constant 1974 prices. The average depreciation rate was computed at 11 per cent and was taken from Mendez and McLean (1999), *Essentials of Jamaican Taxation.*

Index

For Product Safety Concerns and Information please contact our EU representative GPSR@taylorandfrancis.com Taylor & Francis Verlag GmbH, Kaufingerstraße 24, 80331 München, Germany

Printed and bound by CPI Group (UK) Ltd, Croydon, CR0 4YY
01/05/2025
01858461-0004